The Myth of Emptiness and the New American Literature of Place

The Myth of Emptiness and the New American Literature of Place

WENDY HARDING

UNIVERSITY OF IOWA PRESS

IOWA CITY

University of Iowa Press, Iowa City 52242

www.uiowapress.org
Printed in the United States of America

Design by Omega Clay

The University of Iowa Press is a member of Green Press Initiative and is committed to preserving natural resources.

Printed on acid-free paper

Library of Congress Cataloging-in-Publication Data
Harding, Wendy.
The myth of emptiness and the new American literature of place / by Wendy Harding.
pages cm
Includes bibliographical references and index.
ISBN 978-1-60938-279-7 (pbk), ISBN 978-1-60938-292-6 (ebk)
1. American literature—21st century—History and criticism. 2. Emptiness (Philosophy) in literature. 3. Place (Philosophy) in literature. 4. Nature in literature. 5. Discourse analysis, Literary. I. Title.
PS231.E46H37 2007
810.9'3273—dc23 2014010232

For Jacky

CONTENTS

ACKNOWLEDGMENTS

This book has grown out of encounters with places, people, and texts. I first came to the U.S.A. many years ago. After spending my childhood in England, I found my new country unsettlingly innocent of history. Europe spoke to me of the depth of its past, while America impressed me with the expansiveness of its space. That I now believe my dualistic vision of the two continents to be erroneous is due in no small measure to the work of the historians and geographers cited in this study, and of course, to the writers whose works are the focus of my book. The land has its stories for those who are prepared to read and listen to them.

My investigation of the falsity of the myth of empty space has been aided by the generosity of colleagues and institutions. My research on the American territory began when I became a member of the study group on North America at the University of Toulouse in France, where I have been a professor since 2000. Aided by my friend and codirector, Nathalie Dessens, I have organized a number of conferences and symposia treating various aspects of American space-time. Working with the team has been an exciting adventure. Special thanks are due to Nathalie Dessens, Nathalie Cochoy, Aurélie Guillain, Anne Stefani, and the other members of the American Studies group. The former and present directors of the research team on Anglophone cultures ("Cultures Anglo-Saxonnes"), Catherine Lanone and Philippe Birgy, have also been exceptionally supportive. Conducting research at the University of Toulouse would be much more difficult were it not for the devotion of Nadine Aurières, the librarian responsible for interlibrary loans; I cannot thank her enough.

This book would not have been written had I not had the chance to make trips to the United States for research purposes. My interest in the subject began when the University of Montana welcomed me in the summer of 2009. Jill Bergman, Brady Harrison, and David Moore were particularly generous with their friendship and help. In 2011 I had the privilege of being a visiting scholar at the University of Connecticut, where Wayne Franklin encouraged me to pursue this project and helped me with his expertise on the subject. Margaret Higonnet gave me valuable practical advice. Diane Krumrey invited me to talk at the University of Bridgeport that same year, giving me a chance to try out an early version of my ideas. She has been a great friend, always ready to help me with questions about America. In the fall of 2013 I was Visiting Exchange Professor at the University of Idaho. The library turned out to be particularly rich in documents relating to my subject. Scott Slovic gave me immensely helpful advice; his generosity and friendship have been very precious to me. As head of the English Department, Gary Williams did all he could to make me welcome and ensure that I had perfect working conditions. The monthly ecocriticism discussion groups run by Erin James provided great conversation, sugary snacks, and food for thought. Thanks to all the members for making me welcome. Thanks too, to the librarians who have stocked all these university libraries and established the networks that make it possible to obtain books from other institutions. The people at the University of Iowa Press have been immensely professional, helpful, and good-natured. Special thanks are due to Elisabeth Chretien, Charlotte Wright, and Laurel Anderton.

I am grateful to Robert Toedter for permission to include his photograph, *Westside of Cortese Landfill, Narrowsburg, New York* (2006), and for his generosity in providing me with the image. Thanks also to the Ansel Adams Trust for permission to reproduce *Mount McKinley and Wonder Lake, Denali National Park, Alaska* (1947), and to the University of Arizona's Collection Center for Creative Photography for furnishing the reproduction.

The most important influence on my writing and thinking is my husband, Jacky Martin. He accompanied me on all the physical and mental journeys this book required. His intellectual curiosity, research expertise, theoretical sophistication, vast word-hoard, and tolerance of my sometimes argumentative ways of working out problems make him a wonderful guide and sometimes collaborator. I dedicate this book to him with love.

Introduction

From Empty Spaces to Storied Places

Over the past decades, a change has been taking place in the way writers, artists, and scholars represent our surroundings. Sites that were once represented as devoid of human presence, as either wilderness or wastelands, have been newly explored and discovered to be full of the signs of human activity. Though my main focus in this book is literary texts, a rapid comparison of two photographs from the 2011 exhibition *Earth Now: American Photographers and the Environment*, held at the New Mexico Museum of Art,[1] will suggest the extent to which the idea of empty space has changed over the past hundred years.

Ansel Adams's 1947 photograph, *Mount McKinley and Wonder Lake, Denali National Park, Alaska*, offers a stunning example of the way that consummate artist defined landscape photography for most of the twentieth century and, at the same time, offered Americans a particular vision of the national territory.[2] The snow-covered mountain fills the upper half of the frame and extends beyond it, the rugged topography of its surfaces capturing and reflecting sunlight in a diagonal pattern that emphasizes its massiveness. In the foreground, the smooth surface of Wonder Lake outshines the snowy mountain, reflecting bright clouds in its mirrorlike surface so that it seems to contain and re-illuminate the sky that has been dimmed by the mountain. No human presence interrupts the subtle exchange of light between earth, water, and air. The darkness of the sky ensures that the contemplation of the land does not evoke a divine presence either. The natural world is not a conduit for the spirit; it exists in and of itself, apart from us, an imposing, distanced emblem of otherness. The monumental stillness and remoteness of mountain and lake demand respect, even reverence, for

America's remaining spectacular wilderness areas. Not surprisingly, photographs such as this made compelling arguments in efforts to establish national parks and conserve natural landmarks throughout the twentieth century, especially in the American West.[3]

Appearing in the same exhibition, Robert Toedter's *Westside of Cortese Landfill, Narrowsburg, New York* (2006) illustrates the political and aesthetic revolution in photographic responses to the environment that the exhibition brings to the public's attention. The place designated by the title of the photograph is one of the national priority superfund cleanup sites under the jurisdiction of the U.S. Environmental Protection Agency.[4] Toedter gestures toward traditional landscape photography in excluding human figures from the scene, but he also departs radically from earlier conventions. The choice of site is surprising: though situated next to a dangerous toxic dump, it looks like an ordinary American backyard scene, the backdrop for a family snapshot rather than a photograph in an exhibition. The wooded landfill appears sufficiently congenial for a now absent couple to have elected it as the site for their habitation.[5] Their desire for a peaceful refuge "away from it all" is humorously troped by the birdhouses that resemble scaled-down models of traditional American habitations. We are no longer placed in front of nature, looking in from the outside, but confronted with the character of our longing for it, and maybe some of the consequences. Eschewing the detached, transparent pose of the traditional landscape photographer, Toedter has situated his camera close to the scene and seems to be implicated in it. Rather than reinforcing the imaginary split between the civilized and the wild, the photograph blurs conventional distinctions between what is natural and what is human-made, framing the tree in the foreground of the picture with the plastic geese on the left and the two birdhouses on the right. With the traces of human presence, time enters the landscape.

TOP | *Mount McKinley and Wonder Lake, Denali National Park, Alaska* (1947). Photograph by Ansel Adams. Collection Center for Creative Photography, University of Arizona, © 2013 The Ansel Adams Publishing Rights Trust.

BOTTOM | *Westside of Cortese Landfill, Narrowsburg, New York* (2006). Photograph by Robert Toedter. Courtesy of the photographer.

Whereas the unruffled lake and monumental mountain in Adams's photograph seem eternal, the bright turquoise chairs at the center of Toedter's photograph situate the scene in the age of plastic. The Narrowsburg scene is provocatively ambiguous in seeming both empty and inhabited. The two vacant chairs provide a colorful focal point and pose a number of questions. Positioned with their backs to the woods, the chairs make us wonder about the view they are facing outside the frame of the photograph. Toward what kind of landscape are they oriented? Are they turned toward a human habitation beyond the landfill or are they situated in a clearing so as to afford a view of further woods? Are they simply unoccupied because it is winter, or does the picture's context as part of a series documenting the National Priorities List suggest a more sinister reason for their emptiness? In facing the viewer of the photograph, the chairs seem to address these questions to us directly. We are asked not simply to admire the scene from a distance, but to reflect upon our place in the land.

Whereas Adams's photograph invites our admiration and warns us that our place in the scene is only as respectful visitors,[6] Toedter's raises questions about the occupancy of the American territory. Both images are placed under the sign of empty: the emptiness induced by Adams's admiring gaze and the abdication suggested by the unoccupied seats in Toedter's photograph. Both options confront us with a landscape created by omission: a carefully cropped panorama and a deserted backyard in winter. Nevertheless, the two kinds of absence are very different, because the former scene sustains a myth while the latter poses an interrogation.

The writers selected for this study—Rick Bass, Charles Bowden, Ellen Meloy, Jonathan Raban, Rebecca Solnit, and Robert Sullivan—represent a broad cultural movement away from the dichotomous thinking that splits space into zones of plenitude and zones of emptiness. Their books contribute to complexifying a type of writing that is already difficult to classify. They are not autobiographers, though their writing is centered on their own experiences in particular places. They are not nature writers, though their investigations take them into the domain of the natural sciences. They are neither geographers nor historians, though they deal with space and time. They are not travel writers, for they have no interest in stimulating readers' interest in faraway places. In creating hybrids of all these genres, their texts express the complexity of place. My choice of these particular authors may seem, at first glance, somewhat heterogeneous and idiosyncratic, though I hope their coherence as a group will become clear. I have left aside some important contemporary American writers of place such as Susanne Antonetta, Janisse Ray, and Terry Tempest Williams, whose ecological memoirs center personal and environmental histories on chosen sites in compelling ways,[7] since my chosen corpus is more appropriate to an exploration of the myth of empty space. Unlike Antonetta, Ray, and Williams, who are natives of the places they write about and have never held any illusions about whether or not they are inhabited, the authors in my chosen corpus arrive from elsewhere to explore sites that have been placed under the sign of empty. In so doing they reenact the American myth of discovery, only in revealing what lies beneath cultural myths, they reshape attitudes to habitation. In different ways they reveal that there is no such thing as empty space; there are instead interconnected places that are never separate from human activities. There is no place outside human culture and no culture distinct from place. Places are always storied—humanly imprinted—just as stories are placed—given substance through their geography.

Before embarking on the readings of individual works that constitute the central focus of this book, in Part I, "The Idea of Empty," I first review some of the theories addressing our insertion in space and then examine the ways that the conception of emptiness has mutated in the centuries since the first English-speaking settlers arrived on the continent. Chapter 1, "Placing the Land under the Sign of Empty," argues that emplacement has been a central problem for the people whose settlement in the United States displaced America's first nations. America was not a site to which the European colonists and immigrants were bound by memory but a space they sought to claim and inscribe. To accomplish this, they represented the land as empty and therefore available. In reality, there is no such thing as empty space; even the most remote, desolate, and barren locations bear the imprint of humanity. Thus empty is a double-faced sign: it links a mutating decoy—the illusion of emptiness—to an underlying project, an act of appropriation. This introductory theoretical chapter borrows insights from geographers like Doreen Massey, David Harvey, Edward Soja, and Edward Casey in order to explore the question of empty space; nevertheless, the main focus of this book is representations: how space is signified in culture. Hence, this chapter also introduces a new idea about the way these writers structure their texts. I hypothesize that rather than presenting closed patterns, the writers assemble multiple, heterogeneous scripts that suggest the complexity and multiplicity of our relationships to place and thereby undermine the myth of empty.[8]

Moving from theorizing about the sign of empty to illustrating its historical resurgences, chapter 2, "Creating the American Nation from a Vast and Empty Chaos," explores the mutating representations of American places as empty. From the first years of colonial settlement in North America down to the present day, terms like "vacant," "void," "desert," "desolate," and "barren" have competed with a discourse that proclaims the land's bountiful plenitude. The early texts create a new American icon—the wilderness—placing it under the sign of empty and projecting onto it all the settlers' hopes and fears. Initially the settlers characterize the American territory by what it lacks; the immigrants arrive to bring what is needed to complete it. Later, during the period of expansion, America's emptiness offers an antidote to Europe's stifling overcrowdedness. Depending on people's interactions with the land and projects for it, the values attributed to the sign of empty shift. It has proved a versatile cultural construct, but while the attribution of emptiness has been a vector of creativity, it has purged the land of its history, an omission that the new literature of place seeks to correct.

The remaining chapters of this study analyze six of these corrective works. Part II, "Seeking New Connections," considers three authors who represent the transition from the tradition of nature writing, with its emphasis on the solitary individual communing with nature in an uninhabited place, to new forms of writing that recognize the coexistence of human and other-than-human presences in the land.[9] Rick Bass, Charles Bowden, and Ellen Meloy chart a movement from disillusion to discovery and recommitment. They reveal that the virgin spaces they had dreamed of are, in reality, more socially complex and politically imbricated than they had imagined. The large open spaces that fired Romantic aspirations no longer function as foils or mirrors of the solitary self. Emptiness is just an artificial construct, designed to simplify accounts of human interactions with the environment. The writers chronicle their progressive discoveries of the complex histories of their chosen places as well as their struggles to adapt to their revised vision of the land they inhabit.

Chapter 3, "Becoming Committed to Place in Rick Bass's *Winter,*" looks at how the author represents his conversion from solitary adventurer in a land emptied of all signs of humanity to a member of an interdependent community.[10] The book revisits a number of nature-writing tropes and humorously rewrites them. For example, rather than occulting signs of the machine age, Bass describes in loving detail the equipment essential for survival in the harsh Montana winter. He experiences his environment not simply through the gaze but through physical contact that involves penetrating its substance. Participation in the natural world is not restricted to loafing and contemplating; inhabiting the Yaak Valley in the northwestern corner of Montana means engaging in a kind of contract that demands work and struggle and, finally, responsibility. This early work by Rick Bass shows how the birth of a commitment to place exposes an individual to the risks and rewards inherent in relationships with other human beings, with other-than-human beings, and with the land.

Charles Bowden's *Frog Mountain Blues,*[11] analyzed in chapter 4, tackles a broader concern at the heart of the new literature of place: the relations between individuals and communities and their projects for the land they inhabit, and transitively, between the nation and its territory. To give an idea of the complexity of those relations, Bowden brings together a motley assortment of images, texts, and stories about the Santa Catalina Mountains in Arizona. He creates a montage or collage of various inscriptions and traces made by their different occupants, revealing how human appropriation and inhabitation has overprinted the topography of the Catalinas with a barely intelligible welter of human signs. Better than any polemic, the assemblage of those inscriptions and traces reveals the complexity of the struggle centered on the mountains. Looking beyond the text's seemingly haphazard assembly, this chapter considers the different foci or generating forces that are braided together in the weave of the text. These multiple scripts represent a space—Frog Mountain—that is, on the one hand, overrun, assaulted, defiled, and desecrated and, on the other, always unattainable, remote, and secret. The crazed patterning of the book's structure derives from the author's attempt to seize something that remains inaccessible because the land is different for each inhabitant and always in the process of becoming.

In chapter 5, "Suturing the Map of the Known Universe in Ellen Meloy's *The*

Last Cheater's Waltz," I show how the personal struggle that structures Meloy's book also corresponds to a crisis of culture and of representation.[12] *The Last Cheater's Waltz* stages the shift from the impossible dream of an unchanging, pristine desert to the reality of humanity's continuous relations in and with the land. The nature writer's projection of the self onto a landscape that is conceived of as empty no longer works for the protagonist. Moving beyond the circumscribed zone of the self and its projections, she discovers the traces of continuous human activity in the territory surrounding her Utah home. This discovery necessitates a shift from the fantasy of a solitary waltz with a beloved place to the recognition that the desert is not faithful to her alone—it is a cheater. More than a rediscovery of a given locale, the explorations related in this book transform the engagement that the writer establishes with the land. The two apparently contradictory forces of beauty and violence that she finds in the desert are born of energies inherent in the land and its inhabitants. Meloy takes on the challenge of stitching these contraries together; she explores and maps her surroundings piece by piece and then sutures together the disparate fragments.

In Part III of this study, "Retracing Paths and Reassessing Emplacement," the focus shifts from the impassioned lovers of chosen places found in Part II to more detached investigators of American geohistory. From the outset, Jonathan Raban, Rebecca Solnit, and Robert Sullivan hold an unromantic, postlapsarian attitude to the national territory. They give more importance to the history of habitation of particular spaces than to their personal relationships to the land. Places designated as empty contain remnants of past and present activities that have been left unattended, open for inspection. They contain the archives of foregone, partly effaced tragedies that have affected the land. Whether they are the traces of former settlements in Raban's *Bad Land*, or the residues of military conflict in Solnit's *Savage Dreams*, or the buried refuse of urban America in Sullivan's *Meadowlands*, these remnants can be decoded, re-storied, and reconstructed by careful documentation and imaginative empathy. Ultimately, the buried tragedies discovered in these neglected sites need not be repeated. Uncovering them is the first step in reorienting the occupation of the land.

Chapter 6, "The Peopled Shape of the Land in Jonathan Raban's *Bad Land*," enlarges the scope of the habitation issue from the individual's perspective to that of the group. In Raban's book,[13] the land is neither a sanctuary for an exceptional people nor the repository of transcendent values; instead, it is considered in relation to its people, as a co-creation. The "Bad Land" of the book's title (the plains of eastern Montana) merits that appellation only because of bad usage, not because of its intrinsic worthlessness or its malefic intention, as some of the failed homesteaders of the early twentieth century ruefully came to believe. Raban's self-portrayal as alien émigré, initially capable of seeing only "hillocky emptiness" (4) in the plains, is vital in debunking the illusory image projected onto the land. The writer invites readers to learn to see and to learn along with him as he acquires a new vocabulary of landscape. Following in the tracks of the homesteaders, he pores over the texts, images, and stories that they produced in response to their surroundings. His orientation is historical and sociological, but his main concern is the nature of the bond between humans and their surroundings, a fundamental question that he matches with his personal anxiety about settling in a new land.

In *Savage Dreams* Rebecca Solnit breaks with traditional nature writing in focusing not on the exceptional character of the American West,[14] nor on her personal involvement in two particular locations, although both these aspects are touched on, but rather on the relations between the territory and the people that occupy it. She investigates the collective mentality by juxtaposing two places that, for different reasons, are generally represented as empty spaces: a military test site and a national park. As her book reveals, the projection of empty is not an expression of either transcendent or negative values, but a fabrication that masks social, political, and collective aspirations, or "dreams." In chapter 7, "Unsettling Oppositions in Rebecca Solnit's *Savage Dreams*," I focus on Solnit's quest to clear away the layers of forgetfulness, indifference, and falsification that have built up around two sites and to replace them with compelling accounts of some of the varied spatiotemporal experiences gathered there. Her book links cultural memory to the body and the land, assembling scripts that intersect and converge. Within the diptych structure of her book, Solnit assembles fragments in what may initially seem to be a random, crazy-quilt style. Rather than following the strict logic of historical processes and turning this tangle into a straight line, her approach consists in weaving a web of correspondences around events and people in order to express intersections, recurring patterns, and convergences.

More than any other place, the New Jersey Meadowlands illustrate the failure of America's policy concerning lands that are deemed empty. Robert Sullivan's exploration of this area in *The Meadowlands: Wilderness Adventures at the Edge of a City* employs some of the conventions of the literature of place in burlesque fashion in order to critique the dichotomous attitudes to the land that have resulted in the sanctification of certain sites and the abandonment of others.[15] Sullivan's original contribution to the literature of place lies both in the attention he pays to this neglected region and in the comic vein in which he describes his swampland adventures. He stages a discovery of America in reverse, going eastward in space and backward in time. Chapter 8 traces this "reverse spiritual commute." The place it uncovers merits our attention if only because, despite all the abuses heaped on it, life persists there with impressive resilience. Sullivan shows it to be a place of creativity and transformation, rather than a wasteland. In bringing together the organic and the inorganic in surprising combinations, the Meadowlands evince the hybridity that characterizes the world. To describe such a place, Sullivan employs a new ecopoetics of entanglement characterized by humor, indirection, and baroque excess. The aim of this new mode of writing is to stimulate questions about our way of living.

These new writers of place testify to the interactions between Americans and the territory they occupy. If the books studied in Part II, "Seeking New Connections," focus on the relations between individuals and specific places, Part III enlarges the scope of the inquiry to the broader relation of the land to the nation. However, the distinction between those two sections is only a question of differing emphasis. One's personal connection to the land can never be separated from formative cultural mythologies and sweeping geohistorical currents. Investigations of national tendencies take on immediacy in being presented as the testimony of personally engaged individuals.

Generally, these texts offer a response to a crisis in representation. In revising the narratives that tell of place, they work to reshape attitudes toward it. They reject both the objective photographic style of documentaries and the selective cropping or soft-focus idealization of nature writing. They abandon the Romantic obsession with beauty and the sublime, or rather they cite it ironically, since by privileging chosen sites or species it refuses the complexity of contemporary environmental issues. All the books studied here reject the national master narrative that erases difference by figuring parts of the territory as mere surfaces alternatively perceived as empty, blank, and ahistorical or as wasted, barren, and vacuous. That reductive vision effaces the multiple narratives accreted in particular places through time and ignores the complexity and undecidability of the past. All the texts contain a reflection on the limits and abuses of misrepresentation, though they are all more or less critical of their own aptitude to correct such a bias. The inquiries undertaken in these books profoundly affect and transform the inquirers. They realize that they cannot remain in the position of spectators or even that of informed witnesses. They insist that there is no position outside, as the photograph by Ansel Adams flagrantly proclaims and as that by Toedter just as blatantly denies, no safe overhanging position from which to look upon the world, no empty chairs that do not call for responsible occupation.

Whereas Thoreau found in the idea of wildness a useful position from which to critique nineteenth-century American society, these writers see the need to reconnect the social and the natural in order to correct the distortions of dualistic thinking. They call into question divisions like wild and domestic, or nature and society, but this is not their primordial objective in the rendition of place. Concomitantly, they rediscover the complexity of actual spaces and of their layered and ramifying structures. Part of the intricacy of places once thought of as empty comes from their diverse appropriations over time. Their successive palimpsestic layers become apparent through the various stories and human existences that have given them consistency. Space is peopled, storied, and contested. Under the sign of empty each of the writers discovers a profusion of traces that furnishes the material for reconstructing the stories-in-the-making linked to the particular places they investigate.

I.

The Idea of Empty

1

Placing the Land under the Sign of Empty

America's Geographical History

Human beings commonly identify themselves in terms of both their social status and their geographical location. Literature plays a major role in fostering and reinforcing the feeling of belonging to and interacting with a social and spatial environment. Recently, in the wake of Lefebvre's pioneering work,[1] human geographers have systematized these intuitively accepted relations into structural principles constitutive of human space: "all social (and indeed physical) phenomena/activities/relations have a spatial form and a relative spatial location."[2] N. Scott Momaday punningly reminds us that "events take place."[3] Questioning the disciplinary divisions that separate geography from history, Doreen Massey insists that "the spatial is integral to the production of history."[4] One only has to think of all the associations that cluster around the North/South and East/West axes in the American imagination to garner ample proof of that statement. Indeed, according to William Gass and Gertrude Stein, America has a "geographical history."[5] Besides, as philosopher Edward Casey succinctly put it, "Places gather."[6] In bringing together humans, animals, and things, they offer a powerful nexus for collecting evidence of their complex interactions. Places gather most pointedly at certain foci imposed by the land's topography: along the course of rivers, at estuaries, along the passages traced for roads, canals, or railways. Yet while places gather, what they bring together has to be sorted. The stories that assemble there may subsist only as traces, or they may be so tangled that they need to be unraveled.

The literature of place mediates between humans and the land. There would be no literature without the gathering potential of place, but place would remain inaccessible without words and images as intermediaries.[7] Literature puts the land in place. The imaginary sites discourse creates are, if we agree with Robert Pogue Harrison, vital to human habitation: "Without *logos*, there is no place, only habitat, no *domus*, only niche; . . . no dwelling, only subsisting. In short, *logos* is that which opens the human abode on the earth."[8] The literature of the United States shapes the territory into distinct regions and, at the same time, traces dynamic trajectories across the nation. The national literature casts Americans as a nation of exiles, immigrants, and wanderers, whose identification with specific places enters into competition with the lure of the unknown. It evokes the reciprocal action between the attraction of settled and outlying places and the connections between them.

In America, as opposed to the ostensibly less dynamic space of the Old World,[9] the individual's relation to space entails not only the notion of emplacement—finding one's place in a social group and attuning oneself to a locality—but also the idea of adjusting to the extensive national territory. In the cultural imagination,[10] from James Fenimore Cooper through Jack Kerouac and beyond, enjoying the full status of an American does not signify just inhabiting a city or belonging to a region; it means enjoying mobility and transience, being able to travel and migrate across the American continent, entertaining cultural expectations within the national territory but also cherishing the dream of unattached, unfettered existence. The land is not held to be the repository of the values and the cultural memory of the nation from which members must learn;[11] on the contrary, inasmuch as it was held to be undiscovered, the land offered a site of invention and of creation. Rather than the site of the nation's memory, it was (at least imaginatively) the blank medium upon which its dreams could be projected and materialized. For the settlers, the land had a geography rather than a history; its annals began with Columbus. Conceiving the American continent in this way, they tended to disregard what was already there in favor of their visions of what it should be, and the consequences were often unforeseen. In Rebecca Solnit's words, "That history is not only the history of human actions, of causes, but the history of effects, of ecological damage" (47). For those who care to examine it, America is a palimpsest overwritten with various plans for inhabitation. As some of the writers studied in later chapters show, the land also contains the traces of its own resistance to those plans.

The Place of Place in American Literature

Perhaps because of the nation's complex geohistory, place is not taken for granted in American culture. It is not just the backdrop for human intercourse that we find in European novels. For American writers from Cooper, Thoreau, and Whitman to Cather, Steinbeck, and Snyder, it is a major agent in the definition of human relations. This does not mean solely that Americans see themselves as contending with an exceptionally challenging territory, although this is a major consideration, but more essentially that they can fully express and achieve their individual or collective destinies only by coming to terms with their spatial environment and interacting with it. Hence the national literature articulates provocative statements about relations to place. For example, writing about Western literature, Barbara Allen claims, "In their attempts to shape the land to their will and in telling stories about those attempts, westerners create their own identities, coming to resemble the landscape they live in and talk about in deeply marked and ineradicable ways, becoming immutably one with the land."[12] Nathaniel Lewis terms this sort of claim "environmental constructivism." He is skeptical about the assertions Western nature writers make about the impact that the natural landscape has on the shaping of their identities,[13] seeing them as a simple reversal of social constructivism. For him, literature is simulation rather than representation; there is no connection between language and reality. Though this theoretical model is attractive, it seems reductive to limit cultural action to the playful production of simulacra. It denies the importance of the work of imagining a verbal universe in which to situate the subject and of finding the words that offer openings to the real.

The literature of place holds special importance in American letters. It has taken various forms in keeping with the evolution of mentalities. Three overlapping phases can be roughly sketched in the nonfictional writing about place: the first period offers chronicles of discovery and settlement; then a phase of Romantic projection extends from the publication of Emerson's *Nature* (1836) to *Pilgrim at Tinker Creek* (1974) and beyond; and, finally, the more environmentally conscious contemporary period is initiated by groundbreaking texts like *Sand County Almanac* (1949) and *Silent Spring* (1962).

Contemporary literary works suggest that a transition is underway from texts devoted to celebrating the individual's encounter with the wilderness to a new mode that reveals a more historically complex relation between Americans and their environment.

The American literature of place has always been hybrid, at a crossroads between genres such as travel literature, natural history, and autobiography.[14] Recently writers have been orienting it in a direction that requires us to reconsider our insertion in space. Appearing alongside the now familiar pieces of nature writing featuring sanctuaries of natural beauty, we now find works that focus on neglected, even damaged, sites in order to raise new questions about Americans' relation to their land. Starting from the end of the twentieth century, orientations have changed. In some cases, the new writers visit traditional nature sanctuaries but examine them differently, focusing on human as well as natural history. Three common concerns characterize the new focus on disinherited spaces in America. One is the desire to revisit the wild spaces that have been lavishly celebrated as central to the American dream of regeneration[15] but which now appear as lures diverting attention from the exploitative development of the West and the despoliation of indigenous populations.[16] Whether institutionalized or abandoned, in the new literature of place these sites no longer appear pristine but emerge as abused or neglected, and emptied of their people as well as their indigenous plants and animals. The second concern in this new literature of place is to question the duality between culture and nature, inhabited and desert spaces. Formerly accepted as dogma, this split now appears fallacious if not dangerous insofar as it conceals the links of dependence that connect supposedly empty spaces to expanding urban industrial centers.[17] This false dichotomy served to underwrite the exploitation of natural resources and contributed correlatively to the desertification of natural spaces. Finally, the strongest concern in the new focus on disinherited places is certainly the desire to understand and to testify about the past, not in order to accuse or atone, but in order to conceive of a different relation to the land based on the accreted constructions of the past.

In focusing on emplacement in American culture, I have not included works whose sole purpose is to describe sites exclusively from the perspective of the various scholarly disciplines—natural sciences, geography, or history. In the same way I have omitted the fictional and the exclusively autobiographical. All of these discourses may appear in the new literature of place, but none of them is the unique point of access to space. The writers of place I have chosen to study focus on the interactions between individual experience and the collective imagination and between the land and its human and nonhuman occupants. I have also chosen to exclude travel or exploration literature from the selected corpus. Though that dimension figures in most of the texts selected, the objective is radically different from that of more traditional explorations of natural places. The purpose of traveling has changed—space is more a site of commitment than an opening to adventure. The focus is poles apart from the exoticism that motivates the explorer. If exoticism invites us to experience vicariously the foreignness of certain places, the task of the new writers of place is, on the contrary, to integrate alien or unknown places into daily existence. In keeping with my interest in debunking the myth of empty space, the places described in my selected corpus are initially placed under that sign. Moreover, the writers at least entertain the idea of emptiness in order to reject it more convincingly upon investigation. There are other contemporary writers who may share similar insights about the land but develop them from different perspectives. For example, Susanne Antonetta, Janisse Ray, and Terry Tempest Williams braid together personal memoir and meditations on place, choosing to introduce readers to sites that they have known intimately from childhood. Indeed, their bodies bear the traces, sometimes even the scars, of their existence in those places. Although their testimonies are important, I have not included them in this study, for the writers know their territories well enough to ignore the sign of empty that greets outsiders. By contrast, the writers I have chosen to study arrive as outsiders, so that readers can easily join their company on the journey toward a deeper understanding of the places on which they focus. Ultimately, though in different ways, both groups of writers reject the cultural division between empty and occupied places; both emphasize the continuity of space and encourage responsibility to the environment as a whole.

I have chosen to place the texts studied here in the admittedly broad category of literature of place because the designation "environmental literature" does not quite fit them.[18] Although the ecological dimension is an important aspect of the corpus, references to scientific ecology or political environmentalism are not uppermost in it. Instead, these works take the form of individual testimonies issuing from personal investigations addressed to a readership that is ready to reassess its preconceptions. Before being acknowledged as a political issue, place is experienced as emplacement. In dramatizing the individual writers' coming to consciousness of place, these works testify to the necessity of personal awareness in provoking political commitment. At the same time, as I think this study will show, I do not hold with the distinctions made between place and space. The conceptual split between concrete location and formless abstraction, neatly summed up by Laurence Buell in *The Future of Environmental Criticism*,[19] fails to allow for the ways in which places are nodes or knots that cannot be separated from their attachments within more extensive space-time meshworks.[20] This is what Buell discovers when he loses his license plate and spends a day navigating the "non-places" of modern officialdom to recover it.[21]

The Sign of Empty as a Representational Block

To comprehend the ecological damage that the myth of empty space has provoked, it is first necessary to reduce a mode of signifying that has become a cultural block. To correct that block, the writers I have selected revisit abandoned, threatened, or damaged places in order to understand when and how they arrived at their present state. They recapture spatial signification by examining the vestiges of destitution in the hope that an understanding of the vagaries of history will help disentangle the complexities of the present and better orient our relationships with the land in the future.[22] In this, they seem to share Doreen Massey's faith in the performative force of spatial form: "Spatial form as 'outcome' (the happenstance juxtapositions and so forth) has emergent powers which have effects on subsequent events. Spatial form can alter the future course of the very histories which have produced it."[23] In their quests, the new writers of place shun the centers of power that have mobilized cultural geographers' attention[24] in order to concentrate on more remote or disfavored places. They revisit sites that in one way or another have been thought of as empty and hence available. In returning to these places, they expose the cultural illusion of fresh starts.

The selected texts concern certain very specific, sparsely inhabited or uninhabited zones such as mountains (Bowden), swamps (Sullivan), deserts (Meloy; Solnit), prairies (Raban), and wilderness areas (Bass). Despite the fact that they have been represented as empty, these places reveal both where the settlement of the American continent has been focused and where it has miscarried. In the second half of the twentieth century and more decisively at the beginning of the twenty-first with the advent of a global ecological crisis, the idea of empty space has come under scrutiny. Places once viewed as hostile wastelands or untouched, redeeming wilderness sanctuaries become instead terrains of recollection, assessment, and atonement. In the new literature of place, sites once designated as empty cease to be imagined as hostile or unique environments sectioned off from civilization; on the contrary, they are seen to offer exceptional opportunities to decipher and reconstruct the various dimensions of a national crisis in representation.

Throughout this study, I have confronted a terminological problem: How can I use a term that refers to a nonexistent reality? In fact, in discussions of American space, "empty" refers to a double entity linking the unstable projection of emptiness to plans for expansion. The generic term "empty" serves as a sort of cover word or common denominator for all the terms that in the course of American history have been used to designate the same duality. I consider its numerous variants, whether substantive or adjective,[25] words such as "wild," "desert," "pristine," "barren," "wasteland," "wilderness," or "void," as embedded avatars of the notion of empty. There is a certain advantage in looking at spaces represented as empty rather than at those that are generally accepted as socially saturated.[26] Since I posit that there are no such things as empty spaces, and, moreover, that even the most remote, desolate, and barren locations bear the imprint of humanity, spaces described as empty become privileged fields of observation. They reveal the hidden or overlooked traces of human influence and also, paradoxically, its most pernicious effects. A corollary of that proposition is that empty spaces are never dissociated from the active centers of social power. These peripheral, protected, or disinherited spaces become the inverted image of civilization, the return of the repressed of a culture in transformation. Their relation to central social sites recalls Michel Foucault's observations concerning heterotopias as "something like counter-sites, a kind of effectively enacted utopia in which the real sites, all the other real sites that can be found within the culture, are simultaneously represented, contested, and inverted."[27] Emptiness becomes the necessary counterpart of centers of power, permitting both hegemony and creativity. In the sites designated as empty, more than in the geographical hubs, one can perceive both a culture's most uncontrolled divagations and the seeds of its renewal.

As opposed to the challenge of a supposedly virgin continent open to discovery, places once thought of as empty offer the tangible traces and testimonies of foregone times. They may also contain what Kent C. Ryden calls an "invisible landscape of meanings, memories, and associations" perceived only by insiders and imperceptible to the passing traveler.[28] The field of exploration they represent is not the open ground available to free enterprise but the national sites of memories that were suppressed and are waiting to be recovered. Far from offering opportunities for rebirth, they now offer unique points of entry into the motivations and complexities of the national soul. If figuring landscapes is a means of cultivating modes of seeing, designating places as empty is, by contrast, a way to foster modes of unseeing. The new literature of place in America uncovers in these marginalized sites revelatory traces of confusion and perseverance, and in following them it restores visibility to what had been invisible.[29]

The analyses and field studies produced by recent cultural geographers offer a sociocultural spatial perspective that aids in appreciating the specific work done by the writers that I have selected for this study.[30] Empty space, we learn from the writings of the new cultural geographers, does not exist; it is a notion created or constructed by human interactions. Nonetheless, this notion is one of the major ideological operators that has contributed to the structuring of American space and has indirectly played a role in the formation of American identity. The heterodox writers that I have selected, besides their intrinsic value as writers, provide a privileged field of exploration to test this claim. They refuse to blank out portions of the national territory and, instead, set about decrypting the underlying stories. They search for perceptible traces of human occupation so as to reconsider themselves and their culture in the reading of these traces. They reexamine spaces that have been designated as empty in order to resolve a crisis in representation and in national identity.

The new literature of place reveals that there was never such a thing as empty space on the American continent. Like all cultural fantasies, the concept has a public face and a concealed underpinning. The places designated as empty are in reality culturally distinctive sites full of human and nonhuman, cultural and natural traces; however, these traces have been ignored or effaced. Emptiness is always the product of human decisions. As I will argue in the next chapter, from the first days of the colonial settlement, areas were pronounced empty and conceived of as empty in order to serve precise objectives. The practice is directly linked to the settlement situation, and similar ideological constructions can be observed in other colonized countries like Australia, Canada, or South Africa.[31] By contrast, on the European continent, places beyond the city, although viewed as alien, were nevertheless compatible with the presence of other humans, even if they were stigmatized as barbarians. In the American and more generally in the colonial context, what was beyond settlements was seen as "empty." In this form of unseeing, the territory was represented as devoid of human imprint, as inhuman. The land became ipso facto available, even urgently calling for human presence.[32] To put the phantasmal workings of the sign of empty in a comparative frame, it is perhaps useful to compare the open perspective that empty spaces evoke to the obstruction that forests represent in the European imagination. In *Forests: The Shadow of Civilization*, Robert Pogue Harrison argues that because they interrupted men's aspirations, forests became charged with a welter of contradictory impulses. They are places of mystery and exuberant life that put human endeavors to the test. By contrast, the invention of vacant spaces liberated the human spirit, opening unrestricted fields of expansion upon which it was able to exercise its designs. In ideological terms, land designated as empty became inscribable; it demanded to be materially claimed and conceptually informed.

The concept of empty has not served exclusively as a simple factor of expansion, escape, or projection, but also, and perhaps mostly, as a means to deal with the chaotic and turbulent processes attending the formation of a common identity on a newly claimed land. In order to perceive the economy of these processes, it is important to accept that the idea of emptiness was never dissociated from that of fullness. Emptiness and fullness constitute the two facets of a constantly changing, never stabilized national entity. In order to perceive the historical dialectics of full and empty, it is important to make a distinction between three levels of perception of the land. First, there is the referential level of animate and inanimate entities that are classed according to fairly consensual categories such as trees, lakes, mountains, or animals. These categories next filter through cultural representations that instill them with time and culture-bound values; for example, trees can be perceived as impediments or resources and mountains as objects of revulsion or of veneration. At the same time, personal emotions can color socially predefined representations in accordance with each individual's sensibility. Without such distinctions, it becomes impossible to explain how the selfsame place can be perceived from opposed points of view or how the same space can be represented differently from one epoch to the next, much less how private testimonies can report vastly divergent impressions of the same locales. These distinctions also enable us to untangle complex and ambiguous concepts like "wild" or "wilderness" that commute between the realities they denote and the values they suggest. The writers I will study in subsequent chapters pay attention to the unpredictable fluctuations in representations together with their transformative power on the definition of the land.

Associated with the ideas of "emptiness" or "fullness" is the concept of a nation always in need of validation and never quite solidified. "Emptiness" stands for a primal physical void that asks to be reclaimed in order to flesh out the idea of America. America needs to incorporate otherness in order to be complete, but that otherness has to be purified, despoiled of its distinctive differences, in order to be assimilated. In order to shed light on this ideological construct, we could contrast the spaces designated as empty with those institutionalized as sacred.[33] Empty spaces are implicitly marked as inchoate and unimproved; sacred places such as Independence Rock Historic Site or Mount Rushmore become iconic national symbols once they have been overprinted with American symbolism.

There is always a correlation or co-definition between full and empty, so in order to understand their dynamics, we should abstain from projecting onto them dichotomies such as cultural or natural, urban or rural, inhabited or deserted. In the course of American history, in order to further the development of the nation, the values of fullness and emptiness are freely interchanged in references to the territory. As I will illustrate in more detail in the next chapter, the first colonists endowed their fragile settlements with a reassuring substantiality by projecting emptiness onto the surrounding unexplored territories; imagining these spaces to be empty was a means of reinforcing social coherence. During the expansion phase, the space outside the settlements was increasingly seen as underdeveloped and open (variants of empty), and thus necessarily ready to be fertilized by the fullness of the American expansion. The land had to be emptied conceptually to give the nation the impression of plenitude. Later, after the great surge of industrial development at the end of the nineteenth century, a new form of abundance had to be found so as to redeem the ecological degradation resulting from uncontrolled industrialization. The wilderness variant of the sign of empty served that purpose, and so its value came to be inverted.

The dual construction of the sign of empty means that its various avatars cannot be taken at face value. First of all, the sign is highly unstable—it can be attached to deserted, desolate, or out-of-the-way places, but it can also be associated with mountains, lakes, forests, or oceans. Localities are "placed under erasure," so to speak, obliterated by the sign of empty. The inherent duality of the sign does not mean that it is blatantly duplicitous or that it is universally accepted; rival visions of the land can be proposed under the same designation. In the controversy over the Hetch Hetchy dam, for example, the conservationists saw the site as an unused space whose resources of water and recreation could be harnessed for the population. On the other side, the preservationists maintained that keeping the valley as it was would preserve one of the nation's treasures for the pleasure of its citizens.[34] It is also remarkable that, as they were about to transform one of the most complex biotas, homesteaders held contrasting visions of the prairie as barren yet splendid, desolate yet full of promise. When the settlers imposed their perceptions on the land, designations of empty or full were a means to displace and ignore the complexity of the American territory. In the case of the prairies, the perception of emptiness denied the indigenous richness of the grasslands habitat; the definition of fullness was retrieved from the memory of the agricultural landscapes left behind in Europe or the eastern states.[35]

A second reason the sign of empty can never be taken at face value is that its resurgent declensions are always linked to cultural and political projections. In the light of the correlation between full and empty presented above, projections can be seen as the various ways of accomplishing the definition of the always inchoate and embryonic American sign. Projections of the sign of empty involve the imposition of three strategies: predation, inscription, and purification. First of all, predation consists in appropriating what is perceived as either unclaimed or unoccupied. Second, inscription consists in imprinting cultural images on what is conceived of as blank. Finally, in the third strategy of purification, sites representing purity, such the national parks, were often claimed for the nation by removing the indigenous inhabitants, while places conceived as confused or worthless became sites of expurgation, dumping grounds for the unwanted residue of American culture: its outlaws, its religious dissenters, or its nuclear and industrial waste.[36] By means of all these projections, the idea of America is aggrandized, consolidated, purged of its perceived imperfections, and strengthened in its fullness.[37]

A final form of obliteration associated with the sign of empty is the way it permits places to be lifted out of time and seemingly beyond the preoccupations of humans. With the disappearance, the nonrecognition, or the suppression of the traces of human or nonhuman presence, places become timeless, almost insubstantial and nonexistent. Abstracted from human or nonhuman habitation, they are reduced to their pure physical spatiality. In contemporary America this exposes them to transformations that take two opposing forms. They can be elevated, often by legal means, into sanctuaries like the national parks, encapsulating all the transcendent virtues that society attaches to space. Conversely, they can be demoted, almost expelled from the national territory; they can become invisible and unmentionable to the point that they can be defiled by the elements that threaten society—as in the case of the swamps, deserts, and mountains that are used as dumping grounds, missile storage sites, or nuclear testing grounds. In these two extreme cases of spatial obliteration, the imposition of the sign of empty coincides with the desire to control space. This is obvious in the welter of procedures regulating the conditions of access to nuclear test sites or the array of regulations governing the national parks.

Encountering an-Other Space

Paradoxically, the imposition of the sign of empty on the land results in a proliferation of inscriptions that contribute to effacing the traces produced by other encounters.[38] A double semiotic plane is perceptible. On one side are the cultural inscriptions that aim to place the whole of the territory under the same homogenizing icon, and on the other are the numerous traces that the new wave of writers persistently tries to unearth. These traces correspond to the intrusion of otherness in the form of the unexpected, the strange, and the deviant perspectives that run afoul of the imposition of a master plan on the land. The new literature of place recovers the vestigial traces that have been obscured by the enveloping influence of the cultural sign. The writers search for tangible traces, ruins, vestiges, or remains that prove that something existed that has been effaced, displaced, or reconstructed,[39] or they identify gaps and discontinuities in the web of appearances that create entrance points into buried histories.[40] They search for the traces of diverse frequentation that challenge the sterile reproduction of the same cultural sign. In designating places as empty, the dominant culture denies their diversity, but, at the same time, it inscribes that denial conspicuously and brutally on the land. In the stunning expanses of the national parks and the ravaged landscapes of the nuclear test sites, one can visualize the best and worst of what can happen when American territory is placed under the sign of empty.

Yet the writers' quests for traces of otherness are far from simple and, most importantly, far from complete. The questing subjects are not detached observers; they are put to the test and transformed by their experiences. The inquiries they conduct entail the dislocation, or perhaps the relocation, of the American subject; the self has to be reconceived as a permeable entity, open to the experience of otherness. Moreover, the writers' quests are protean and uncertain, for they have shifted onto new ground, or rather onto new configurations of time and space. In anthropologist James Clifford's words: "We ground things now, on a moving earth. There is no longer any place of overview (mountaintops) from which to map human ways of life, no Archimedean point from which to represent the world."[41] Inquiries into the past progressively shift to perplexed reconsiderations of the objectives of present-day America. Finally, interrogations of empty spaces pose the problem of the opportunity and the means available to define the other-than-self, or rather the conceptual status to give to the other-than-self or the unknown. Is the other friend or foe, helper or foil, approachable or ultimately unknowable? The writers' doubts can be heard in titles like *Bad Land* or *The Last Cheater's Waltz*. Behind the spatial explorations described in these books lies the postmodern search not so much to assign meaning to otherness—that seems to have been the moderns' obsession—but to admit the existence of unaccountable, irreducible entities.

Though the books frequently relate quests, these are not ends in themselves; frequently, they cannot be justified by their results in terms of elucidating traces and vestiges.[42] The writer's project is not simply archaeological, even though the investigation of the past is a discipline imposed on the reader. In Rebecca Solnit's words, "It is a refusal to merely flee, forget, and survive. To walk toward the problem is an act of responsibility, an act of return, and an act of memory" (377). The land has to be deciphered in all its discrepancies and upheavals, then exposed and accepted as such. Some of the books studied here do not go beyond that objective. Nevertheless, the very manner in which the writers design their processes of rediscovery is indicative of further intentions; the demystification of the land is also a blueprint for its reinhabitation. Their investigations open up spaces that have been sealed off by the sign of empty, making them available to other possibilities. Their inquiries unlock "an-Other world," described by Edward Soja in relation to Lefebvre's philosophy as "a meta-space of radical openness where everything can be found, where the possibilities for new discoveries and political strategies are endless, but where one must always be restlessly and self-critically moving on to new sites and insights, never confined by past journeys and accomplishments, always searching for differences, an Otherness, a strategic and heretical space 'beyond' what is presently known and taken for granted."[43] In contrast to empty space, which seems to be waiting passively for an impress, an-Other space is located at the intersection of multiple trajectories and becomings, all of which contribute to giving it shape.

Reconnecting with the "beyond" and the "other" also becomes a means of revising the respective values of interior and exterior spaces that had been largely biased in favor of the subject in nature writing's Romantic phase. By opening herself to other geohistories, Solnit is able to perceive "lines of convergence" (23) not only tying the various constituents of a site into a readable text but also installing the subject in a new role, that of a witness, the position that Toedter's photograph invites us to adopt. The witness is neither the explorer nor the adventurer, nor the solitary individual trying to approximate Emerson's "transparent eyeball," nor Bordo's problematic "specular witness" whose gaze "testif[ies] to the condition of wilderness by marking itself as being there at the site of the wilderness";[44] instead, she becomes a responsible actor implicated in her surroundings. These new witnesses merit their roles as guides not by virtue of their association with transcendent values but insofar as they are able to hold together all the contradictions and connections—and to perceive contradictions as connections—in the outside world and in themselves. As Solnit declares in connection with the Nevada Test Site: "Such places bring together histories which may seem unrelated—and when they come together it becomes possible to see new connections in our personal and public histories and stories, collisions even" (24). The spaces the new writers uncover are indeed sites of collision, not of fusion, but out of these collisions comes a new form of energy. The most evident results of that new burst of energy are the books produced. They offer a radical reconditioning experience, but they are also events in themselves as meaningful literary artifacts.

In their attention to imagining new configurations of otherness in places where they had been blanked out, these writers are concerned not with seeking the inaccessible transcendental entity that founds Levinas's ethics[45] but with responding to a more concrete and intractable margin of difference at the very heart of human relations. Despite the imperiousness of the individual's desire to claim all he sees that Bass comically admits to in *Winter*, these writers come to acknowledge that the same space is shared by others with equal rights to occupation. The evidence of this coexistence undermines the discoverers' claims to being the sole agents and operators in sites that are reduced to timeless, unmarked surfaces. They uphold Massey's claim that space is "the condition of both the existence of difference and the meeting-up of the different."[46] The transcendental, pantheistic celebration of self-expansion gives way to more humanly diverse and relativistic interactions in which multi-affiliated individuals encounter difference. Acknowledging the relatedness of everything that shares space means submitting to new ethical and ecological imperatives. We are invited to think beyond the duality of self and other to what Patrick D. Murphy names "anotherness, based on the Another—not the Alien and not the Stranger, but the brother, the cousin, the sister, and not just the human ones, but all the creatures with whom we share the planet."[47]

Writing beyond Dualism: Disclosure

These writers adopt a hermeneutic approach to space implying several related assumptions: space is not self-evidently accessible through description, nor can it be exhaustively revealed; it requires the intervention of implicated observers in order to be deciphered, but these observers cannot be defined as unitary entities. Since they need to be open to the experience of otherness, their identities have to be fluid and porous. We experience places through layers and strata of representations that do not contain a core; they are neither fixed nor immutable. Places change all the time and are bound to be affected by the process of investigation, in the same way the investigator undergoes an existential change as a consequence of his or her inquiry.

These new writers try to express the "betweenness of place," to borrow Entrikin's term;[48] that is to say, their evocations of place are neither wholly objective nor subjective. Indeed, such dichotomous modes of representation are shown to be impossible, since the subject is formed in and by its surroundings in a process of co-creation. These books do not aim to provide either a picture (the lures of perspective) or a subjective appropriation of space, but to chart a more complex dual process in their discovery of zones of convergence and interaction that attest to the land's history. Place is not a tangible material object apart from human subjects but rather a geotemporal palimpsest; subjects are no longer unitary but rather the nexus of multiple responses to and reflections on the things they encounter.

The writing subjects reveal themselves in part through the evocation of their processes of investigation. In this sense their texts may seem to evoke earlier texts chronicling America's discovery; nonetheless, if the discourse of exploration is occasionally cited, it is to comic effect, as seen most notably in *Meadowlands*. If these books deal with discovery at all, it is in the sense of uncovering the traces of the many lives lived in the land. In contrast to the texts relating the discovery of virgin territory, these books take as their mission the disclosure of the complex geohistories that give human sense to place. Discovery supposes that land was pristine and unoccupied, without history and devoid of human trace, while disclosure presupposes the contrary. Discovery seeks the expansion of the subject and the nation, while disclosure aspires to encounters with otherness. Discovery aims at dispossession and appropriation. Disclosure responds to difference by opening to otherness.

The disclosing strategy is double. The writers first reveal what was concealed and relate it to the land's present state; in so doing, implicitly or explicitly, they address a political message to the nation. Their disclosures are never simply backward looking; they always contain a message addressed to the future. Such messages do not pretend to reveal any final and definitive truth about American culture. They are always context and time bound and necessarily provisional. They take part in the nation's ongoing dialogue with its territory.

Disclosure of place takes several forms and modalities. In their initial phase of disenchantment, writers may shift from Romantic expansion and projection upon wild spaces to the depression, indignation, or anger that Bowden and Meloy express. The writers then offer assessments that recapture and analyze the facts that have been suppressed in order to recreate a more complete picture. Sometimes these assessments include indictments that identify responsibilities. Finally, in a reconfirmation of their emplacement, the writers perceive in the alternating processes of erasure and inscription discovered in empty spaces a reason to believe in the exuberance of the American sign and a confirmation of the possibility of renewal.

Along with the historians, geographers, philosophers, and sociologists mentioned in this study, these writers are part of a contemporary cultural movement to rethink humanity's emplacement in the world. Their recognition of the complexity of that emplacement, as both being and putting in place, might be mistaken for a lack of commitment to environmental issues. Nevertheless, the protective, conservative position in which humans were taken to be outside nature although responsible for its stewardship has proved to have only limited effectiveness. In the context of the wilderness movement, this dualistic thinking has provided the rationale for forestalling a number of destructive projects, but it has reached a dead end in the deep ecologists' claim that nature is best left alone. This radical position implies that humans are not natural, that they do not belong in the world.

The writers studied here, especially those treated in Part III, reevaluate the errors of modernity. They are sensitive to postcolonial critiques of the self-serving ideologies that served as the motors for expansion. The dualistic modern divisions of culture and nature, time and space, and fullness and emptiness have driven the colonial enterprise in the past and allowed the exploitation of resources to benefit a fraction of the human species.[49] These writers are descendants of the European peoples who colonized the Americas, but they now understand the exploitative intentions concealed under the dualistic tenets of imperialism. Their attitudes are self-critical and attentive to the complexity of the places they investigate and the mind-sets of other inhabitants. Their role in contemporary debates on the environment is not the charismatic, castigatory position of figures like Edward Abbey. Instead, they have chosen to be the new griots for an amnesiac nation, reminding readers of all that has been suppressed in depictions of the land as empty.

Since theirs is a literary contribution, this study of their works will try above all to account for the ways that they translate spatiotemporal complexity into writing. Two important modes of literary complexity are apparently working in opposition in these works: one tends to establish connectivity; the other aims at creating interruptions and gaps. These centripetal and centrifugal movements correspond to the two vectors of a relation to space that Limerick has described as a constant process of disorientation and reorientation.[50] Taken together, these two antagonistic but intersecting textual movements deconstruct the superficial unilateralism of empty. They disrupt monolithic ideology by introducing relativity.

Scripting Place: Space in and of the Text

Situated at the intersection of a number of discourses, the new literature of place raises certain questions for literary scholars. Is there a literary form of meaningfulness beyond the geographical, polemical, or historical dimensions of these works? Do the authors' personal commitments justify considering their works as artistic achievements? Can the literary critic estimate the value of these works by referring to formal aspects such as structure, intertextuality, and style? New critical categories are needed to respond to these works that weave together multiple discourses into multicentered, polyvocal texts.

Since the aim of this study is to examine how space signifies in the new literature of place, I do not intend to evaluate the correctness of the writers' geographical descriptions, their scientific accuracy, or the political orientations of these texts. Indeed, such a goal would counter my conviction that there is no exterior, objective position from which place can be observed. This is one of the "modern" illusions that Bruno Latour has exposed in *We Have Never Been Modern*.[51] While I cannot ignore the sociocultural theory that explains in generally accepted terms, in the wake of Michel Foucault, how cultural representations of social space reflect the past and present economy of social and political forces, my main task is elsewhere, not because I ignore the dialectic of space as social practice—a topic well documented by contemporary specialists in the geography of social spaces[52]—but because I approach representation from a different angle. I focus on representations *of* space and on representations *as* spaces, not as mere projections of a sociocultural substructure. Writing, just like maps or architectural blueprints, both references real space-time and is itself a constructed space. These works are spatiotemporal constructions whose complexities, puzzlements, unidentified references, and gaps are not to be taken as imperfections but as attempts to convey the undecided, ambivalent quality inherent to the experience of space. In a more immediate, personal, and compelling way than that of the new geographers, the new writers of place capture the vibrant complexity of the sites they write about. Their works prepare us for a new experience of space. In reading them we follow some of the trails through the geohistorical networks that they evoke. As a matter of fact, my own readings can be considered as the marking of trails rather than the definition of patterns. Ultimately, just like the earlier discourses that worked to reduce the complexity of space-time and to represent sites as blank surfaces, these texts will have material consequences. In revising cultural attitudes to the land they will have an impact on the way we live in it.[53]

The new writers I study here manage to reconcile the contradictory objectives of creating an open, labile space on the one hand, and generating a sense of coherence on the other. They create trails leading to and from the sites that are the focus of their works and make temporal references that spiral out of the text's present moment, thereby giving their literary spaces the dynamic quality of the places themselves. Their books seem to follow the precept that Paul Klee discovered in his art and formulated in what he termed "the elementary theory of creativity": "What is good is form-giving. What is bad is form. Form is the end, death. Form-giving is movement, action. Form-giving is life."[54] Like Ellen Meloy's "Map of the Known Universe" in *The Last Cheater's Waltz*, the books give the sense of being explorations in progress. Like all open texts, they invite readers to join in their making, and their performativity as texts is felt even more strongly than in works of fiction. They refer to experiences that we are asked to believe have actually taken place. Instead of being required to suspend our disbelief, we trust that we could enact bodily the same process of discovery that we encounter imaginatively. Hence these texts are guides to enriched encounters in the national territory.

In order to address the vital force of these texts, this study works from the hypothesis that they deploy various scripts rather than forming finished patterns. In other words, they gather events, people, ideas, and places into a textual montage. The unpredictable textual sequencing of scripting offers an alternative to the linear unfolding of history, although that too can be a structuring feature of the literature of place. Writers may follow spatiotemporal continua, but they also break away from them to range more widely and freely through time and space. By compiling multiple scripts, the writers avoid the stasis of straight description and the linearity of autobiography; instead, they construct auto-bio-geo-graphies in which references to actual places are fertilized by human experience, and conversely, mental activity is fashioned by interaction with other-than-human elements. Specific scripts may center on humans to a greater or lesser extent, and their orientation may be referential or conceptual, subjective or objective, but when brought together in the texts studied here, they create a situation of tension and interaction that produces a concerted effect on the reader.

The function of scripting in the new literature of place is not primarily to clarify or formalize issues, to fix agendas, or to define political action. Other texts perform these tasks more effectively. Scripts combine in these works in order to mirror the complexity of the issues involved in our insertion in the world;[55] they suggest that the reversibility of arguments and the relativity of positions always precede the definition of solutions.

"Scripting" designates the writers' practice of reconstructing space-time as text. The term emphasizes both the performativity of textual constructions and the formal specificities of writing about place in a geohistorical mode. A script can be seen as any set of signs or symbols—verbal or pictorial, historical or contemporary, private or public—patterned into a meaningful arrangement. The multiple scripts found in these books form the necessarily unstable assemblages of selected narratives connected with any given space. They stand in direct opposition to the blanking-out process associated with the word "empty." Scripts assume different forms that can cover a spectrum of discourses from "objective" renderings with theoretical and methodological underpinnings to "subjective" evocations relating personal experience in space. The practice of scripting consists in organizing and focusing the discourses that can be or have been produced in response to particular places. Dispersed, erratic, discursive elements are gathered into personally angled texts to produce original representations of those places. The discourses brought together might be myths, anecdotes, newspaper articles, or references from geography, history, or science, but these inquiries are never pursued for their own sake. What counts in scripting is not the resolution of a plot sequence as in novels, nor the collection of exhaustive information as in documentary texts, nor diagnosis and guidance as in political or ecological pamphlets, though these might be the aims of some of the composite types of discourse. Instead, what is vital is the connectivity introduced between the chosen scripts and the infusion of an orientation that produces a degree of coherence in textual space.

As practiced by the new writers of place, scripting is neither a fictionalization of the past nor an explanation of the past from a historical perspective. No attempt is made to make the relics of history hang together to produce a streamlined and conclusive story. The aim is to connect without excluding. The emphasis is on bringing loosely connected things together on the model of Meloy's multileaved "Map of the Known Universe." The resulting texts suggest spatial realities that are based on the rich complexity of networks rather than on hard facts and statistics, dates and decisions, causes and events. The writers do not search for initial causes or teleological or linear developments. Instead they produce something approximating hypertexts in which all the versions of a given event and all the possible interpretations could be fitted together. Like the hypertext, their versions of place suggest an ongoing process that never achieves stasis; everything could have been different previously and everything could be altered from the present onward, and everything will be seen differently depending on the "space-time" that the viewer inhabits. As Mark Tredinnick insists in a discussion of Barry Lopez's work, "Places are never still; they are composed of sets of constantly shifting relationships, including the one between the moving witness and the landforms and lifeforms of the terrain. Places are dynamic, right down to the level of geology and atoms. . . . Lopez's writing makes his places feel alive because he keeps his engagement with them mobile."[56] The writers studied here are also mobile, but they do not simply dynamize their texts by relating their personal trajectories; their scripting introduces movement by shifting temporal and spatial reference points as well as styles, angles of vision, or modes of discourse.

Scripting gathers various strands of space-time into webs of meaning. Writers collect the fragments of stories, fill in gaps, and restore continuity to signs that have ceased to signify. They also investigate erasures and reconstruct the various narratives that have been overprinted by a confusion of superficial signs. They restore variability and indeterminacy to sites that have been fixed or simplified. In suggesting the reach of the various discourses gathered around a particular space, they restore the connections between the local and the global. Their work embraces a hybrid conception of reality that participates in the same intellectual current that Latour or Haraway represent in other fields. Scripting opens texts, aerating previous constructions, interrupting the logic of continuity in order to allow the possibility of otherness, unexpectedness, and unpredictability. By definition alterity cannot be conceived through reproduction of the same; it is what is excluded or de-territorialized. Since it cannot be incorporated as such it must be given space to be anticipated by the readers. In introducing relativity, openings, and multiple perspectives, the new writers demand readers' participation in the making of textual space.[57]

Scripting is a way of resisting fixity while still allowing for connections among multiple points. Of course everything in language is already connected and ready to be reconnected. In that perspective scripting would bring nothing new. But when it comes to representing space, language tends to revert to commonplaces, and phrases simply fall into place. Scripting permits the topical, accidental, and idiosyncratic rendering of an individual's or a community's very specific relation to a place, revealing the stories that it contains or the experiences that it has occasioned. Scripts combine to permit original readings and interpretations of the land. They connect the heterogeneous components—physical, mental, spiritual, or philosophical; concrete or intangible—that converge in lived experience. The imaginative textual connections they allow result in multilayered "mental geographies" that will never be identical for different readers.[58]

Scripting is the least formalized critical concept that can be imagined. Instead of referring to a theory that inevitably becomes the main center of interest, scripts are the itineraries sketched out by the writer and organized by the interpreter. They emulate William James's idea of the mobility of consciousness: "flights and perchings."[59] Like the aleatory movement of consciousness, scripting does not focus arguments toward a conclusion; it regulates the various passages and intervals between noticeable points in texts. Writers can combine scripts at will like the strands in a textile; the thicker the weaving the closer they cling to the multiplicity of experience. In following scripts readers can resist the teleological orientation of texts and instead conceive of them as places to be explored, crisscrossed by the trails the writer has followed.

In responding to these writers' idiosyncratic maps of America's uncharted geohistorical spaces, we confront the contradictions that Massey describes: "Real space (space-time) is indeed impossible to pin down. But anyway, the argument should not really be about content (some patently vain attempt, in an evocation of a simultaneity of stories-so-far, to enumerate each and every one of these trajectories). Rather, it is a question of the angle of vision, a recognition of the *fact* (not all of the content) of other realities, equally 'present' though with their own histories."[60] As readers we respond to the multiple "stories-so-far" gathered in the new literature of place. As a critic one of my aims is to identify the literary techniques that work to suggest the other realities concealed beneath the sign of empty. I will also map some of the paths taken in my reading of the texts and signpost some of the connections and convergences toward which the scripts lead.

In the multiple narratives brought together in these texts there are necessarily discrepancies and contradictions, omissions and deviations. Stories reflecting human interactions cannot be unitary and coherent. Gaps and contradictions create space for the otherness that master narratives occult;[61] they also implicate readers in the construction of new meaning. In their deployment of multiple scripts, the new writers of place reproduce the complexity, the diversity, and the inconsistencies of human adjustments to space. In their postmodern and postcolonial explorations of space-time, a patchwork of discordant, partial, fragmented stories displaces the official national accounts. Besides, there are disparities, overlaps, and always interplay between imaginary and real places, between mythic and commonplace narratives, between collective and individual perceptions of space. There are no global readings of spatial situations, no "world-as-exhibition" according to Derek Gregory's judicious phrase,[62] but rather the collage of a multiplicity of microsituations relaying, interrupting, or reorienting the course of events in order to produce sometimes unpredictable consequences. Taken together these multiple causes and results might give the impression of a global picture. Yet as Patricia Price justly remarks: "The resulting dislocations, discontinuities, and disjunctures work to continually destabilize that which appears to be stable: a unitary, univocal place."[63] In a number of studies sweeping, global statements still prevail because they produce the reassuring impression of being on top of the situation.[64] This is precisely what the new writers of place refrain from doing. Their approach to spatial reality also predicates a shift from the global to the local in the treatment of space. There is no hierarchic progression from local to global, from actions to consequences, or from cause to effects, or even from one historical age to the next; instead, everything is connected in chains of loaded and complex representations that come close to Massey's concept of "throwntogetherness," which she sees as compounded of "multiplicity, antagonisms and contrasting temporalities."[65] The problem with representations is that connections tend to be ruptured, simplified, or subsumed into overarching scenarios that obfuscate the issues. To differing degrees, the writers studied here try to reconnect representations in keeping with the places they consider—hence the emphasis on scripting. They resist the temptation to generalize from the local to the national level. They remain at ground level, where complexity is maximal but also observable.

In bringing together works that treat different sites and situations, I do not mean to suggest that they are carbon copies of the same problem—far from it. Nevertheless, they are all avatars of a complex situation always in process: the mutation of the dual and duplicitous sign of empty. Ultimately, the revised representations of place offered in these texts suggest not only better conceptions of the different localities, but, more importantly, ways to reconnect with the land. Understanding the complexity and multipolarity of our relationship to space is the first step toward finding ways of reinhabiting it, without perpetuating the cycles of emptiness and fullness that have been projected onto the land in the past.

2

Creating the American Nation from a Vast and Empty Chaos

No one would contest the fact that the American continent features geographically distinctive places with a rich variety of natural and cultural habitats. Nevertheless, it is also a fact that from the first years of colonial settlement in North America down to the present day, words like "vacant," "void," "desert," "desolate," "barren," or "uninhabited" have been used to describe the land, vying for place with contrasting descriptions of its bountiful plenitude. The linguistic perplexity that the territory seems to provoke cannot be attributed simply to the disorientation induced by the encounter with novelty.[1] The profusion of signs indicating both the emptiness and fullness of the land bears witness to the European settlers' struggle to inhabit America, to come to terms with its strangeness, and to find their place within it. Emptiness is by no means a geographical feature; it is, instead, a cultural construction that is constantly revised as the settlers' interactions with the land change. By looking at the changing values associated with emptiness and fullness, we can see how the settlers and their descendants adapted their representations to their existence on the continent and, reciprocally, how the continent shaped their culture.

The Colonizers' Invention of Blank Spaces

Generally, the discourse on territorial emptiness formulates projects of colonial expansion. Joseph Conrad's well-known evocation of the phenomenon in *Heart of Darkness* elegantly evokes the way colonization is predicated on conjuring up blank space. Marlow's excursion into Africa has textual origins: "Now when I was a little chap I had a passion for maps. I would look for hours at South America, or Africa, or Australia, and lose myself in all the glories of exploration. At that time there were many blank spaces on the earth, and when I saw one that looked particularly inviting on a map (but they all look that) I would put my finger on it and say, When I grow up I will go there."[2] In Marlow's fantasy of reciprocal determination—"I will go there"—the explorer's presence brings definition to territory that was previously unidentified, while the act of occupation distinguishes the self. The blank space triggers the desire to become a definer, a namer. Entering the territory, even through the imagination, he asserts himself as subject; he creates himself in his interaction with the map and the territory that it delimits. Justifying himself through the mapmakers' division of the world into known and unknown territories, the European colonizer represents himself not as an invader of occupied places, but as the surveyor of emptiness.[3] Depicting space as blank renders it available and in need of human presence. It becomes inscribable; it asks to be claimed and named. Of course the values that are projected onto empty space change according to the definer. Conrad challenges the hegemonic narrative by revealing a "heart of darkness" that mirrors back the savagery at the core of the colonial enterprise.

In the American context, designating space as empty is not exclusively a prelude to expropriation;[4] it is also a means of addressing the difficulties inherent in forging a cohesive society in a newly colonized territory.[5] By defining and redefining what is empty and full, the colonizers construct communities, shape identities, and create projects for the future. The values attributed to the sign of empty shift as the settlers' interactions with the land change. In periods of entrenchment, when what is outside the community's habitual boundaries is considered threatening, emptiness and fullness are dichotomized. In periods of expansion, what was once considered as alien becomes desirable, and the values of fullness and emptiness tend to fuse or invert. From the interaction of the complementary facets of projected emptiness and fullness emerges the constantly mutating, never stabilized national entity. America has always been in process, subject to revision and debate, and hence always in need of validation.

The earliest accounts of the territory that came to constitute the North American colonies are fraught with contradictions, with the land being characterized as both cornucopia and wasteland. Emptiness and fullness converge in the accounts of the first explorers, as the blank space on their maps becomes filled with the projections of their desire and ideals. John Smith's account, *A Description of New England* (1616), admits that the land is mostly "vnknowne,"[6] yet to attract investors, he stresses the land's bounty, even though he admits that his voyage has little to show in the way of profit. Enhanced by his fertile imagination, the coast of Maine holds out "incredible abundance of most sorts of fish, much fowle, and sundry sorts of good fruites for mans vse,"[7] while that of Massachusetts offers "Free stone for building, Slate for tiling, smooth stone to make Fornaces and Forges for glasse or iron, and iron ore sufficient, conveniently to melt in them."[8] The land appears as a source of raw materials for the kind of industry that would make it into a more productive and attractive replica of the Old World.[9] Thus, the blank space of the unknown continent serves as a screen on which to project dreams of prosperity.[10]

For the people who went on to found some of the first English-speaking settlements in New England, emptiness and fullness quickly became dichotomized. When the Puritans arrived from Europe, they brought with them a mode of life that they hoped to implant in a purified form on the American soil. To become Americans the new settlers needed to assimilate an unfamiliar place by first blanking out its particularities and then projecting onto it their own aims. Idealized forms of plenitude took on substance when juxtaposed to a negative void that could be either excluded or reclaimed and transformed. The Puritans saw themselves as leaving behind a corrupt continent to found a model community in a virgin land. To achieve this dream of perfection they needed to imagine their adopted place of residence as a blank page on which to compose their exceptional history. Rather than projecting fullness onto an unknown terrain as John Smith did, the Puritans describe an unpopulated wilderness in need of their civilizing presence to bring it to fruition. In his *History of Plymouth Plantation*, William Bradford writes retrospectively of the settlers' expectations about their destination: "The place they had thoughts on was some of those vast and unpeopled countries of America, which are frutfull and fitt for habitation, being devoyd of all civill inhabitants, wher ther are only salvage and brutish men, which range up and downe, litle otherwise then the wild beasts of the same."[11] Whereas John Smith had described "a goodly, strong and well proportioned people,"[12] Bradford depicts only "wild beasts." This designation contradicts the more complex portrait of Native Americans that appears elsewhere in his *History*, but portraying the land as empty—"devoid of all civill inhabitants"—is the necessary prelude to introducing the "civill body politick" of the Mayflower Compact. That text aimed to fill a legal void—the absence of a patent to settle in New England. Recontextualized within the *History of Plymouth Plantation*, the agreement appears as more than just a charter for governance; it supplies the "human" presence that the wild land calls for.

Thus the early texts create a new American icon, the wilderness, placing it under the sign of empty, and projecting onto it all the settlers' hopes and fears.[13] This "desert" space is ambivalent, since it is both the unredeemed negation of their Christian faith and its new proving ground. This duality is evinced in a document addressed to potential settlers, "Reasons and Considerations Touching the Lawfulness of Removing out of England into the Parts of America" (1622).[14] The text, signed by R. C.,[15] expounds the arguments in favor of leaving England to settle in the new colony, which the author depicts as "a vast and empty chaos."[16] This portrayal evokes the formless matter out of which God shapes the earth in the creation story from Genesis. The term denies the American continent any past and instead establishes it as the unformed material with which to make history. America is a blank slate on which to write a new text.

In identifying their projects for the new land, the settlers contribute to the palimpsestic process through which Americans define themselves in relation to the space they inhabit. An exegetical passage from R. C.'s "Reasons and Considerations" justifies the colonists' designs on the land by advancing the biblically sanctioned motive of "the conversion of the heathens." In this vision of events, the community of immigrants imports its ethics into the "empty" continent to redeem it through proper use:

> Now it seemeth unto me that we ought also to endeavor and use the means to convert [the Indians], and the means cannot be used unless we go to them or they come to us; to us they cannot come, our land is full; to them we may go, their land is empty.
>
> This then is a sufficient reason to prove our going thither to live lawful: their land is spacious and void, and there are few and do but run over the grass, as do also the foxes and wild beasts. They are not industrious, neither have art, science, skill or faculty to use either the land or the commodities

> of it, but all spoils, rots, and is marred for want of manuring, gathering, ordering, etc. As the ancient patriarchs therefore removed from straiter places into more roomy, where the land lay idle and waste, and none used it, though there dwelt inhabitants by them (as Genesis 13:6, 11, 12, and 34:21, and 41:20), so it is lawful now to take a land which none useth, and make use of it.[17]

The writer represents the immigrants' Christianizing mission as a transfer from a full land on the old continent to an empty one on the new. Though bringing the Christian faith to the empty land should be "sufficient reason," the writer adds the argument of the Europeans' project to use the land industriously.[18] He depicts America as full of "commodities," which are said to be laid waste without the virtuous presence of the settlers. This argument anticipates Locke's justification of property rights in terms of the labor invested in the land,[19] as well as later laws governing homesteading and other territorial policies in America. The document suggests the settlers' fears about moving as well as their anxiety about making claims on the American territory. They were certainly not unaware of the question of the indigenous people's entitlement.[20] Their response was to depict the land as wild, barren, and empty, and to advocate the superior claim of those who could extract profit from it.

Emptiness as Opportunity in the New Republic

Given the emphasis in early texts on the idea of proper stewardship and the virtuous use of American space, it is not surprising that agrarian ideals should come to loom large in discourse related to the land. Representations of the earliest settlers as good husbandmen mutated into the Jeffersonian ideal of the yeoman farmer. Moreover, America's independence from Britain brought about a change in the values attributed to emptiness and fullness. The land's emptiness came to signify the promise of opportunity that was stifled in Europe by overpopulation. In *Notes on the State of Virginia*, Jefferson contrasts the Old World, where "the lands are either cultivated, or locked up against the cultivator," to the new Republic, which promises "an immensity of land courting the industry of the husbandman."[21] Jefferson's voice chimes perfectly with that in *Letters from an American Farmer*, in which J. Hector St. John de Crevecoeur depicts Europe as "a crouded society, where every place is over-stocked."[22] For both men, the enticing image of the new

Republic is projected onto a space represented as open and freely available. For de Crevecoeur, America's vastness defies description: "Many ages will not see the shores of our great lakes replenished with inland nations, nor the unknown bounds of North America entirely peopled. Who can tell how far it extends? Who can tell the millions of men whom it will feed and contain? for no European foot has as yet travelled half the extent of this mighty continent!"[23] Though it strains the capacity of language to "tell" about it, the vast expanse of the continent now seems infinitely more inviting than threatening. Like the blank space on Marlow's maps, the "unknown bounds of North America" seem to lie open for the taking. A fertile and freely available land offers itself to the immigrant: "Does he love a country life? pleasant farms present themselves; he may purchase what he wants, and thereby become an American farmer. . . . Does he want uncultivated lands? Thousands of acres present themselves, which he may purchase cheap."[24] In this account, there are no legal or moral restrictions on occupying the American territory;[25] the settler's desire seems to be the primary justification. Effacing the seller's action, the reflexive construction "present themselves" gives the illusion that the land yields itself to the buyer with the bounteous liberality of the naked allegorical figure of America in early depictions of the continent's discovery by Europeans.[26]

Europe no longer offers a template for constructing a community; instead America has become the model. In a reversal of the initial dichotomy, European fullness now equates with corruption whereas American emptiness leads to virtue. For Jefferson, the new nation's "vacant lands" are the key to a virtuous republic founded on agrarian values: "I think our governments will remain virtuous for many centuries as long as they are chiefly agricultural; and this will be as long as there shall be vacant lands in any part of America. When they get piled upon one another in large cities as in Europe, they will become corrupt as in Europe."[27] In de Crevecoeur's eyes Europe is deficient, its territory defined by negation:

> A country that had no bread for him, whose fields procured him no harvest, who met with nothing but the frowns of the rich, the severity of the laws, with jails and punishments; who owned not a single foot of the extensive surface of this planet? No! urged by a variety of motives, here they came. Every thing has tended to regenerate them; new laws, a new mode of living,

> a new social system; here they are become men: in Europe they were as so many useless plants, wanting vegetative mould, and refreshing showers; they withered, and were mowed down by want, hunger, and war; but now by the power of transplantation, like all other plants they have taken root and flourished![28]

The commonplace metaphor of planting, historically used to describe colonization, now naturalizes emigration. Whereas in Europe the majority of the population has "not a single foot" of land and is allotted only the space of the jails, in the ample space of the new republic, these "useless plants" thrive and metamorphose to "become men."

For the early commentators on the American experiment in democracy, the land offered a blank space on which to compose a new, egalitarian society. Alexis de Tocqueville follows the textual tradition of placing North America under the sign of empty. In terms that echo those of the first Anglo settlers and affirm Jefferson's agrarian model, he discounts the Indians' claim to their homelands: "North America was only inhabited by wandering tribes, who took no thought of the natural riches of the soil, and that vast country was still, properly speaking, an empty continent, a desert land awaiting its inhabitants."[29] Unfettered by the claims of custom and precedent constraining European societies, the New World offers the perfect terrain on which a democracy can grow. Its virgin soil allows humankind to begin anew, absolved of all past errors but endowed with the wisdom gained from them: "When man was first placed upon the earth by the Creator, the earth was inexhaustible in its youth, but man was weak and ignorant; and when he had learned to explore the treasures which it contained, hosts of his fellow creatures covered its surface, and he was obliged to earn an asylum for repose and for freedom by the sword. At that same period North America was discovered, as if it had been kept in reserve by the Deity, and had just risen from beneath the waters of the deluge."[30] In its exuberant fusion of Christian teleology and modern political analysis, *Democracy in America* erases the bloody history of invasion, conquest, and colonization.[31] America arises from the seas to greet Columbus; its origin derives from its discovery. Furthermore, "nature herself favors the cause of the people" by offering them her bounty and allowing them to "spread peaceably . . . over those fertile plains."[32] At almost the same moment that Emerson published his essay "Nature," Tocqueville celebrated the United States as a nation favored with the necessary conditions to make democracy flourish. It is nature's nation,[33] an organic product of the soil, liberated from the messiness of human history.

The Invention of the Frontier

In spite of the fabulous promise of opportunity America holds out, the spacious territory of the new republic is not free of menace. The zone on the border between the settlements and the uncharted territory beyond them becomes the focus of American anxieties and aspirations. The dichotomy between full and empty space gives rise to a new hybrid formation: the frontier. Like the idea of empty, the concept of the frontier is a cultural projection. Contemporary historians, notably Patricia Nelson Limerick and Richard White, have explored the much more tangled reality behind the myth.[34] Nonetheless, from an early stage in the nation's history, the frontier began to take on specific contours in the public imagination. De Crevecoeur warns of the threat it poses to the agrarian way of life:

> Now we arrive near the great woods, near the last inhabited districts; there men seem to be placed still farther beyond the reach of government, which in some measure leaves them to themselves. . . . The few magistrates they have, are in general little better than the rest; they are often in a perfect state of war; that of man against man, sometimes decided by blows, sometimes by means of the law; that of man against every wild inhabitant of these venerable woods, of which they are come to dispossess them. There men appear to be no better than carnivorous animals of a superior rank, living on the flesh of wild animals when they can catch them, and when they are not able, they subsist on grain.[35]

At the boundaries between European settlements and uncontrolled wilderness, the guiding influence of the community and the authority of its laws weaken. For de Crevecoeur, these border territories become dangerous zones of contact where humans risk succumbing to the influence of the wild and reverting to an animal state. In descriptions of this frontier society, the negative strains of earlier discourses on the savageness of empty space seep into otherwise affirmative representations of the new republic. The values associated with America's openness and Europe's saturation become unstable at the frontier, and the wild and free lands beyond the settlements threaten to dehumanize those who venture into them.

In the nineteenth century, under the pressure of America's expansion, the values of empty and full became unstable once again. With the prospect of the new republic doubling in size thanks to the Louisiana Purchase in 1803, debate over the wisdom of acquiring the new territory centered on a struggle over its definition.[36] For the Federalists, whose support was in the cities and in New England, the new territory represented a threat to the status quo and a menace to the nation. They depicted Louisiana as an empty wasteland, the home of animals and savages: "an untrodden waste for owls to hoot and wolves to howl in," "the realm of alligators and catamounts."[37] For Fisher Ames, Louisiana was a contaminated space, occupied by a "Gallo-Hispano-Indian *omnium gatherum* of savages and adventurers," no more capable of respecting laws than otters.[38] Like the alien inhabitants who dwelled there, the vast and largely unexplored territory to be added through the Louisiana Purchase was seen as a threat to the very identity of the new republic. Ames eloquently expressed this fear through a spatial metaphor: "We rush like a comet into infinite space. In our wild career, we may jostle some other world out of its orbit, but we shall, in every event, quench the light of our own."[39] In the former congressman's imagination, America becomes a shooting star extinguishing itself in the empty space west of the Mississippi. He imagines the republic breaking away from its foundations and destroying itself in the process. On the other side of the debate, those in favor of the treaty employ hyperbole in a more positive vein. For them the empty territory promises only benefits for the new nation. Louisiana is seen as an "inestimable territory" that presents a "golden opportunity" offering "immense," even "numberless advantages."[40] Thomas Jefferson reconciled these contrasting visions by suggesting that the newly acquired territory would allow the new nation to be purified and consolidated by assigning the indigenous peoples to the new lands, while Euro-Americans could continue to settle East of the Mississippi.[41] In the debate over how to use the newly acquired lands, a new function is assigned to land designated as empty; it becomes a dumping ground for what America refuses.

Later in the century, once the nation became caught up in the excitement of the exploration and development of the vast Louisiana Territory, westward expansion seemed not just judicious but divinely ordained. Occupying the vast expanse from the Atlantic to the Pacific coast was seen, in journalist John O'Sullivan's famous words, as "the fulfillment of our manifest destiny to overspread the continent allotted by Providence for the free development of our yearly multiplying millions."[42] Perceptions of the extensive American territory in the West were shifting from images of emptiness to those of fullness. At the same time, the outer fringes of westward expansion started to mutate in the public consciousness from the danger zone feared by de Crevecoeur into a proving ground for American values. Rather than a threat to American identity, the frontier came to be seen as constitutive of the nation's character. O'Sullivan's influential 1845 article on the annexation of Texas described how the "Anglo-Saxon" settlers were wresting a domestic space "from the wilderness by their own labors and dangers, sufferings and sacrifices." On the frontier, the struggle to occupy and domesticate empty space earned one the right to membership in the American nation.

The Sacralization of Empty Space

At the same historical moment, though, another vision of empty space was in the making. Just as Americans were bringing their vast territory under control by mapping it, parceling it up through the grid system, and constructing roads, canals, and railroads to traverse it, dissenting voices began to question the value of saturating the national space with signs of civilization. A new mutation in values was underway in which uncultivated territory would come to represent a diminishing American treasure to be defended against civilization. Like the European Romantics, America's Transcendentalists found spiritual value in the natural world. Empty space became sacred space, rather than simply the raw material for the making of the nation. One of the best-known expressions of the new reverence for uninhabited places is found in Emerson's 1836 essay "Nature":

> Crossing a bare common, in snow puddles, at twilight, under a clouded sky, without having in my thoughts any occurrence of special good fortune, I have enjoyed a perfect exhilaration. I am glad to the brink of fear. In the woods too, a man casts off his years, as the snake his slough, and at what period soever of life, is always a child. In the woods, is perpetual youth. Within these plantations of God, a decorum and sanctity reign, a perennial festival is dressed, and the guest sees not how he should tire of them in a thousand years. In the woods, we return to reason and faith. There I feel that nothing

> can befall me in life,—no disgrace, no calamity, (leaving me my eyes,) which nature cannot repair. Standing on the bare ground,—my head bathed by the blithe air, and uplifted into infinite space,—all mean egotism vanishes. I become a transparent eye-ball; I am nothing; I see all; the currents of the Universal Being circulate through me; I am part or particle of God. The name of the nearest friend sounds then foreign and accidental: to be brothers, to be acquaintances,—master or servant, is then a trifle and a disturbance. I am the lover of uncontained and immortal beauty. In the wilderness, I find something more dear and connate than in streets or villages. In the tranquil landscape, and especially in the distant line of the horizon, man beholds something as beautiful as his own nature.[43]

This passage rewrites the American discourse on empty space, making "bare ground" a place of elevation rather than degeneration, a site for spiritual rather than material development. Confounding earlier divisions between the uncultivated, unregenerate wilderness and sites redeemed by humanity's civilizing influence (the plantations), Emerson christens the uninhabited lands the "plantations of God." What was formerly abject becomes sublime, inducing in the speaker a strangely liminal state: "I am glad to the brink of fear." In this state, apparent contraries become reconciled: "In the woods, we return to reason and faith." Or they are overturned, so that the familiar becomes "foreign and accidental" and the alien becomes "connate." In uninhabited places, being extends outward into "infinite space," and the subject sees himself reflected in all that surrounds him.

The revalorization of wilderness was not simply a way to revitalize the self or to renew contact with the transcendent; restructuring the values commonly assigned to the empty and the full was also a means to critique the utilitarian mentality of nineteenth-century capitalism. This aim is central to Thoreau's writing. Conscious of going against the national current, he begins his essay "Walking" with what he calls an "extreme statement" proclaiming the value of wildness over civilization: "I wish to speak a word for Nature, for absolute freedom and wildness, as contrasted with a freedom and culture merely civil."[44] Thoreau becomes the advocate of the remaining uncultivated spaces around Concord that his neighbors either shunned or converted to utilitarian ends. Inverting their values, he treasures the "little oases of wildness in the desert of civilization."[45] So, in the preface to *A Week on the Concord and Merrimack Rivers*, he acclaims "the barren sands of a desolate creek." In "Walking" he is the prophet of swamps: "Hope and the future for me are not in lawns and cultivated fields, not in towns and cities, but in the impervious and quaking swamps." Reversing the idea that the advance of civilization means progress, Thoreau finds promise in the resilient vitality of the wetlands. Land condemned as empty and barren becomes full of life in the eyes of Thoreau the naturalist.[46]

Does the Transcendentalist vision of empty space represent a complete revolution in American values? Not entirely. Though often in conflict, the discourses of the Transcendentalists and the Expansionists also echo one another at times. After all, the barren wilderness allows Emerson's spirit to extend outward toward the horizon. In "Walking," Thoreau revels in the idea of moving westward toward freedom. He casts himself as a frontiersman, on the border between the settled and the wild: "Let me live where I will, on this side is the city, on that the wilderness, and ever I am leaving the city more and more, and withdrawing into the wilderness."[47] Nonetheless, Thoreau discovers the limits of the appeal of wilderness in climbing Mount Katahdin. There he finds a form of emptiness that excludes him.

Writing about the experience in *The Maine Woods,* Thoreau delineates the limits of Nature's accessibility to humanity. Above the tree line, among the "hostile ranks of clouds" and "cool bare rocks," the wilderness becomes a threat to humans: "Vast, Titanic, inhuman Nature has got him at disadvantage, caught him alone, and pilfers him of some of his divine faculty. She does not smile on him as in the plains. She seems to say sternly, Why came ye here before your time. This ground is not prepared for you. Is it not enough that I smile in the valleys? I have never made this soil for thy feet, this air for thy breathing, these rocks for thy neighbors. I cannot pity nor fondle thee here, but forever relentlessly drive thee hence to where I am kind."[48] Far from the nurturing woods of *Walden,* in a much more extreme version of the wild, the pleasurable diffusion of self in Nature becomes a painful, even life-threatening depletion: "Some part of the beholder, even some vital part, seems to escape through the loose grating of his ribs as he ascends."[49] Rather than sending him back a reassuring image of himself, the "vast and drear and inhuman"[50] landscape empties him of his substance. Thoreau self-consciously reverts to an older discourse on empty space, depicting the mountain as "a place for heathenism and superstitious rite—to be inhabited by men nearer of kin to the rocks and wild animals than we."[51]

Romantic appreciation of the sublime seems to topple over into the old distrust of emptiness, though this echo of the Puritans is certainly a rhetorical flourish. For Thoreau, Mount Katahdin is too remote from human habitation ("The ground is not prepared for you"[52]); its barrenness allows no room for humanity.

In fact, on the mountaintop Thoreau has perceived something new that he cannot fully articulate. His encounter with land that has never been inhabited and appears truly uninhabitable demands a revision of the valorization of emptiness. Humanity finds a home in places that, like Walden, are already imprinted with the traces of former occupation. Mount Katahdin is devoid of any mark: "Not even the surface had been scarred by man." The emptiness that is indispensable to the definition of America is situated at the interface between settled and unsettled lands; it is incompatible with terrain that is unreclaimable for human life. It is in this sense that we can read the exclamatory passage that concludes the account of the Katahdin adventure: "Talk of mysteries! Think of our life in nature,—daily to be shown matter, to come in contact with it,—rocks, trees, wind on our cheeks! the solid earth! the actual world! the common sense! Contact! Contact! Who are we? where are we?"[53] Although the highly elliptical quality of the fragmented syntax makes the meaning of these lines elusive, the human imprint on the land appears vital for Thoreau. The answer to the questions "who are we?" and "where are we?" is suggested in the imperative "Contact!" Americans need to be grounded to answer both questions; and the barren rock of Mount Katahdin allows no foothold.

By the end of the nineteenth century, emptiness and fullness are no longer opposed as the contrasting zones of wilderness and civilization; they are combined into new formations in which the one fertilizes the other to create new icons of Americanness. New hybrids like the half-savage figure of Natty Bumpo; like Thoreau, bragging "lustily as Chanticleer";[54] or like Whitman, with his "barbaric yawp,"[55] compete for pride of place with the pilgrims or the yeoman farmers. These new hybrid figures find official recognition in Turner's thesis that the settlers' encounter with the land forged this new identity:

> The frontier is the line of most rapid and effective Americanization. The wilderness masters the colonist. It finds him a European in dress, indus-

> tries, tools, modes of travel, and thought. It takes him from the railroad car and puts him in the birch canoe. It strips off the garments of civilization and arrays him in the hunting shirt and the moccasin. It puts him in the log cabin of the Cherokee and Iroquois and runs an Indian palisade around him. Before long he has gone to planting Indian corn and plowing with a sharp stick, he shouts the war cry and takes the scalp in orthodox Indian fashion. In short, at the frontier the environment is at first too strong for the man. He must accept the conditions which it furnishes, or perish, and so he fits himself into the Indian clearings and follows the Indian trails. Little by little he transforms the wilderness, but the outcome is not the old Europe, not simply the development of Germanic germs, any more than the first phenomenon was a case of reversion to the Germanic mark. The fact is, that here is a new product that is American.[56]

With the dangers of the frontier past, the former apprehension that contact with the wild stripped people of their humanity has disappeared. Going native is no longer a hazard to be avoided, but a necessary step in occupying the land. Retrospectively, the encounter with unmapped territory becomes the rite of passage that turns Europeans into Americans. Curiously, for Turner the wilderness becomes an actor in the Americanization process, finding, taking, and stripping the newcomer. Yet while the historian gives the land its due, he ignores the human complexity of occupation, occulting the collaborative role that the Indians played in this adaptation process. At the frontier his settler finds a wilderness emptied of human occupants.

Paradoxically, as the values associated with emptiness and fullness shift, the changes that would earlier have signaled the triumph of civilization come to be seen as losses. At the end of the nineteenth century, the overcrowded cities become a blot on the American landscape and a new topos emerges, the "city wilderness."[57] Published in 1899, Robert A. Woods's book bears this oxymoronic title and describes the poor quarters of Boston's South End as "fit haunts for the depraved and vicious. Evils of all kind find here a congenial soil and produce a rank growth."[58] Numerous remedies are put forward to cure America's teeming slums. Perhaps one of the most surprising is Thomas Seton's *The Gospel of the Red Man,* which revives the figure of the Indian—ironically at the very moment when he is thought to have vanished from the territory—in order to indict the failure of the American system.[59] For Seton, the ideal is not the "pioneer and plainsman"[60] but the indigenous people whom they displaced. With the frontier "closed" and the last battles against the Indian tribes behind them, Americans could begin to appreciate a way of life they had destroyed. By following in the tracks of the Indian, Seton suggests, a failed society can restore itself in the wild.[61] The Indian is to be a guide back to perfection: "Him, therefore, I proclaim as the model for an outdoor life, our travel guide of the fourfold way that leads to perfect manhood."[62] Seton's rejection of the figure of the pioneer represents yet another radical revolution in the values associated with American space. After being acclaimed for bringing European civilization to America, the settlers began to be blamed for their destruction of a pristine continent.[63]

Nostalgia for the Blank Spot on the Map

In the twentieth century, with the signs of the modern age imprinted all over the national territory, the value of emptiness mutates once again and Americans look back nostalgically at the virgin land described by the early explorers. In "The Green Lagoons," Aldo Leopold describes a canoe excursion he took with his brother in 1922 into the delta of the Colorado River. In a characteristically American fantasy of discovery, the brothers imagine themselves retracing the footsteps of the first European explorers of the continent: "For all we could tell, the Delta had lain forgotten since Hernando de Alarcón landed there in 1540. When we camped on an estuary which is said to have harbored his ships, we had not for weeks seen a man or a cow, an axe cut or a fence."[64] Like the early explorers, the brothers name the landmarks they encounter: "The Delta having no place names, we had to devise our own as we went."[65] Nevertheless, Leopold frames this youthful excursion with a nostalgic evocation of loss. To begin with, the place is enshrined in memory: "It is only in the mind that shining adventure remains forever bright."[66] The lagoons cannot be revisited, as they no longer exist:

> I am told the green lagoons now raise cantaloupes. If so, they should not lack flavor.
>
> Man always kills the thing he loves, and so we the pioneers have killed our wilderness. Some say we had to. Be that as it may, I am glad I shall never be young without wild country to be young in. Of what avail are forty freedoms without a blank spot on the map?[67]

In Leopold's revised history of the land, the uninhabited estuary represents a lost paradise and the later agricultural development becomes a form of desecration that has deprived Americans of their birthright. In the twentieth century, America's most prized heritage has become the "blank spot on the map." This blank spot no longer has the same value as Marlow's in *Heart of Darkness*. Whereas in earlier times emptiness called for a civilizing presence, it now evokes the nostalgic memory of a paradise lost. As Jennifer Ladino remarks in describing Rachel Carson's evocation of the pastoral, this rhetorical trope "takes advantage of imperialist nostalgia, the longing of first world countries for the very thing—either a culture or an environment—they have destroyed."[68] These "eco-memories" can be mobilized against new forms of exploitation.[69] Leopold is a case in point: his nostalgia for the plants and animals that once populated his exhausted Wisconsin farm inspired the restoration work he chronicles in *Sand County Almanac*. This effort to reinhabit the land contrasts with the wilderness projects that seek to empty certain places of all traces of human habitation and to create sites that evoke the land as it is imagined to have been at the time the Europeans arrived.

The twentieth century sees yet another turning point in attitudes toward the land and yet another mutation of the values attributed to empty and full. Empty space became institutionalized as an American ideal in the laws instituting the national parks, national forests, and finally the wilderness areas. The utilitarian arguments that once served to justify the occupation of the territory were turned to new purposes in the debate over America's lands. Conservationists like Gifford Pinchot argued that the value of unoccupied terrain came in part from the commodities that it could furnish for society. Wild lands were to be managed, ostensibly in a rational and sustainable fashion. By contrast, preservationists like John Muir opposed the exploitation of the land's resources for any purpose other than recreation, arguing that civilization benefited from its very wildness.

With the creation of the first national parks, "empty" places became national treasures. Emptiness was no longer merely a term to designate sparsely inhabited spaces; instead it was a condition deliberately and systematically imposed on designated spaces where development was proscribed. At the moment of their constitution, the land within the parks' boundaries was purged of its inhabitants.[70] The people who had for centuries hunted on the grounds of Yellowstone, Yosemite, or Glacier National Parks were banished from them. The emptying out of the land was the prerequisite for its reconversion into zones of natural beauty for the delight of the nation's civilized inhabitants and the promotion of a tourist industry devoted to that purpose.[71] John Muir voices this new philosophy in his defense of the Hetch Hetchy Valley against the project to build a dam for the city of San Francisco: "The making of gardens and parks goes on with civilization all over the world, and they increase both in size and number as their value is recognized. Everybody needs beauty as well as bread, places to play in and pray in, where Nature may heal and cheer and give strength to body and soul alike."[72] By the end of the nineteenth century, then, in a reorganization of earlier values associated with emptiness and fullness, the creation of uninhabited areas, American "gardens and parks," became a mark of civilization.

Quickly, though, it became clear that the national parks did not satisfy the twentieth-century American longing for untamed nature. Due to the spread of automotive transport and the ensuing democratization of tourism, their attempt to reconcile emptiness and fullness was doomed to failure. The plenitude of the transcendent sign of nature birthed a different sort of abundance: crowdedness. A movement arose to create wilderness areas that would be protected from mass tourism. Americans began to imagine a purified space completely emptied of the social. Wallace Stegner argues eloquently for this new configuration in his 1960 "Wilderness Letter": "We simply need that wild country available to us, even if we never do more than drive to its edge and look in. For it can be a means of reassuring ourselves of our sanity as creatures, a part of the geography of hope."[73] These words represent an anxious modern departure from the Transcendentalist vision. Humans, God, and Nature are no longer composed of one and the same stuff. The natural and human worlds have split apart, and the rift between them constitutes a form of madness. Stegner's remedy for this modern malaise consists in preserving natural spaces empty of humanity, to whose periphery the majority could "drive" up and "look in" (presumably through the car window) to palliate the sickness caused by civilization. Groping for a rationale to keep wild spaces free from the taint of humanity, Stegner arrives at the inspiring phrase "the geography of hope," endowing empty space with a projected value for the future.

After centuries of discourse denigrating emptiness, demonstrating the utility of keeping wilderness areas free of development of any kind was a daunting challenge. The commodity value of natural resources remained a strong argument in favor of their exploitation. A reply had to be found to claims by ranchers and representatives of various extraction industries that unused land should be kept available rather than "locked up" against them. Hence the 1964 Wilderness Act begins with a passage emphasizing the usefulness of undeveloped land.

> In order to assure that an increasing population, accompanied by expanding settlement and growing mechanization, does not occupy and modify all areas within the United States and its possessions, leaving no lands designated for preservation and protection in their natural condition, it is hereby declared to be the policy of the Congress to secure for the American people of present and future generations the benefits of an enduring resource of wilderness. For this purpose there is hereby established a National Wilderness Preservation System to be composed of federally owned areas designated by Congress as "wilderness areas", and these shall be administered for the use and enjoyment of the American people in such manner as will leave them unimpaired for future use as wilderness, and so as to provide for the protection of these areas, the preservation of their wilderness character, and for the gathering and dissemination of information regarding their use and enjoyment as wilderness; and no Federal lands shall be designated as "wilderness areas" except as provided for in this Act or by a subsequent Act.[74]

The act gives a legal sanction to the split between the natural and the social. At the same time, paradoxically, it implies that wilderness is as much a cultural creation as its binary opposite, civilization. This creation becomes institutionalized through the 1964 act, which redefines wilderness not as a source of commodities to be extracted, but as a potentially inexhaustible resource that can be enjoyed only if left to regenerate itself. The usefulness of wilderness lies in its remaining unused, a paradox that is a sure sign that the duality of empty and full has no stable referent on the plane of reality and that the terms have begun a new mutation in the nation's collective imagination.

The Wilderness Act promises "opportunities for solitude or a primitive and unconfined type of recreation," available on land "retaining its primeval character and influence, without permanent improvements or human habitation," and "appear[ing] to have been affected primarily by the forces of nature, with the imprint of man's work substantially unnoticeable." The new wilderness areas should "appear" as blank and inscribable as the continent once was in the eyes of the first European discoverers. In this simulacrum of emptiness from which all traces of humanity have been expunged, the children of the pioneers can eternally renew the wonder of encountering a virgin continent. The contradictions in this latest avatar of emptiness are perceptible from the outset. It places human beings in the impossible position of being both the saviors and the enemies of the wild.

With this later twentieth-century development in representations of uninhabited territory, the image of Americans' relation to empty space also had to be modified. They needed to be depicted as defenders of wilderness rather than its conquerors. Thus Lyndon B. Johnson announced a new kind of American pioneer, whose purpose was "to preserve some remnants of that wilderness from the onrush of modern civilization."[75] These words suggest a complete reversal of earlier cultural values, since settlement has come to represent a threat to the American territory. The nation now endows its empty spaces with its highest values and measures its own worth by its capacity to preserve them. We can measure the extent of this change in national identity by looking at the speech that Howard Zahniser, one of the primary architects of the Wilderness Act, delivered to the Sierra Club Wilderness Conference in 1951: "We are part of the wilderness of the universe. That is our nature. Our noblest, happiest character develops with the influence of wildness. . . . With the wilderness we are at home."[76] Repudiating the civilization Americans spent centuries creating, Zahniser internalizes the value of emptiness. Home no longer has to be defended against the wild; humans are "at home" in the wild. Paradoxically, in promoting the ideal of pristine land, in which "man himself is a visitor who does not remain," the Wilderness Act seeks to protect this new American "home" from its very owners.[77]

Empty Land as Dumping Ground or Artist's Canvas

Of course this new model of idealized empty spaces does not preclude the resurgence or the mutation of earlier constructions of emptiness. In the debate over the areas to be chosen as dumping grounds for the Nuclear Age, all the negative terms associated with emptiness resurface, to be countered by discourses that affirm wilderness. The Euro-American prejudice against arid lands as incompatible with human culture serves as an argument for concentrating nuclear waste in the Nevada desert. The old, negative terms deny the area any value other than its utility as a repository for all that civilization rejects. In a study of newspaper articles reporting the debate over using Yucca Mountain to stock the nation's nuclear waste, Larsen and Brock found that the farther away the readers lived, the more their local newspapers resorted to negative clichés such as "'desert,' 'remote,' 'desolate,' 'isolated,' and 'barren.'"[78] By projecting emptiness onto certain lands, contemporary consumer culture creates wastelands in which to dispose of unwanted refuse.

The desert is also a privileged site for the new constructions of and in space that are subsumed under the term "land art." Some practitioners of this art interact with the land in ways that are compatible with the new wilderness ideology, leaving no permanent traces of their activity. Generally, though, the willingness to create completely ephemeral artworks is found more readily among European artists.[79] In a tendency that is reminiscent of earlier ways of responding to the territory, American land artists use the land as a blank surface available for transformation, often with the kind of heavy equipment used in extraction industries. These are the artists that interest William Fox in his book *The Void, the Grid and the Sign*. Fox represents the Great Basin landscapes as blank pages ready for human inscriptions.[80] For Fox, Michael Heizer is one of the consummate artists of desert places, and his work opens a metaphysical space to observers: "It articulates the void and allows us to enter it."[81] Whether the sculptor shares the same view is debatable. Heizer explains that he chose Nevada as his worksite "not . . . because the mountains are pretty, but because it has the materials I need, the rock and gravel and sand."[82] The signs Heizer creates are ambivalent and controversial. Do they represent an enhancement or a desecration of the landscape? Are his gestures merely self-serving or do they hold meaning for his fellow Americans?[83] How significantly different are they from the exploitative operations carried out in the desert whose traces on the desert's surface Fox describes as "in your face and horrifyingly beautiful"?[84] In the face of this ambiguity, perhaps the value of Heizer's art resides in the questions it raises about Americans' relationship to their land.

From Blank Page to Palimpsest

From the early texts describing the wonders and terrors of the newly discovered continent to the latest controversies about what to do with "deserted" lands, the concepts of emptiness and fullness have shifted and mutated in America's ongoing debate about the nation's territory. Though it has never described an actual situation, the discourse on emptiness has served as a basis for the culture's projections. It has produced the central cultural topoi of the wilderness and the frontier, though the meaning of these imaginary spaces has never been stable. Imagining the land as empty has been a way of starting over, of creating new projects and new definitions of what it means to be American. The idea of emptiness has underwritten the worst predations but has also inspired the noblest aspirations. Necessarily, it has nurtured the national tendency to amnesia, for it requires the blanking out of traces of past interaction on and with the territory. The American discourse on emptiness is hostile to the recollection of the multitude of stories-in-the-making that constitute space.

Calling a place empty liberates it for new inscriptions, occulting previous signs of habitation and making it available for new inventions. While the process sanctions America's forgetfulness of other inhabitants and of its own past, it ensures the nation's legendary inventiveness and mobility. The trouble with the American fascination with the idea of emptiness is that it makes habitation problematic. Getting to know a place means acknowledging that it is not a blank page but a palimpsest, shaped by successive layers, folds, and intersections of historical activity. As geographers and historians have come to recognize, land is not simply spatial; it is spatiotemporal. The markings inscribed on its imbricated strata are not effaced after each inscription; instead, they produce accretions of meaning that demand a new conception of fullness.

The idea of space constituting a blank page is an untenable proposition. The layers of occupation do not efface those that have preceded, nor can they be considered as radical rectifications. They overwrite one another, producing a complex, palimpsestic text that, when read attentively, permits the study, interpretation, and re-envisioning of past and present problems of inhabitation. In that perspective, the sign of empty becomes an invitation to discover accumulated vestiges of former occupation and to arrive at a humbler but truer appreciation of one's own place. To begin to imagine an ethical relation to the land, Americans need to explore the complex palimpsest it offers and to discover there the imprint of past relations. To address the problem of competing claims to the land, they need first to consider it in its full complexity. In this new way of thinking about space, the traces of the past, whether in the form of texts, stories, or material remains, are vital in retrieving the evidence of those interactions with the land that the representations of fullness and emptiness have tried to obliterate.

This rapid sampling of the many layers of discourse on America's empty spaces hints at the land's complex history of occupation. However, a much vaster enterprise of excavation is necessary to expose the problems pertaining to the concept of empty. This is the task that the new American writers of place confront. Increasingly, American writers are choosing to look beyond the sign of empty attached to favored or neglected sites and instead to pay attention to the complex interweave of discourses and inscriptions that overlay them. In so doing, these writers create new ways of relating to place. Site by site they are replacing the dualistic signs of empty and full with more complex geohistorical mappings. I will now turn to a selection of these works in order to investigate the new trend in American representations of space.

II.

Seeking New Connections

3

Becoming Committed to Place in Rick Bass's *Winter*

From the Transcendentalists onward, nature writers have advocated the withdrawal to America's unsullied empty spaces as an antidote to the ills of society. The belief in the salutary effect of such places has affected political decisions governing the territory: first, the establishment of the national parks, and then, the creation of the Wilderness Act. In protecting selected pristine natural sites from the corrosive effects of modern industrial life, the argument goes, America guarantees its citizens places of escape, liberation, and fulfillment. Rick Bass's adventures in Montana, recounted in *Winter*, begin in this spirit; he and his girlfriend, Elizabeth, set out to find a remote spot that will be "the ideal 'artist's retreat'" (1), a place of isolation and personal expansion. Shaped like a writer's journal, *Winter* relates the experience of finding the ideal spot and of breaking away from a typically modern life, only to discover, paradoxically, that contrary to the ideology of personal development through isolation, individual survival depends on creating new bonds. *Winter* is not about living alone in an empty space, but about discovering the need for neighbors and for an attachment to a place. In the Yaak Valley, humans and nonhumans form an interdependent community of interests. Thus, in contradistinction to the wilderness ideology, rather than opposing nature and society Bass describes how he learns to fit into the ecology of the Yaak. Instead of simply reversing the traditional split, *Winter* tentatively points the way to a transformation of the perception of space in contemporary America. Humans are not separate from the natural world, faced with the options of either preserving it by leaving it alone or else destroying it. On the contrary, they are profoundly involved in the definition and transformation of the land, while, at the same time, the particular conditions of the biotope foster specific social formations.

The search for new ways to inhabit the land goes hand in hand with the pursuit of new ways to write about it. At first glance, *Winter* seems to emulate the form shaped by John Muir in *My First Summer in the Sierra*:[1] it concentrates on a single season spent in one place, and it contains daily entries relating selected experiences. There are many differences, however. Whereas Muir focuses on how the immediate encounters in the California mountains connect him with what he takes to be the eternal truths of nature, Bass deals rather differently with time. His dated entries are somewhat more sporadic and his thoughts often spiral back to the past and to other places. Encounters with fellow humans and engagements with tools figure as much in his book as meetings with the many entities that Muir calls "Nature's . . . people."[2] Within the journal format, Bass arranges multiple scripts that produce something very different from an individual's communion with the natural environment. *Winter* relates a person's adjustment to an environment, and it shows how the many encounters that take place there reshape the individual. The book's multiple scripts do more than describe a single season; together they cohere into something like an environmental bildungsroman or an apprenticeship in habitation. Initially, Bass casts himself as an explorer and discoverer, but he maintains an ironic distance from his dream of finding virgin territory to occupy. Then, he stages his discovery of the networks joining people, plants, animals, and things that all have their place in the ecology of the Yaak Valley. In so doing, he suggests the personal changes brought about through his interactions with the community. In the course of a season he begins to understand what it means to become responsible to a place.

The Dream of an Empty Valley

The script that opens *Winter* is suffused with the self-mocking humor that characterizes Bass's autobiographical work. The first-person narrator sets the account of his move to Montana with Elizabeth in the frame of America's romance with westward movement and the dream of finding unsettled land. Nevertheless, his ironic self-reflexiveness subverts this clichéd cultural scenario. The couple's quest takes them across the map of Western states—Texas, New Mexico, Arizona, Colorado, Utah, Idaho—but they are initially frustrated, finding that places are either too crowded or too forlorn. Finally, in Montana, they penetrate "deeper and deeper into the last and largest spot of unroaded green on our highway map" (5). They are drawn to the blank space on the map, so dear to Aldo Leopold and to other Americans before and after. Like so many writers before him, most notably Thoreau, Bass admits to feeling the magnetic attraction of the wild: "We wanted a place of ultimate wildness" (1). He humorously undercuts the uncompromising exuberance and the naive absolutism of that desire in the subsequent remark that "if there was an indoor swimming pool and maybe some tennis courts on the premises and a little garden, well, that would be all right too" (1). This sybaritic wish for some of the comforts of civilization is partially granted in their discovery of the Fix ranch; indeed, the couple finds a place that offers plenty of room to live and write in exchange for caretaking responsibilities. Still, the prologue voices their Romantic longing to escape from society and to renew contact with nature.

In scripting their exploratory journey Bass invites readers to share vicariously in their first view of the valley. The text unveils the place in the form of an epiphany. After moving laboriously through the landscape ("driving, climbing"), the couple halts before a sudden, miraculous vision:

> We kept driving, climbing, and then we came down off the summit and into the little blue valley.
>
> There was nothing but a mercantile and a saloon, one building on either side of the street, and a slow winding river working through the valley (a cow moose and her calf standing in the river behind the mercantile)—and still no sign of life, no people. It was as if they had all been massacred, I thought happily. We knew immediately that this was where we wanted to live, where we had always wanted to live.
>
> We had never felt such magic. (5)

Like Moses looking into the Promised Land, Bass first sees the Yaak Valley from a mountain summit and immediately falls under its spell. The poetic words that describe "the little blue valley" transmit its magic to readers. The apparent emptiness of the place is partly what enchants him; he exults in the absence of any sign of life, even humorously relishing the thought of a massacre. Nevertheless, this description also makes the falsity of the impression readily apparent, for the buildings announce the human presence in the valley. The dream of emptiness is clearly an illusion or a willed distortion, induced by the dismissal of the marks of human presence.

The "dream" script draws on the lexicon of romance to express the dizzy intoxication of discovery. Blind to the reality of the place, he is buoyed up by the first rush of love and anticipation, and flooded by elation: "I felt freer and fresher and more daring, more hopeful than I can ever remember feeling. . . . It was like going into a battle, or falling in love, or waking from a wonderful dream, or falling into one: wading into cold water on a fall day" (7). The clash of conflicting sensations and the mixture of the oneiric and the real alert readers to the contradictions at work. The writer strains to convey the newness of the situation; he seems to return to a state of innocence in which experience cannot adequately be put into words, and yet the words he finds—"battle," "love," "dream"—are the familiar motifs of romance.

Initially, the feelings of elation that Bass describes seem perfectly attuned to those expressed by Muir in his most lyrical writings. In fact, in one of the early journal entries (September 25), he endorses Muir's description of the water ouzel from *The Mountains of California*, exclaiming, "Exactly! In a hundred years—in this narrow canyon in extreme northwestern Montana, anyway—ouzels haven't changed. I feel spirited back in time, whisked away into the past. This is why we have come up here, to find an unspoiled ouzel" (32). This passage almost seems to echo the Romantic idea of a bird representing eternal, unchanging nature, except that Bass's ouzel is more threatened than Keats's nightingale; it is confined to a contracted space, and the assertion that it is "unspoiled" suggests that elsewhere wildlife is diminished. This admission tacitly expresses the modern attitude to wilderness evoked in the preceding chapter; protecting selected spaces from the destructive influence of humanity is a way to preserve a small part of America as it was in the past, before the incursion of civilization.

In passages like this, one might be tempted to consider Bass as a conventional nature writer, but that would be a mistake. First of all, the sense of loss pervading these lines mitigates their expansive celebration of the natural world. Second, Bass's own description of the ouzel has a radically different tone from Muir's. He describes the bobbing bird with metaphors drawn from the modern industrial world: "There is one water ouzel, just one, who sits on the mossy boulders and bobs up and down, exactly like—the Romantics, whoever they were, would slay me for thinking this—the movement of an automatic stapler, straight up and down like the little bird in a cuckoo clock, a rhythmic, mechanical curtsy. It's as noticeable a movement in the still, heavy woods, among the swirl and confusion of the waterfall, as a neon billboard" (31–32). The writer brings contemporary frames of reference to bear on the things he sees. In grafting the mechanical onto the natural, he makes the bird into a comic hybrid. He thereby positions himself in relation to the past with a postmodern playfulness, displaying both self-reflexivity and self-derision.

If one considers only the themes that he touches on, one might erroneously consider Bass to be in agreement with previous nature writers, as suggested by Peter Matthiessen's words quoted on the book's jacket: "A joyful celebration of solitude . . . a marvelous book in its unpretentious marveling at self and nature."[3] Nevertheless, the apparent similarity does not account for the subversive hints found in Bass's allusive discourse. His "dream" script plays on two registers: his obvious elation at emulating his nature-loving predecessors is often shadowed (and enriched) by the doubts, vague inklings, and contradictions that make *Winter* so intriguing, revealing, and authentic. The impressionistic, fragmented diary charts an individual's growth, but it also yields up a confession that reveals as much through its fumbling formulations as through the ideas and themes developed. *Winter* contains the tangible traces of a mutation that the writing "I" experiences and observes but never completely explicates.

Rather than the transparent subject communing with nature, feeling part of the cosmic whole, Bass's autobiographical "I" is divided and prone to doubts. The "unspoiled ouzel" makes him happy because it transports him away from his quotidian cares, yet those concerns resurface continually. The natural and the social are not separate in spite of the cultural imperative to split them into a binary pair. The experience of the self in nature is felt as a loss of the social self, yet the two poles are ever present in the writer's mind, as we discover in untangling the complex intertextual play in this script: "It's better than reading a novel, this spinning sense of loss, of good loss, of transport to other worlds—and it's certainly better than writing one" (32). In spite of the affirmation that he is transported away from the world of writing, the "spinning sense of loss" refers back to Bass's reflection on Raymond Carver's poem "Looking for Work," in which the speaker wakes out of a blissful dream of a waterfall into his everyday life. In Bass's reversal of this opposition, the ouzel he finds swimming in the waterfall transports him away from his everyday work of writing. Ironically, though, the journal entry brings the writer and the ouzel back into the realm of words. Moreover, in Bass's recounting of his solitary hike to the waterfall, the sense of escape is temporary; it brings on a return of what has been repressed, and other thoughts intrude: "I watch the ouzel for so long, and with such pleasure, that I begin to feel guilty" (32). The clock is ticking as the writer contemplates the bird, and his conscience calls him back to other concerns.

Indeed, Bass does not depict himself solely as the solitary subject that Matthiessen sees; his identity is more complex and relational: "Muir wrote that the ouzel is usually found alone, and that's what this one is. I'm alone too, having left Elizabeth back at the cabin, and am both missing her and exulting in the emptiness, the deep wilderness" (32–33). In a confession that is uncharacteristic of nature writing, Bass admits that his mind is in two places at once, both in "the emptiness" and "back at the cabin." Indeed, the thought of solitude brings on a yearning for sociability. The couple's impressions of plenitude and self-expansion in empty space are mitigated by inexpressible sensations of loss: "And sometimes, being human, Elizabeth and I have to ask, What are we missing? Usually the easy answer, the quick one, is not a damn thing. But some days—here, as everywhere, I think—a longing sweeps into the valley like a haze. But we can't define it, can't pin it down—and it passes soon enough" (40). This hazy longing, at times strong enough to fill the whole valley, points to something that is absent from traditional nature writing, not explainable in terms of the ideology that holds up the empty space of wilderness as the prime site of individual fulfillment. By evoking the inexpressible, Bass suggests that the wilderness philosophy he has inherited leaves something unaccounted for.

The account of the couple's ardent quest for emptiness and solitude contains an undercurrent of misgivings that surfaces from time to time from beneath the ebullience of their euphoria at finding the place of their dreams. The double dimension of their paradisiacal retreat in the Yaak Valley appears at the outset, when the woman showing them the ranch announces that she and her husband are looking for a couple to replace them as caretakers. Bass can hardly contain his joy; the offer seems too perfect: "Was some sort of trick being played on me? My heart was racing and I could barely speak, and when I did, my voice did not sound like it belonged to me" (7). Nevertheless, the ranch resembles Arcadia only for the newcomers, not for the family about to leave it; the woman's husband is unsuccessfully seeking work in the neighboring town while she tries to scratch out a living by keeping a vegetable garden and raising chickens that are inexplicably dying on her. Their decision to leave the ranch is not surprising. In retrospect, Bass recalls something strange about the person who shows them the ranch: "Thinking back on it now, I realize that the woman seemed a little frantic, delighted for the company, and often seemed to be addressing some third party, which sometimes appeared to be just in front of us and at other times just behind us. She never seemed to get the perspective of eye contact and spoken sentences down correctly" (6). The choice of emptiness seems to have produced a phantom "third party," representing all that has been excluded or occulted. This ghostly absence anticipates the haze of longing that Bass discovers later.

The newly arrived writer (not the perceptive, retrospective chronicler of his adventures) persists in caressing his dream of joyful inhabitation and literary creativity: "What a wonderful place that greenhouse would be to write in" (6). Nonetheless, the ambivalent issues are raised and the scene is set for the progressive education of the young couple into the reality of place. What strategy will enable them to fend off the fate of the departing couple? What are the right ingredients for their successful installation? *Winter* is a kind of accelerated bildungsroman in which the protagonist reconstructs himself through his interaction with place. Despite the fairly familiar scenario in which the individual leaves his position in society to test himself in a remote spot, *Winter* blazes a new trail through the myths and stereotypes about the American wilderness. In facing the challenge of overwintering in his Montana retreat, the writer finds himself more and more involved in the community and the country around him. The book reverses the plot of the social romance; instead of staging the hero's entry into society, it depicts his rediscovery of his social engagement in fleeing from it.

The experiences described in the book reverse or rewrite many of the traditional themes of nature writing. The first idea put to the test is the illusion of emptiness. The young couple's initial impression of the valley as containing "no sign of life, no people" (5) is deliciously naive and thus indicative of Bass's ironic distance from the discovering personae: "It was as if they had all been massacred, I thought happily" (5). The desire for emptiness is acknowledged here but exposed as both selfish and symptomatic of blinkered vision. Continuing in this vein of retrospective irony, the writer expresses his careless insouciance about the human community in which they have taken up residence. The entry for September 24 describes the neighborhood of the ranch, with the tiny town of Yaak nearby, the river flowing through it, and, to the south, the slightly larger mill town of Libby. Speaking of the road that connects them to the bigger town, the writer exults in the thought that in winter it fails to function as a route: "The lovely thing about the road to Libby—the road to the big city—is that, so I'm told, it's often impassable in winter. Our valley can become marooned, snowbound" (28). In his desire for isolation, he ignores the concerns of other residents. The exaggeratedly selfish wish to preserve the newly found haven continues in the discussion of the Noranda Mining Company's plans to open a silver mine nearby: "If and when the mine goes in and Libby begins to fester and boil, it'll all be over on the other side of the mountain from Yaak. We'll be back up in the woods, Elizabeth and I, up in the snow, unable to see what's going on and trying to put it out of our minds" (29). In both these examples, snow serves as an image of the blanking-out process that maintains the illusion of a flawless natural site from which the polluting effects of civilization are excluded.

Emptiness is clearly an invention, a false impression that depends on cropping out unwanted elements, as in landscape photography. Bass's *Winter* works both to produce the illusion and to expose it as such: "I am starting to breathe fast. This doesn't belong in a journal of winter, a journal of peace" (28). The contradictions in the couple's position are readily apparent. For example, even though they want to cut themselves off from the aggravations of the town, the couple happily use the unattended tennis courts on the outskirts of Libby, enjoying the Indian summer and exulting in their good luck: "We have stumbled into the pie, Elizabeth and I, finding this valley, this life. We have fallen into heaven" (30). The illusion of paradise depends on their selectivity; they will take Libby's tennis courts but not its silver mine. Moreover, even the Yaak Valley bears the marks of intensive human use that the writer admits to at rare moments. Fish are scarce in its picturesque river because the gravel bed has silted up, making it inhospitable to trout eggs: "Massive clearcutting up on the north fork of the valley has washed sediment into the river" (25). The clear-cuts and the mines mentioned in this section of the book undo the illusion of a pristine environment, untouched by humans, an empty wilderness.[4] They also refute the idea that there could be a place away from it all, cut off from civilization. The Yaak Valley is connected to other sites through complex ecological and social networks.

It soon appears that the place of their dreams is far from being empty or deserted; instead, it is a sparse but thickly knit community of neighbors with a social center, the Dirty Shame Saloon, and the towns of Libby and Troy in the near distance. More important than its situation is the way in which the locale and the rigorous climate have given rise to a social group: a specific community that integrates privacy and independence, individuality and cooperation. As a matter of fact, because of their ignorance and their inexperience, the newcomers appear as the weak link in a network of relations that is entirely self-supportive. Progressively, as they become accustomed to the place and its inhabitants, the couple come to appreciate the proximity of people, the density of their presence, their stories and lives, the warmth of their periodic get-togethers for football matches or communal events like the hilarious Thanksgiving dinner (93). Nevertheless, these collective events are few and far between. The reduction of social niceties throws into relief the common bond of humanity among the people of the Yaak Valley. The country's rigorous winter reduces socializing to a minimum, exposing all the more clearly the mutual lines of dependence. Language, the primary means of communication, disappears as if the snow could muffle human voices and prevent all unnecessary intercourse, reducing existence to its bare essentials: "A country of mutes, but also of doers, not sayers" (128). Help is spontaneously given rather than solicited: "Actions are the way to communicate, not words. It's simple. If someone *wants* to tell you what time it is, or *wants* to pull your truck out, he will" (128).

Instead of the split between society and wilderness that initially shaped the site of his dreams, the writer discovers a new form of inhabitation allying humans and nonhumans. Progressively, he abandons the dream script for new forms of discourse that acknowledge the exchanges between people, their tools, and the land that are necessary for survival. The inhabitants of the Yaak Valley govern their actions by observing everything around them: "The consensus, unanimously so, is that this is going to be a fierce winter: fuzzy deer already, men's beards growing faster, old people feeling it in their bones, their hearts; the way stars flash and glimmer at night; the way trees stand dark against the sky" (18). The whole of the environment appears animate, interrelated, and responsive, with men, deer, stars, and trees reacting together. Moreover, in addition to needing each other, the inhabitants depend for their existence on the trees and animals in the surrounding territory.

Making Connections

In a clear departure from the ideology underpinning many nature texts, individuals in the Yaak Valley have not forsaken society; on the contrary, they rely on it to continue. Civilization and its advantages are not only necessary for survival; paradoxically, they are also as indispensable to independent living as the valley's natural resources. Although the writer confesses that he is a defector—"I'm hiding up here—no question about it" (92)—he encounters a number of people with the kind of experience that he does not have, and he is hungry for their knowledge. After meeting one couple (Tom and Nancy Orr), he admits: "I want to ask both of them questions all day long, all winter—about dream hoops, about ravens, about trapping" (17). The animal population educates him too; their changing coats warn him of the coming winter: "I think that I can learn" (18). Indeed, Bass is not a loner but a learner taking advantage of others' experience, gathering the information he needs to survive in the valley.

More than a group of dissenters, the people of the Yaak Valley are a community of disgruntled idealists who try to recreate a different form of collectivity. Their aspirations are formulated in very tentative terms: "We've all had run-ins with society, with crowds. We've all always been able to hear something better, something different, whizzing just above our heads—a sort of buzzing feeling in the back of our minds, sort of a crackle—and for a long time we did not know what it was, weren't sure what was going on. It was always up there, though, just beyond us, just always out of reach" (96–97). This realization of the group's shared but inexpressible aspirations comes during the account of the Thanksgiving dinner, when the scattered individuals come together for a festive celebration. The implication is that whatever unnameable thing had been out of reach in the past, it is now attainable. Since that "something different" was not available in society at large, the

English language lacks the words to describe it. It can be evoked only with unintelligible sounds and motions—"whizzing," "buzzing," "a crackle." It seems, though, that the group has found what it was seeking in the "country of mutes," in the community that needs no words to bind it together.

With time, Bass realizes that his beloved solitude is not so much an escape as a roundabout way of reconciling him with humanity by putting him in contact with similar souls: "I'm supposed to be a hermit, but what a half-assed hermit I'm turning into: running away to the woods in order to discover that I love people, friends" (99). Far from being a hermit, he discovers that he identifies closely with the place and its people: "It has everything to do with people, as well as the land, up here—even though there's only thirty or so of us. It's like we're a *herd*" (68). The herd does not admit of individuality but only cooperative membership aimed at accomplishing the same purpose of surviving in their given habitat.

Rather than representing himself as the typical nature writing protagonist—the isolated individual communing with the land—Bass constantly refers to a social network that extends all the way back to his family in the South. He discovers the Yaak with his girlfriend and dogs, sharing his experiences and emotions with them. The prologue ends with his apprehensions on leaving his Southern home, comically shared with his canine companions: "The dogs I could tell were worried too, and missed Mississippi. I could tell they thought I was making a mistake" (8). Fittingly, the book concludes with a visit from the Southern family, a sign of the general acceptance of the couple's new emplacement. Bass voices his awareness of people's need for social grounding, for example when he buys Elizabeth a local newspaper and, after watching her read it through twice, concludes: "I'll have to keep an eye on her, take care of her. We'll have to take care of each other" (106). Far from bringing independence, then, the new setting makes the writer aware of people's interdependence and their responsibility for one another.

In another significant departure from the nature writing tradition, in *Winter*, the writer's connection with the natural world is not restricted to the senses (and primarily the eye). A vital mode of contact comes through the possession and the correct handling of tools and machines. Indeed, at times the book reads like a catalogue and instruction manual for all kinds of necessary implements for the rugged outdoor life. There is a wealth of details about the nature, structure, and use of equipment like CB radios, generators, transmissions, and pickups—accessories that are never mentioned in nature writing but which become essential in the Montana context. Bass has a particular affection for his chain saw. The entry for October 5 begins by declaring its make and number, its color and its origin. Its mystique comes from its power—"It's big and strong, a wild horse, and I'm scared to death of it"; from its technical perfection—"My Stihl starts like a fine car, fuel-injected, and rumbles nicely with a throbbing, rattling purr when it's set on slow idle"; and from its mechanical intricacy—"It's complex and has all sorts of tricks and gimmicks" (61). Such descriptions, as well as several long, highly technical sentences quoted from the user's manual, introduce a form of discourse that is alien to contemporary paeans to empty spaces. Usually, the only equipment admitted in nature writing texts is of the low-tech variety: backpacks, sleeping bags, at most a canoe. Thoreau needs a little more than that to build his cabin at Walden Pond, but he makes it a matter of pride to manage with as little as possible. By contrast, Bass discovers that possessing a good stock of equipment is essential to his peace of mind: "Own two of everything, says the landlord, and Elizabeth and I are taking him up on it: two trucks, two axes, two radios, two generators, extra food, extra light bulbs, extra gloves for when one pair is wet, extra boots, extra tire chains, extra firewood, and extra luck" (120).

Besides being characterized by the richness of its flora and fauna, life in the Yaak Valley is conditioned by the strict execution of a checklist of "Things to do" (16) and the adherence to a set of rules. In one of the early journal entries, the writer draws up a list of the indispensable accoutrements of a logger (16), information that is certainly unusual in any discussion of wilderness. Near the end of the book the writer reflects on what his winter experience has taught him: "It's taken me a long time, but I'm finally learning" (151). What follows is a list of the necessary equipment and gestures to ensure survival.

All these technical details sound particularly unromantic and even coarsely materialistic, like a Sears catalogue, but they are fundamental to understanding Bass's new approach to the environment. His willingness to mention them may seem like either artlessness or provocation to readers accustomed to the traditional nature writers' raptures. Yet emphasis on equipment and protective clothing demonstrates that contact with the elements and the land is not a hedonistic adventure; it is on the contrary a chastising experience in which one is made conscious of one's body through direct and frontal contact with reality. The writer mentions bruises, accidents, injuries, aches and pains: "No one up here has a full set of teeth" (116). These wounds are the tokens of humanity's necessary intercourse with the world, and the resulting marks and scars constitute the record of initiation and acceptance.

Similarly, the writer seems to fully experience the Yaak's trees and animals not by detached observation but by direct, head-on confrontation. Tools are an extension of his body and a means of access to the living substance of other beings. The writer relishes the sensuous contact that they afford. He even fantasizes about cutting into the center of larches and consuming the wood: "The heart of these felled trees is a luxuriant amber-orange, like pumpkin meat. The wood burns hot and good, clean and fast: nothing burns like old dead dry larch" (41). As the tree yields up a substance as life giving as food, the comparison to pumpkin meat is doubly appropriate. At the end of winter, Bass exults in the pleasure of drawing a hoe through the earth, a guilty indulgence because it feels like "an act of infidelity" to winter (158). The tool permits the sensuous entry into the womb of the earth: "The motion of it: pulling the sharp hoe through the earth, the earth furrowing and rising, a trail appearing, and then chopping at the earth, and the earth turning up, loose and willing, soft, under the surface, piling up, ready to be planted" (158). The syntax dissolves the subject-object relation into an interactive duet in which the earth is both actor and acted on. The world is caressed and revealed thanks to the transformative power of human tools.

Unlike that of Transcendentalists and their descendants, Bass's participation in the natural world is not restricted to loafing and contemplating but demands work and struggle. The writer shares a discovery that mirrors Richard White's insight that "our work—all our work—inevitably embeds us in nature, including what we consider as wild and pristine places."[5] Living in the Yaak Valley requires labor. In admitting this fact, Bass distinguishes himself from the many nature writers who represent their engagement with the land as a series of leisure-time excursions during which all practical cares appear to have been set aside. Even Thoreau, in laboring to be as self-sufficient as possible, depicts his task of "making the earth say beans instead of grass" as more like a gentleman's hobby than hard work.[6] Bass, on the contrary, has to adhere to a grinding, repetitive daily schedule: "type, cut wood, split and stack" (47). Gathering wood is an obsession and a necessity, just like writing. To be able to write, Bass needs to keep himself warm: "Green logs pop and bang against the sides of the old tin stove in the greenhouse, where I'm writing" (69). Both writing and splitting wood are forms of ascetic practice that the intellectual follows assiduously. They are equally demanding tasks that are carried out with rigor and discipline. The writer's and the woodcutter's crafts are means of exploring the fundamental materiality of the world, the "thingness" that differentiates it from the subject.[7] At the same time, they are ways of bringing the human and the nonhuman into an interactive relation.

Wood gathering permits direct physical contact with the exterior: "I'm thinking about how I love getting wood. I moan about it . . . and yet I really, really enjoy that feeling: lifting the great logs, loading them into the car, bringing them home, splitting them, stacking them, the pile growing higher, the fortress, the protection against the cold, the currency of the North already down in the woods, waiting for me to pick it up, and free for the taking. I'm sure a psychiatrist somewhere will be reading this and clucking his or her tongue, going 'Tsk, tsk, tsk,' but that's the way it is, the way I feel" (69–70). It would be easy to dismiss this self-revelatory passage with its reference to "the currency of the North" as proof of an exploitative relation to nature, yet the accumulation of the actions seems as important as the amassing of wood. In delineating all the stages of the activity, Bass emphasizes its constructive and transformative dimension. Gathering wood is a way of both demarcating interior and exterior space—of building a "fortress" against the elements—and of bringing the outside in.

Bass never casts himself as a detached observer in his descriptions of the Yaak. *Winter* has a confessional dimension, and the writer connects all the more with readers by revealing his doubts and contradictions. He is always fully implicated, in a complex emotional engagement whose interwoven strands he attempts to unravel and examine, even though he is conscious of exposing himself in the process. He confesses to having "hard dreams," like the vision of the horse with "his face iced over with snow and sleet" (19). This example illustrates the mix of empathy and apprehension that his arrival in an unfamiliar territory inspires. He dreams of an angry ghost visiting him for many nights in a row (59) and imagines it to be the spirit of the ranch's former owner, haunting the person who has usurped his place. His delight in his surroundings thus seems inseparable from fear. These contrasting feelings may seem superficially to match the response to the sublime identified by Burke.[8] For Burke and for subsequent commentators on landscape,[9] distant, majestic spectacles overwhelm the senses and inspire awe. Since they are remote from human experience, they cannot be adequately represented.[10] Despite the apparent resemblance, Bass's emotions on discovering the Yaak Valley are of a slightly different order. At first, his apprehension arises from his ignorance of the place: "I knew nothing about winter. I had never seen it before, and I felt dizzy with fear, giddy with wonder, anticipating it" (8). The heightened language of this confession evokes the volatility of new love. The mix of wonder and terror signal the beginning of an attachment. As his connection to the land deepens, he uses the metaphor of marriage to describe it: "A lot of the trees are getting bare now. This is like a marriage. Something is coming on. I hope I can do this" (78). By the end of the book, his emotions are still mixed, but the delight and fear derive from his growing understanding of the place and the commitment that he has made to it. What had once seemed most alien about the Yaak has come to stand for that which he loves most:

> I can feel spring's coming, and I'm almost frantic, almost frightened, to realize winter's going. Sometimes I want summer and green grass to come, but sometimes I feel I like I've committed my life to winter, moving up here, and what's more, I've fallen in love with it, and have gotten used to it, and can't picture there not being snow under my feet.
>
> I feel I've gotten dependent on it, the way we always do with a thing we love. The natural terror of that thing not always being around. (156)

Winter has become a metonymy for the valley itself, hence the importance assigned to it in the book. The seasons' mutability signifies the potential destructibility of the environment. Bass's commitment to the place exposes him to the same risk as that which comes with human relationships—the risk of losing a cherished being.

The writer's involvement with the land has another dimension that may trouble environmentally conscious readers; his passion is closely associated with and even indistinguishable from the desire to grab and possess. In *Winter* and even more so in some of his other books, hunting is an important activity that places him at the interface between the self and the world; he expresses his exultation in the act of culling a living creature as proof of his appreciation and recognition. Such is the meaning of the wild and robust feeling expressed in the description of his encounter with a grouse: "I've been taking my shotgun with me when I go up the mountain for wood, in case I see a grouse. Yesterday I saw one. I got out of the car and followed it into the woods, running, and flushed it, shot it as it was flying golden, into the sun—a heavy ruffed grouse, like a villain in one of Shakespeare's plays" (63–64). The unbroken continuity between the pursuit, the vision of beauty, the shot, and the literary association is surprising but revealing.

That feeling of discovering and enjoying the land's riches is similar to his experience on a hunt for overlooked larch stumps: "These huge carcasses are like hidden, forgotten treasures, rotting in the silent woods" (41). Besides arguing the practical necessity of stockpiling fuel against the winter months, Bass admits to taking pleasure in seizing and consuming what catches his eye for its beauty. Moreover, handling and burning wood places him within a cycle of life in which he willingly participates: "It's fun to chop, and I like to watch the flames, watch the erratic, pulsing heat it gives, and I like the snaps and pops, and when I'm dead and gone, I'll be glad I used it" (21). The "pulsing" heat that the burning wood emits seems to sustain the writer's vitality, while its extinction makes him think without regret of his own. Cutting wood is also an occasion to discover the nature of wood and manage his relation to the resource around him. Wood gathering is a way of adapting to the circumstances, like the rabbits changing their coats (18), doing what should be done in harmony with the changing season. It is more a question of instinct, the instinct to adapt correctly to one's surroundings. Yet even the argument of adaptation does not quite satisfy him, and he returns to the pleasure of confronting and consuming the natural beauties around him. His desire to contemplate the felling of the last giant larches, which he admits to loving profoundly and being unable to cut down himself, is at the same time embarrassing—"It's sick, it's perverted" (42)—and intensely personal. His confession that "I do not think I would be able to turn away" (42) testifies to a deeper and stronger participation in nature, a consummation rather than an enjoyment, a kind of Nietzschean *amor fati* that, instead of abstaining from destruction, gets involved in it in order to share its devastating force.

The writer's obsessive wood gathering seems an affront to the most basic wilderness precept: take nothing but pictures and leave nothing but footprints. Of course he is aware of the contradiction between his ecological leanings and his excessive consumption of wood: "If everyone in the world burned as much wood as I am going to this winter, the planet would be obscured, one great wood-smoke cloud"; "Maybe I am a moron for using wood for fuel rather than the similarly priced propane." Nevertheless, he accepts the contradiction and justifies it with arguments that are at the same time provocative and naively resigned: "We're all dirty, but we're all sweet!"; "We all have dirt in us"; "(and we are all the same, always have been) and there is wood lying all around, wood everywhere, and it is free, and I have a life to live" (21). He represents his actions as an expression of his own nature: like the wood smoke, he is dirty and sweet; like the wood, he is free and alive. Implicitly, his wood burning inserts him in the life of the forest, even as it makes him a consumer and a producer of waste.

In *Winter*, in contradistinction to many nature writing texts, the writer is not a transparent, registering instrument recording the glories of nature and taking on substance and subjectivity by virtue of the encounter;[11] instead, he brings to the Yaak a complex, contradictory personality that needs to be chastened into coherence by its encounter with the new environment. At times he entertains the illusion of starting afresh, for example in the exhilarating descent of a snow-covered mountain, "like running down Olympus—Zeus as a boy of seven, perhaps" (85). Still, these intimations of immortality are far removed in tone from Wordsworth's tranquil contemplation. Bass is at the same time more boisterous and more naive, more careless and more violent. He compares his transformation to the destructive and vigorous force of an avalanche: "It's not avalanche season, but I could picture what one would be like: the whole mountain beginning to slide beneath me, coming to life. I'm coming to life myself up here in this valley; I've taken a broadax to my life. Zeus, at the age of seven. I know I won't live forever. Why does it feel as if I will?" (85–86). The comparison suggests his insouciance and recklessness, but at the same time it proclaims his authenticity and the fundamental character of the change taking place within him.

The writer is not so much projecting or expanding himself in contact with his environment as discovering himself through engagement with it and accepting what he finds. The calling of birds in the woods sounds like an interpellation, a message coming both from outside and from within: "My life seems about to *speak* to me, that sense of waiting, of promise, is so strong" (72). His commitment to the Yaak Valley brings a new clarity, as if he needed the place to express his character: "I'm discovering things about myself up here, things I should have known by now, but don't. I don't think this reveals a complex personality so much as a simple mind, but it's the only one I've got, and I'm glad to have it out here, away from town" (116). Accepting this reduction to the basic elements of human existence has its compensations. At several moments in the book Bass expresses his joy in participating in the cycles of nature. In a sharp departure from the usual anthropocentric appropriation of animal lives by nature writers, he compares himself to animals. The rabbits teach him the necessity of preparation for winter and the snow makes him "feel" (134) and act like an animal: "I am like an animal—not in control of my emotions, my happiness and furies, but in charge of loving the snow" (90).[12] Feeling animal does not mean resorting to barbarity but observing the seasonal rhythms, being attuned to and participating in the plenitude of natural transformations.

In Bass's universe, animals are neither projections of nor foils to humanity; instead, provided one has abdicated all human pretentions to distinctiveness, they are companions in existence: "The [coyotes] catch mice the way I gather wood. We're all close, we're all tied together" (36). In that state of Lawrentian collective mindlessness, the writer is able to experience an organic process of mutation; his growth is not rational or deliberate but slow and progressive, following the natural rhythms of existence. In the new place, the writer retrieves a fresh perspective that most adults have abandoned: "But if you remember to look at the snow like a child, or a Texan—gazing up, trying to see where it originates—then the slowness into which it falls, the paralysis of its journey, will drop you immediately into a lower, slower state, one where you're sure to live twice as long, and see twice as many things, and be two times as happy at the end" (133). This surrender to the specificity of the world does not diminish, but rather enhances, consciousness. The adjustment is sometimes demanding: "It is hard to fit nature. A seam is coming up. I am going to have to step from winter into spring. I must do it gracefully" (158). Trying to "fit nature" might sound like the traditional pathetic fallacy—fitting nature to the moods of man—but in *Winter* it has a completely different meaning; instead of projecting oneself onto nature, it means merging into the flux of seasons.

For all its magic, the Yaak Valley is not entirely benign and bountiful; its inhabitants are exposed to brutal and unpredictable extremes. The land is not a virgin site to be penetrated, explored, and captured in prose; it is a closed, obstructive, intractable reality that demands adjustment and compromise. Winter is the ultimate eraser, blotting out the features of the landscape: "If it's snowing, you go out to the woodshed with a rope tied around your waist, . . . then at least you can find your way back to the cabin" (120). Winter teaches: "Take nothing for granted" (134). If a storm rolls in, an outing can become a mortal risk: "The road narrowing and narrowing between the baroque, towering drifts (so high above the truck that if they collapsed, in an avalanche, we'd be swallowed, and the road truly *would* disappear) until there's barely room for us to fit" (152). In contrast to the illusion of emptiness derived from his first glimpse of the valley, the blankness Bass describes here is not a terrain for imaginative projection; rather, it forces an encounter with the real. Winter and snow are the real heroes of the book. They blot out other considerations, reducing the land and its inhabitants to the simplest form of existence.

Faced with winter's onslaught, the writer acknowledges his adversary's superiority: "Forty below. We're a little frightened. We're at the mercy of the cold. We hope for mercy. It's as if the brutal cold is looking for something, passing over, searching. I hope it doesn't find what it's looking for here" (123). Preparing for the coming of winter is like preparing for war, for the ultimate ordeal that will put one's existence to the test. In confronting an unpredictable force and possibly risking extinction, the writer feels, paradoxically, in the presence of a life-affirming power: "What a good sound the wind is making. What if this is the sound you hear after you lie down and die? I am not ready for that but I am ready for this" (79). The winter wind conjures up death but allows it to be considered from a distance; in the sentence just quoted, it is "that," and it allows "this"—the present moment—to be savored all the more fully. Accepting the cold is like pledging allegiance to something bigger than oneself, something destructive that both fulfills and transcends one's destiny. Rather than heroism or tragic choice, like a religious vocation it demands an act of submission.

Globally, all these departures from earlier themes in nature writing signify the end of a specular relation to the world and the delineation, albeit in a tentative and sometimes humorously naive manner, of a new interactive conception of the human bond with nature. In *Winter* this connection remains a private emotional attachment more than a full-blown commitment to the environment. However, the new bond forged in the winter season becomes the basis for a newfound responsibility. Not surprisingly, in subsequent books about the Yaak, Bass goes on to delineate his political engagement to protect the region he has come to love.

At the end of the book, the writer is no longer a rolling stone "happy just at being on the landscape" (1); he has become a rooted, emplaced, acclimatized individual. The book's last sentence is intriguing: "I won't be leaving this valley" (162), as if the decision to stay is the outcome of a long reflection, a final fateful choice, but also, curiously, as if the writer feels secretly that the Yaak should not be abandoned, that it needs his protection. A reciprocal bond seems to have been contracted between the writer and the valley. This bond is the product of the experience in awareness and awakening that is described in *Winter*.

Growing into Responsibility

In scripting the lessons in reality gained from his Montana experience, Bass guides the reader toward a kind of rebirth that contains the premises of a new conception of emplacement in America. This understanding becomes available if readers follow the writer's trail through a series of impalpable realizations released in very simple, nearly imperceptible increments associated with a number of telling moments that are barely analyzed, always left open ended, sometimes thrown out of context. They are enclaves of narrative in a welter of disconnected notations, vignettes of vivid and colorful actuality in a flow of free associations. These events have the logic of dreams in the winter that he calls "this dream season" (159). Because they are always unexpected, they may appear negligible, but they are also all the more suggestive. Usually they come as flashes, visions about something that cannot be expressed in words but was experienced in real life and only approximated through language. Suggestive incidents mark the stages in a process of maturation, without showing the transitions or the mechanics of that evolution. These scenes are situated between the act of forgetting and that of acquiring. They are dense but enigmatic, as if the writer picked them out of a stream of reminiscences and was suddenly intrigued by events that pricked his curiosity but remained partly sealed. They can only be offered as they stand; hence the peculiar importance of these anecdotes that testify to phases in the writer's evolution. Their elliptical nature invites readers to reconstruct or simply fill in the things they suggest.

Among these anecdotes, the one accorded the most importance, perhaps because it gives clues as to how to read all the others, is the story of Breitenstein's wire fence. In itself, the incident may strike the reader as relatively insignificant. The writer opens his neighbor's fence in order to bring out the larch that he has bought from him. In the cold, the barbed wire contracts, making it impossible to close the fence. After struggling for a long while to close the gap, Bass rigs up a "larger makeshift loop" (144) to attach the fence, leaving the wire much looser than he found it. A lengthy bout of self-castigation accompanies the anecdote, as well as an extended comparison between closing fences and the work of writing. Thus the development surrounding the simple anecdote demands that the reader reflect on both its importance to the protagonist and the light it sheds on questions of interpretation.

This passage permits the most extended reflection on the process of writing in a work that is already fairly self-reflexive due to the journal format. The writer compares his upbringing in ranching country to his training as a creative writer:

> In Texas, going from ranch to ranch, . . . I was taught never to leave a gap open: never, not for any length of time, because as sure as anything, an animal would get out. In writing I've been taught the same thing: always close your gates—unless, of course, you *want* something to get out, escape into the next chapter, perhaps, or even into the night, never to be heard from again. The things that count, however—the goods, the story, the livestock—those you always keep the gap closed on, or at least close it when you are through with them. (143)

The rule for wire fences is a hard and fast one, as the repetition of "never" indicates. For writing, however, the situation is much fuzzier, for the writer is absolute master of the textual space and can decide whether or not to close the gaps. If leaving an open gate is always a grave fault on the ranch, in writing it can be an artistic choice. Leaving open spaces allows meaning to circulate in the text, to "escape into the next chapter"; it creates zones of mystery, allowing things to disappear "into the night, never to be heard of again" (143). Such gaps, as Umberto Eco has shown,[13] allow readers to participate in the construction of meaning, leaving zones of indeterminacy that continue to reverberate. In concluding the episode, the writer shares with readers a reflection that he could not disclose to Breitenstein: "I wanted to tell him about my father, and about closing gaps in great novels, how the good ones were strung so tight they would stand forever" (147). By implication, readers should look for both openness and closure in Bass's work, for gaps and tight lines. *Winter* has rigorous linearity, since the sections follow the progress of the calendar, and also a form of closure, since the book focuses almost obsessively on the subject announced by the title. Nevertheless, there are also gaps in the form of missing days, absent details, and omitted explanations, and sometimes these aporia stand out, demanding readers' attention.

In fact, the anecdote of the fence creates a visible rupture in the text, and the writer's insistence on the importance of linearity and closure makes his departure from these rules all the more significant. The entry for January 17 begins with the mention of a Jim Bridger legend about trappers' frozen words that leads to an anecdote about a moose that Bass had witnessed "the other night" (141). Clearly, the linearity of the journal is not being respected; in fact, these anecdotes prepare for the revelation of something else that the writer has omitted writing about. After the moose story comes the confession of the fault of not properly closing the fence the night before, up to now omitted from the text: "I'd been dreading Breitenstein's passage, unable to get it entirely out of my mind, and from a long way off my ears picked up the ragged-smooth sputtering of his old red truck coming up from the valley. Guilt washed in like a cabin door left open on a cold night" (142). The gap in the text functions rather like the process of secondary elaboration in Freudian dream theory; the most significant details are those that have been forgotten. Guilt returns with the sound of the truck, through a metaphor that gives away the fault before he can confess it. At first the obsession with tight fences seems to be solely Breitenstein's, and the writer's own opinion seems to be in opposition: "I prefer the gaps to be loose and a little floppy—easy to open, easy to close." (143). After a long disquisition on fences, with three line drawings as illustrations, another reason for the writer's concern leaks out: "I kept imagining what my father would have done, back in Texas" (145). The memory of his father serves the role of superego, prompting the writer to leave his work and go in search of Breitenstein, "as if controlled from above" (145). This delayed disclosure reveals much more than the simple desire not to vex a neighbor. The gap in the fence shows a stage in the protagonist's development as a man. When, contrary to his expectations, Breitenstein reacts favorably to his inept efforts to close the gap, he feels that he has managed to get through an important test: "I . . . thought of how my father had gotten me through another day, 2,500 miles from home, and of how, eventually, soon perhaps, I would be floating—until then I was sometimes a boy, only imitating a man—it might take years, but I was on the right track, and I could see up ahead where I was going" (147). This introspective reflection concludes the anecdote and, at the same time, guides our interpretation of the text. Keeping afloat in the new environment by surviving the Montana winter and learning the customs of the country is an essential rite of passage to manhood. This comment hints that the book will conclude "eventually, soon perhaps" with the writer's transformation from youth to adult.

Keeping this pattern of development in mind as the tight line that holds the book together, we can look at the way apparently random incidents contribute to the writer's growth. The humorous episode of the missionaries' visit in which an odd couple, children in tow, try to make him a convert to their half-baked new religion, becomes a test of his mettle. After five minutes of polite listening, the writer sends them packing: "He was taking advantage of me. I told him I was typing, and I had to get back to work" (102). He resists the temptation to listen just to hear another human voice, "a visitor of any kind" (103), in his isolated Montana hideout, yet the significance of his firmness is only implicitly suggested by the odd conclusion to the anecdote. First, the writer exults in the hope of winter's transforming power: "Perhaps all the snow in the world will fall, burying everything, such silence, and then I will come out of it in the spring, different, cleaner, not born again so much as built up. I'll laugh at more things, and not get so angry at decadence, at laziness, at deceit and the theft of time" (103). Instead of making him vulnerable to the claims of any visitor, his isolation gives him an ironic distance from the world. The snow, with its insulating qualities, mutes all the vain theories and consolations devised by men to reassure themselves. It leaves him alone to mature in the silent struggle with words and the rigors of winter. Rejecting the illumination the missionaries have found in their haphazard reading of the Bible—"not born again"—he chooses the more difficult path of becoming "built up" by experience. Nevertheless, this is not the final word on the problem of silence and isolation. The episode finishes with the allusion to an odd sound made by a pulley in the barn: "a squealing, almost mocking sound in the wind, a sort of yes-no, yes-no, yes-no, squeak, so loud it can be heard over the high wind. I could go to the barn and climb up and oil it. But it's really the only other thing out there, between here and the woods. It's a grating sound, not normally pleasant, but I almost like it this morning" (103). The decision to let the metallic grating continue is one of the unexplained gaps in the text that readers must fill. There is perhaps a double-edged humor in the mention of the "yes-no" sound: on the one hand, the writer prefers it to the missionaries' vapid preaching; on the other hand, he is not yet so inured to the silence of the woods that he cannot find a modicum of consolation in the sound of human-made objects.

Living in the Yaak means learning to value actions more than social discourse. This seems to be the point of a seemingly unimportant anecdote about leaving the ranch and forgetting to check whether the generator is turned off (133). This episode breaks the linear unfolding of the book in that it harks back to an earlier trip out of the valley. The writer has forgotten the destination; what sticks in his mind is the friendly willingness of one of the Yaak's residents to drive to his house to check the generator. The neighbor reassures Elizabeth that the generator is indeed turned off, and the writer quotes the tail end of their brief verbal exchange and follows it with his own observation:

> "It's snowing hard here," Elizabeth said.
> "It's snowing hard here too," Nancy said.
> The world can be so safe in winter. I was homesick for Yaak, and we had barely left. (133)

The two women's very ordinary and obvious comment on the weather, repeated in nearly identical words, suggests that language can be superfluous. Everything that needs to be said is expressed through the neighbor's reassuring act of comprehension, solidarity, and friendliness. The anecdote affirms the importance of what is not said but implied and of the feelings transmitted by other forms of expression; its apparent simplicity is a clue to the poetics of *Winter.*

The book's final anecdote demonstrates the writer's personal development with the quiet understatement that has become his hallmark. It seems that over the duration of the book's writing, the baroque exuberance of the preface has given way to a quiet assurance that emerges when the superfluous is stripped away: "I felt like I'd waited all my life to peel off my city ways, city life, and get into the woods—molting, like an insect or a snake" (160). A visit from his father permits the writer to measure the degree of this transformation. The importance assigned to paternal judgment has already been demonstrated, yet when the father appears in person it manifests itself in a very undramatic way:

> "You've changed," my father said, not uncomfortably, as he mended his line. . . .
>
> "No I haven't," I said, just as comfortably, still casting to the little fish. . . . I suppose I was pretending that I had always realized what I needed—deep, dark woods, and a quietness, a slowness—and that I hadn't been floundering for thirty years trying to figure this out, trying to get along in cities, trying to move fast. (161)

The conflicting interpretations of father and son counterbalance one another, and the truth hovers unspoken and yet implicit, somewhere between the two. In shedding his skin the son has changed and become more truly himself.

Although it happens on the personal plane, a change of attitude takes place in the course of *Winter* that is consonant with the new perspective on place found in the other works we will study. The Yaak Valley is not the empty space of projection found in earlier nature writing but an existential proving ground whose dense reality demands human interaction. The writer must either become deeply committed to his surroundings or resign himself to being one of the fair-weather visitors who does not stay. He does not seem to be perfectly in control of his situation, nor does the world around him appear controllable. Instead, he needs to "fit nature" (158), to find the right adjustment between himself and the place. He relinquishes a portion of his autonomy but acquires an instinctive understanding of what is right for himself and for his environment. His adaptation is as irrefragable as the curious assertion he adds at the end of one of his entries: "Water, on this side of the Divide, flows to the Pacific" (116). This cryptic declaration may evoke the pull of the West in American culture, but if so, Bass rewrites the recurrent cultural narrative in which the protagonist avoids civilization and adulthood through flight. In the Yaak, Bass takes a stand—"I won't be leaving this valley" (162). He represents himself in *Winter* as a molting, changing individual who becomes increasingly clear about his objectives in life—the aim is neither escape nor self-aggrandizement but integration, commitment, and responsibility.

4

The Storied Mountains of Charles Bowden's *Frog Mountain Blues*

As opposed to Rick Bass, whose explorations in the Yaak Valley extend only to its present-day residents, the other writers whose works I will study prolong their search into the past, discovering the complex histories of inhabitation hidden under the sign of empty. In fact, the remaining books treated here show how the attribution of emptiness has allowed successive waves of inhabitants to write their own stories on the land. The new writers of place seek out the traces of occupation and gather the stories scattered throughout the territory in the interwoven scripts that make up their books.

The scripts that Charles Bowden brings together in *Frog Mountain Blues* blend reenactments of his personal explorations of the mountains that overlook the city of Tucson, where he lives, with the many stories that he unearths in the process. Along with Jack W. Dykinga's photographic images of the mountains, the book contains, albeit in an unconventional form, a history of the settling and occupation of the Santa Catalinas. From the seventeenth-century tales of discovery to the contemporary struggle between conservation and preservation, the mountains' history perfectly illustrates the evolution of the cultural projections of emptiness and fullness found in the discourse on the American territory. Instead of surveying the history of the mountains' settlement in chronological order, the book presents in nonlinear order a series of scripts showing the haphazard interplay of causes and consequences that shaped the land. Rather than presenting a single clear-cut image, Bowden's mountain emerges through a maze of traces gathered from oral accounts, from documents, and from the land itself. The book's multiple angles of vision mirror the divided attitudes to the land that Bowden inherits as an American. The mountain referred to in the book's title (Bowden has restored the Indian name to Mount Lemmon, the highest of the range) emerges not as a single mountain, but as one that is as manifold as its inhabitants and admirers.

The Mountain as Palimpsest

The scripts and photographs presenting Bowden's and Dykinga's explorations of the mountains record the effects of human interaction with the land. Successive modes of appropriation have transformed the mountains, leaving behind their traces. The earliest signs of human presence are the Indian ruins, "Hohokam relics left from the time of Christ" (60). The Spanish missionaries who came at the end of the seventeenth century left traces of a different kind in the legends of the city they built and in the saint's name they gave to the mountain range. In the nineteenth century, miners and loggers descended on the site, leaving behind the "lacerations" of mines, trails, and tree stumps, though the steepness of the slopes curbed their efforts (26–33). Ranchers and homesteaders put up buildings, and their livestock cropped the vegetation, further eroding the soil. In the course of a century, they radically transformed the land, so that, in the words Bowden quotes from Aldo Leopold: "Much of the beauty is the beauty not of life, but of dissolution" (81). Then, when the new twentieth-century romance with the automobile met the old longing for freedom and escape, roads, cabins, hotels, and ski runs appeared on the mountain. Finally, the pressure to protect the natural environment from these recreational installations led to the sectioning off of wilderness areas. The history of the human occupation of the Santa Catalinas is thus readable in the marks it has left on the land.

Frog Mountain Blues links these physical transformations that have come about over time to cultural representations of the American territory. Just as "the constant story of the West" (6) permeates American discourse, so that story has been inscribed in a particular way on the Santa Catalinas. The "constant story" assigns emptiness to the American territory and then makes it a field for projections:

> The gnashing teeth of our hungers have chewed their way across this continent, and now the mountains, all the mountains lording it over all the cities,

> all the wild ground our ancestors called trackless wastes—now these spots are our last memories of a better world where the landscape once hammered us into a new kind of people. All the words and catch phrases we pray live in our bones—Never Give An Inch, Self-Reliance, Waste Not Want Not, Every Man For Himself, No Free Lunch, Suck In Your Gut We're Goin' To Whup It!—all our boasts and sweet dreams of freedom beckon from the rough slopes and still promise to nurture us. (6–7)

Packed into this passage is a condensed history of the mental constructions accompanying the settlement of the American continent. In the first phase, the "trackless wastes" reflect the settlers' initial fear of the unknown land. That fearful image gives way to the heroic legends of westward expansion, "where the landscape once hammered us into a new kind of people." The popular clichés conveying the pioneer spirit of that second phase reflect the organizing power of the frontier myth on the American imagination. This cultural legend was raised to the status of history in Frederick Jackson Turner's frontier thesis. Bowden's part ironic, part nostalgic scripting of this story demonstrates its power and persistence. In the most recent phase of the American romance with the territory, the projections of fullness and emptiness are reversed: the settled land has been devoured by the "gnashing teeth of our hungers," while the remnants of wild ground contain the "last memories" of that national history. At the same time, the nation's hopes are projected onto the remaining "empty" space, which still promises to nurture the enduring dreams of fulfillment.

In Bowden's eyes, something is lost when people's dreams and desires are translated into public policy and concretized in space: "All over the West, there are remnants of that time, places that still offer the Big Lonely and days without walls. We try to talk about these matters, but the words always come out as categories like National Parks or National Monuments or National Forests or Wilderness Areas. Or sometimes as summer cabins, ski lodges and resorts" (7). In listing the unsatisfactory ways of talking about "the Big Lonely," Bowden reveals the warped connection between the cultural field of representations and the different transpositions of those projections onto the mountains. Bowden is a transitional figure among the new writers of place in that he still wants to believe in the latest avatar of the dream of empty—"the Big Lonely"—even though he is dissatisfied with the effects it produces. He perceives that the same impulse that drives the building of roads and the development of resorts also motivates the fight to preserve the land as an official Wilderness. All of those transformations come from the cultural reclassification of the mountains as "something called nature" (76).

At the end of the nineteenth century the Santa Catalinas became the site of a local struggle, reproduced all over the nation, over the right ways to manage land. The first federal laws restricting the exploitation of mountains "were considered a nuisance and blithely ignored or gotten around" (75). The resistance to government control was perfectly consonant with the stance of rugged independence adopted by the frontiersmen: the miners, loggers, and ranchers who first made their living in the West. Voicing the early American hostility to land that lay "waste," they validated their relation to the land in terms of the wealth they extracted from it. With the advent of the idea that nature could constitute a value in and of itself, that old way of living off the land gave way to a new form of development, as speculators put up the first vacation cottages and cabins aimed at the Tucson city dwellers. The first step in protecting the mountains from development was made in the 1920s when a state legislator, F. E. A. Kimball, oversaw the creation of the first local nature reserve, the Santa Catalina Natural Area. Yet the desire to preserve nature for the people led to a development that Bowden shows to be a contradiction. The same man who sponsored the Natural Area was one of the most ardent promoters of the construction of a road that would give the public better access to the mountain. The switch from representing the "empty" mountains as a site of extraction to seeing them as a site of recreation paradoxically accelerated their development. The chapter ironically entitled "The Last Resort" describes the changes brought by the building of the road. First the ski runs arrived, then "the radar station came, and observatories on Mount Bigelow, and a forest of radio towers and new picnic areas and more recreation areas" (84). This accumulation of substantives, along with the repeated conjunctions, conveys the impression that civilization has overrun the mountains in the name of nature.

Against the pressure of this recreational development, Bowden adopts the polemical position that he sums up in the new afterword added to the 1994 edition: "The book's tender and moderate thesis had been to blow up the only paved highway leading to the mountain and then leave the mountain alone to heal" (160). Despite his resistance to "categories," (7) Bowden finds himself pushed by his own preferences and the force of circumstances to place himself in one of them. He admits that environmentalist discourse somehow sounds hollow to him:

> The modern environmental movement is a messianic mission to save wild ground and at its heart—at spots like this unnamed canyon where we sit on a rock and eat while a cold front beats against Putsch ridge—it always seems to me that the center of the movement is a kind of empty barrel. The barrel at first looks full, in fact, overflowing with slogans, calendars, environmental impact statements, critical habitat lists, natural area plans, mitigation schemes, and big shovelfuls of tradeoffs. But after sorting through this barrel I never find much that explains why I come to spots like this unnamed canyon. (53)

Whether scientific, political, or promotional, the various sorts of official discourse do nothing to express the significance that the mountains hold for him. Its abstract terms have the contrary effect of distancing speakers from the land. Bowden offers his more personal, idiosyncratic scripts as both an antidote and a complement to these institutional forms of discourse.

Nonetheless, the environmental literature suggests an idea that resonates with his own feelings about the mountain: "But I hear a kindred echo in this cumbersome word biocentric and accept the idea as something similar to what I feel, only all dressed up in Sunday-go-to-meeting clothes. I think much ground must be spared and left to forms of life as a place where they can fashion their own futures. And I think the Santa Catalinas are one such place among many" (127). The many accounts of human life in the mountains leave out the point of view of other life-forms. The environmental literature tries to correct that imbalance, but its distanced, scientific tone proves alienating, in spite of Bowden's sympathy for ecological arguments. His timid admission of militancy becomes full-fledged in the afterword, where, describing his contribution at a Forest Service hearing to the debate over a new ski run, Bowden tries out other forms of address to plead the mountain's cause. He casts himself, albeit with humorous self-mockery, in various activist roles: first, "the Panderer" (163), then "the Rude Boy" (163), and finally "Chuck the Baptist" (164). These ironic nicknames underline his discomfort with polemics. In concluding the afterword, he pleads for collective repentance and love, recognizing that something is left out of the formal debate. Indeed, as a writer, he seeks to move beyond clichés and instead explore the contradictions in cultural representations of the land.

The polemical position Bowden adopts in the political conflict over the Santa Catalinas does not reflect the ambivalence expressed in *Frog Mountain Blues*. His personal contradictions and his empathy for other points of view do not quite fit with the militant opposition to all signs of human occupation on the mountain voiced in the afterword. In the opening pages of the book, the dream of effacing all traces of humanity seems "pure fantasy," (6) and the urge to "save the mountain from ourselves so that we can keep it forever" (8) appears blatantly self-contradictory. Although the indignation that ignites his quixotic defense of the mountain is one of the tones heard recurrently in the book, there is also the mood of despondency expressed in the "blues" of the title. This half sweet, half painful bluesy feeling emerges from the book's representation of an intricate web of competing convictions about the right way to love the mountains. These contradictions in the narrator's self-portrait demand that readers engage actively with the text. Instead of the neutral objectivity solicited from readers of historical or geographical studies, Bowden's book urges attachment to the speaker and, vicariously, connection with the place he describes. The appeal to affect is one of the strengths of the new literature of place; through this strategy, the writers seek to reconnect us to places that were empty abstractions.

The main orientation of the book is not simply the future of the Santa Catalinas. *Frog Mountain Blues* tackles the larger concern at the heart of the new literature of place: the relations between individuals and communities and their projects for the land they inhabit, and transitively, between the nation and its territory. In order to give us an idea of the complexity of those relations, Bowden brings together a motley assortment of images, texts, and stories. He creates a montage or collage of various inscriptions and traces made by those who have occupied the mountain and its surroundings, as if the book were a multidimensional reply to the two-dimensional map that appears in its opening pages. *Frog Mountain Blues* reveals how human appropriation and inhabitation have overprinted the physical map of the Catalinas with a barely intelligible welter of human signs. Better than any polemic, the assemblage of those inscriptions and traces reveals the complexity of the struggle centered on the mountains.

The book's montage effect is evident at first glance in its alternation of black-and-white photographs with blocks of text of varied typefaces and spatial layout. The autonomous media of text and image enter into dialogue with each other; the ironic clashes captured in Dykinga's photographs are further complicated by Bowden's patchwork of competing discourses. The photographs present startling contradictions between human and non-human elements in the land. In the book's prefatory image of Tucson, different visual planes contrast with one another. In the center of the picture, the geometrical concrete blocks and vertical lines of the modern city are in sharp focus. These human-made structures contrast with the softer outlines of the grass in the foreground and the hazy curves of the mountains in the background. The perspective makes the city look larger than it is, so that it seems to be reaching up to compete with the huge granite mass behind it. Depending on the viewer's point of view, the contrast speaks of achievement or hubris. The photograph of a new high-rise construction site makes a similar statement, as its dark outlines create stimulating vertical, horizontal, and diagonal patterns against the textured, soft gray expanse of the mountain behind it (144).

Some of the photographs show the destructive effects of human occupation on plant and animal life. In the picture of a development near Sabino Canyon, fragments of broken cacti surround a solitary standing cactus, propped up by a stake. In a picture captioned "Along Oracle Highway, north of Tucson" (152), cars, blurred by the effect of speed, head into infinity, while a dead deer lies in the foreground, its body stiff with rigor mortis and twisted into an unnatural position; a highway sign provides the ironic legend "El Conquistador." The photographs allow voiceless things to communicate with readers, insisting on their presence in the land and their right to consideration.

Though the mountains seem in retreat in most of the photographs, a few hint at the tenuousness of humanity's control of the land. A firefighter armed with only a shovel contemplates the blazing undergrowth of a forest whose tall, densely packed trees tower over him (88). An image of a ruined house, with its windows and most of its walls gone (54), suggests the huge gap between the impermanence of humanity's works and the mountain's endurance. These photographs could equally be perceived as emblems of human irresponsibility. The image of a graffitied National Forest sign, in which the slogan "Land of Many Uses" has been altered to "Land of Many AB-Uses," (10) could be taken as a metatextual comment on all of Dykinga's photographs. The effect of the numerous, juxtaposed textual segments that make up the book is more ambivalent. Somewhat idiosyncratic conventions seem to govern the placement of the varied fragments of discourse, so that readers have to find their way through the textual maze.

Each chapter has an epigraph that seems to represent an authoritative voice commenting on the mountain. However, by virtue of their lack of unanimity, the different discourses (for example, a nineteenth-century Arizona newspaper, an anthropologist's transcription of a Papago song, a cowboy's lament, and Aldo Leopold's convictions on wildlife) compete with one another to define the mountains and the right relation to them. No voice really has the last word. Even the name of the mountains is contested. The first epigraph describes an old Papago Indian who "peers through thick lenses at the Santa Catalina Mountains" and names the highest peak "Frog Mountain." Bowden affirms this designation by using it in the title of the book, and as the title and closing words of one of the chapters. Nevertheless, certain aspects of this scene of naming undercut the Papago's authority. He offers no explanation for the name; moreover, his vision is failing, his legs hang uselessly from his wheelchair, and "he wants a shaman fetched from the hot desert to the west." A few pages later, the epigraph to the first chapter, printed in a bolder typeface, tells another story of naming. Quoting from a book entitled *Arizona Place Names*, it tells how Fr. Kino, a Spanish missionary, named the mountains after the saint on whose day he first visited the place (3). The map that prefaces the book bears the Christian toponym, applying it to several landmarks, whereas the name "Frog Mountain" is absent. Thus, the fragments of quoted discourse dialogue with one another to open up the discursive field and allow multiple interpretative possibilities to emerge.

Another convention governs the textual fragments that appear within the chapters, indented from the main text and either centered or right justified. Some of these are presented as evidence to support a point made in the text;[1] others have no introduction, and, in breaking the flow of the text, they ask the reader to make sense of them. At times this collage pattern creates ironic parallels; for example, Bowden juxtaposes his account of meeting present-day gold seekers to an 1881 newspaper clipping that compares the promise of gold to "an *IGNIS FATUUS*" (16). At times, the indented quotations form an ironic counterpoint to the main text; in the "Heart of Gold" chapter, for example, indented pieces of the lost gold mine story break into Bowden's account of hiking in the mountains. Whether they authenticate or contradict the main text, these indentations always open up a distance that makes Bowden's voice appear more real, closer to life as lived.

Even without these inserted fragments, the main text is far from monologic. It incorporates childhood memories, biographies, conversations, and interviews, sometimes relating action directly and sometimes diffracting it through memory or history. Moreover, the text deliberately mixes references to time and place. Stories of gold mining lead to an account of the emblematic life of Buffalo Bill Cody, who spent his final winter in the Santa Catalinas (26–28). With its deciduous trees, the Cañada del Oro evokes "the feel of the Wisconsin woods of [Bowden's] childhood" (16). The text spirals from present to past, spanning the American territory, and mixing present-day explorations and encounters with historical scenes and intimate childhood memories. These unannounced shifts in focus add to the disjunctions of the textual collage; they draw attention to the multiple scripts that demand readers' active participation in the construction of meaning.

The text's subtle montage of different scripts conveying a multitude of perspectives produces a vision of space that is erratic and contradictory, both multilayered and multicentered. This very multiplicity and irregularity are the subject of the book. Though Charles Bowden stages himself as the central persona, he does not pretend to possess an all-seeing, all-knowing camera's eye; rather he presents himself as a versatile, vacillating center-of-consciousness, permeable to other voices and opinions and attempting to espouse in his vision the complexity and contradictions of his investment in the mountain. Characteristic of the narrative voice in the new literature of place, Bowden eschews the detached, omniscient perspective that controls the text and orients the reader; instead, the central persona relates a quest to discover multiple stories involving other points of view, with all the risks to the authority and the integrity of the self that this implies.

Although, on a first reading, the kaleidoscopic assemblage of textual fragments may have a disorienting effect, a number of distinct strands come together in Bowden's reconstruction of the story of the human occupation of the mountains. The text can be read as a braid of scripts rather than a haphazard assembly. Different foci or generating forces emerge, producing an initial impression of randomness, prolixity, and unpredictability. Combined together in the weave of the text, these multiple scripts represent a space—Frog Mountain—that is, on the one hand, overrun, assaulted, defiled, and desecrated and, on the other, always unattainable, remote, and secret. Hence, the crazed patterning of the book's structure: Bowden is trying to seize something that remains inaccessible.

To analyze the book's meshwork structure, I will treat separately the scripts that Bowden juxtaposes and intertwines. His composite picture of the Catalinas is unlike those unified, complete images produced by superimposing transparencies in medical textbooks or trick photography. Instead, Bowden's scripting of the mountains reveals the tensions and the contradictions in the multiple representational layers. If they can be unified by any common theme, the force tying the different scripts together is probably the shared passion evoked in the book's opening and closing passages. The dedication refers to the maternal belief that "love is always the answer," while the last hope of the afterword is that our species can find a way of living in the world that will merit the love of all those with whom we share it. Still, that ideal state of harmony is a distant, though dearly hoped for, goal. What that new way might look like is beyond the scope of Bowden's book. Suggestions can be found in Aldo Leopold's idea of a land ethic, Michel Serres's natural contract, and Bruno Latour's parliament of things; all work toward establishing the philosophical foundations for more ecologically responsible relationships with place.[2] In showing a concern for other-than-human interests, Bowden's book begins to shape the sense of responsibility toward the environment that these philosophers advocate. Though the mountain dwellers' competing discourses hold the floor in the debate the book stages, the mountain itself is at its center. The different scripts on the mountain show that people's fascination with it not only produces divided factions but also radically alters the space in question. At the same time, the mountain determines the activities of the dwellers. The scripts assembled in the book rehearse the mountain dwellers' different projections onto the American territory, and together they illustrate the complexity of relations in time and space.

The Papagos' Frog Mountain

The first of the recurrent scripts projecting an image of the mountains reconnects present-day America with its pre-Columbian past. The book's title resuscitates the almost-forgotten name given to the highest peak by the Papago Indians. Bowden revives the name and suggests different reasons why it fits. Names are inevitably traces of some form of human connection with the environment, but Bowden has to find his own way to link the name to the place because the Papago who supplies the old name gives an English translation from "the tongue of his people" and offers "no further explanation." In the book's opening epigraph Bowden hints at a resemblance between the old man and the mountain itself, a correspondence that goes beyond nomenclature to suggest the Indian's deep somatic identification with the land. Like the old man, the mountain seems to need the healing ministration of a shaman. The taciturn dignity of the paraplegic Indian mirrors the somewhat diminished grandeur of the "maimed stone god" that towers impassively above the city. The absent but much-needed shaman bears some relation to the radical cure Bowden desires for the mountain in that they both promise to restore past integrity. The misty longings attributed to the Papago echo Bowden's own desire to revive Frog Mountain; "Chuck the Baptist" is a voice crying in the wilderness, unheard by the officials who decide the mountain's fate, but hoping to be the forerunner of some charismatic savior who will usher in a new age of love.

The old gods seem to have withdrawn from the site. The tutelary spirit, Navitcu, who made the plants grow and "gave the desert people their first gourds" (120), no longer appears on Frog Mountain. Like the Papago, he has been cast aside in favor of a different way of life that diminishes him: "Like so many things on the mountain, he has been sapped of power by his brush with the might of our machine driven world" (122). Contemporary America worships a different kind of might, represented by the roads and the machines that create them and use them, yet the old pastoral ideals persist in ironic contradiction with the machines,[3] just as memories of the old gods haunt the mountain. Bowden deploys the script centering on Frog Mountain to suggest that humanity has broken its former spiritual bonds with the land and in the process has diminished the vigor of living things.

This sense of decline permeates the story of Bowden's encounter with

Eleasar Celeya, a Sand Papago, one of the few remaining members of the group. Though Bowden describes the old man oxymoronically as "a kind of living fossil" (104), he represents people whose way of life was shaped by the land. Celeya has experienced the kind of connection that Bowden longs for: "He was raised inside the wild country that I can only know in fantasy" (104). The old man's guide to that lost place was his great-grandfather, a man who hunted and prayed like his ancestors, "flourish[ing] in a desert of three to seven inches of rainfall a year" (105). After the great-grandfather's lessons in what Celeya calls "simply, The Way" (105)—as if there were no other—the child is sent to Indian School in California. Motivated by the federal policy of assimilation,[4] this imposed exile attenuates his connection with the place. When he returns, his great-grandfather tests him with a forty-two-mile run through the desert, concluding at the end that the boy is "soft" (106). Nonetheless, Celeya wins the narrator's admiration. Even though at the time they meet, he is a fat, coffee-drinking smoker, Celeya has intimate knowledge of the wild that the narrator lacks. That understanding has diminished, though, from age to age. The old man lives in a different world from that of his great-grandfather, and the knowledge he has is slipping into the past: "He could not give me this knowledge. He himself can barely retain it, his office swirling with blueprints and that ringing phone. For him it is a memory, for me a world I can only know by report" (107). The modern world has cut humans off from the land, relegating the old knowledge to memory and report. "Spirit Mountain," a text by Mariposa poet Ralph Cameron that Bowden quotes, confirms this sense of disconnection. The speaker compares himself to "A tree half fallen down with its roots / showing" (56), but still, his roots keep him in life and tenuously connected to place.

Bowden's Frog Mountain script only illustrates the impossibility of the narrator retrieving the kind of intimate contact that the indigenous people once enjoyed with the land. No matter how he admires it, it cannot be his: "I am not an Indian and I cannot think like a mountain" (56). Still, like the symbol of the half-uprooted tree, the stories he threads together inspire a form of hope as well as dejection. Bowden refuses to concede that Navitcu is dead: "Perhaps he waits under the cliffs in the upper canyon" (122). Through the logic of association characteristic of scripting, Bowden connects the old god to the sluggish frog found immobile on a rock during his hike in the chilly April sunshine. In juxtaposing references to the two entities at the end of the "Frog Mountain" chapter, he suggests that just as the frog could revive in warmer weather, the god and the mountain could recover their former strength. Following the traces of the old knowledge, Bowden discovers "a place that mocks the safe limits of our own imagination" (148). In spite of everything that separates him from the old ways, he recaptures some of the reverence for place that the modern world has lost. The Frog Mountain script points back to a time before the land was marked with the sign of empty; nevertheless, the Way is closed to the narrator.

The Mountains of Legendary Wealth

The magic of the place persists in another cluster of stories threaded through Bowden's book, the white people's legends of the mountains. These legends encapsulate the whites' desires and fears about the territory, revealing the changed relation to land placed under the sign of empty. The central legend, from which all others ramify, is the story of the mine with the iron door, an opening to the unimaginable wealth at the heart of the mountain said to have been sealed off by the Jesuits who exploited it in the distant past. The legend takes form bit by bit in Bowden's book, cited in newspaper clippings from the turn of the nineteenth century (15, 18) and personal testimonies (20–22, 31–32, 34–35), all garnered from a modern-day treasure hunters' manual. The dream of limitless wealth haunts early and latter-day miners, furnishes the plot of a 1923 novel (36), and persists even in the name of a restaurant "planted on the edge of [a ski] slope" (93). Bowden tracks this legend through its different variants to arrive at his skeptical explanation of its origin: "When the Jesuits entered this area, they introduced irrigated agriculture with European crops like wheat. Using Indian labor they built big churches out of mud. The Americans who came a century later refused to believe so simple an explanation for the large ruins" (35–36). From the ruined remnants of Spanish occupation, the legend arose to attribute value not to the mountain itself, but to the extractable wealth it promises for those with the luck or skill to take it.

For Bowden, the fabulous legend of the mine encapsulates all the "dreams of the main chance" that infuse American culture. Gold is the ultimate lure for "a nation propelled by money" (19). Bowden enumerates some of the phrases that encapsulate the popular fantasy of striking it rich in the West: "the Big Rock Candy Mountain, the Days of '49, the Diamond As Big As

The Ritz, the Glory Hole, the Bonanza, Paydirt, the Big Strike" (19). The list reminds readers how the dream of discovering a land of fabulous wealth has driven westward expansion and permeated stories, songs, films, television, and the American vernacular. In Bowden's account of his trek through the Cañada del Oro, his hiking companion is not immune to the imaginative tug of the legend of the lost gold mine. The desire to extract wealth from the land is not limited to mining. Jack's fantasy of taking gold from the mountain evokes the writer's memory of a winter spent on a New England farm, where two neighbors voraciously felled trees and slaved in their sawmill to convert the surrounding woods into a saleable commodity (23). The linking threads of avidity and extraction connect different stories into a web that ultimately explains environmental destruction.

In its immoderation, the settlers' hunger has a heroic dimension. One of the mountains' legendary figures is Pierre Charouleau, killer of bears and lions (17); another is Ben Lilly, a man reputed to have killed a grizzly with his dagger (89). Their deeds are set in the context of the extermination of those animals, so that the celebrated hunters themselves now seem "as remote as the days of megafauna when mammoths wandered Southern Arizona" (91). These men recall national legends like Daniel Boone (91) or Buffalo Bill Cody, who is one of the men drawn to the Catalinas in search of its "heart of gold" (26–28). Like the legend of the iron door, William Cody's rise to mythic status illustrates how covering exploitation in an aura of romance can seem to redeem it.[5] Cody was a truly American genius in his ability to wrap himself in a web of fantasy and illusion and gain wealth by putting his invented persona on stage. He helped put a heroic face on the national history of rapacity and destruction. Having been inspired as a boy by such tales, Bowden understands their appeal. He also understands their cost to the land. Thus the heroic legends are set against a diminished present. The iron door now leads to a ski lodge restaurant, one of the most recent avatars of the quest for gold. The epigraph to the "Frog Mountain" chapter quotes Frank Norris's demythologizing characterization of the adventurers of the West: "To get all there was out of the land, to squeeze it dry, to exhaust it, seemed their policy. When at last the land, worn out, would refuse to yield, they would invest their money in something else; by then they would all have made their fortunes" (117). Bowden shows both the appeal and the destructiveness inherent in the myth that betrays those who respond to it. On the one hand is a yearning for freedom and open space, on the other, an inexhaustible voracity that leads to the disappearance of everything of value in the land.

Both the story of Frog Mountain and that of the fabulous gold mine are centers of fascination in Bowden's book. The scripts centering on these subjects generate great intensity even though they make them appear patently unreal. They refer to a past that has now become legend. They endow the mountains with an aura of fascination, but they also point out their despoliation. The Indian legends relaying the earlier, harmonious vision of a sacralized land provide a counterpoint to the settlers' tales that reimagine the mountains as empty of spiritual value and available for exploitation. Complementing these scripts are others that reveal the ways in which cultural projections have guided human activity and shaped the mountain.

The Beleaguered Mountains

Bowden's representation of his initial encounter with the Santa Catalinas could be taken as emblematic of the settlement of the American territory. It all begins with the lure of the blank space on the map:

> I unfolded the thing and the city spread before me as a maze of thin blue lines tracking streets and highways. To the north the lines thinned and then ended. I asked the old man why this void suddenly appeared in the neat gridwork of the roads. He said there was a mountain, a big one called the Santa Catalinas.
>
> Snow lay on the ground outside the Chicago apartment, and the clouds hung slate gray. I sprawled on the floor of the living room puzzling out the nature of the thing in the blank space on the map, wondering over a force that could stop a city in its tracks. (146)

This empty space on the map of Tucson has a double significance. On the one hand, it demarcates the boundary between the settled ("the neat gridwork") and the wild ("this void"), showing the resistance of the towering granite mountains that "stop a city in its tracks." On the other hand, since that force appears conflictual in the eyes of the young American puzzling over the representation, the blank space issues a challenge to inscribe it with the marks of human occupation.

The script tracing the city's contest with the adjoining Santa Catalinas employs personifying metaphors that depict the history of development as a titanic struggle. Tucson appears as a devouring monster always intent on absorbing, destroying, or transforming the mountains. The collective hunger for what the land offers seems inexhaustible and deadly: “This is the constant story of the West, the region that people pour into seeking some bleary eyed vision of freedom, the region we all want to possess and then seem to maim with our endless appetites” (6). Bowden reworks the old topos of America as an alluring virgin in a new way, representing modern settlement on the mountain as a devastating assault on a living body. Mines are “lacerations” (32); an electric line is a “wide scar” (37); signs of a new development look like a disquieting “hot spot on a lung X-ray” (16). Whereas the mountain is personified, the metaphors depicting the settlers’ incursions dehumanize human activity and give agency to objects and institutions, thereby breaking down the binaries that justify exploitation. Prospectors form a “wave” that “slammed against the mountain” (33), “dream homes nibbl[e] . . . at the National Forest boundaries” (6), and the commodities market is a “mystery beast” with “a deep itch to gorge on . . . metal” (34). In this script contemporary Americans are part of a hybrid monster, a machine to make war on the land, capable of wiping out mountaintops (68) and routing the land (6). The Santa Catalinas are the latest victim in the epic of westward expansion that had previously left the Midwest “a forgotten battlefield,” “ground zero” (74) strewn with “carnage” (72).

Anticipating the case Jane Bennett makes for the vital power of things, Bowden’s script endows the material substance of the beleaguered mountains with agency.[6] The mountains represent something older and bigger than modern humans and they evade efforts to control them. Though they are victims, they have a certain resiliency. Thanks to the steepness of its slopes, the mountain range “saved itself from these hungry saws and axes” (26). In spite of the maps that efface it, in spite of all the efforts to refashion it for human purposes, Frog Mountain endures: “The pulse is slowing, the breath comes with increasing difficulty, and the body is scarred and wounded, but the thing is still alive and can be brought back to full vigor” (148).

Bowden’s personification of the mountains and his depersonalization of the region’s human inhabitants are more than simply rhetorical flourishes. In breaking down the dualities of modern thought,[7] this script suggests the possibility of a different kind of relationship with the land. It suggests a reciprocal exchange between the land and its inhabitants. The mountains give substance to the lives of those who live in their shadow: "The range is the heart and soul of this community. . . . We do not know who we are until we look at the mountain" (6). *Frog Mountain Blues* laments the destruction of the mountains in the hope of protecting them. The narrator imagines taking their side in the struggle: "What would you do if there were no holds barred?" (4), he asks his drinking companion in the book's opening chapter. Dreaming together, the men formulate a plan for healing the scars of human occupation. In spite of the extravagance of their fantasy—"There is no Bill of Rights for mountain tops" (4), observes Bowden's companion—the book points in that direction.

The Beloved Mountains

Alongside the script that presents human interaction with the beleaguered mountain range in terms of a war, Bowden places the testimony of those who have enjoyed a more intimate relation with it. Paradoxically, the lovers of the Catalinas are the very same people who have abetted their destruction: "As they toil on the mountain chasing gold or cattle or sizing up trees for lumber, they tend to fall in love with the place" (24). The users of the mountains get to know them so intimately that Bowden finds his own sporadic relationship superficial in comparison: "I cannot take in everything because, because I have never been a user. A visitor, yes, a person of the book stuffed with the lore written by scientists and naturalists. A hiker, a hunter, an idle wanderer. But never a user. The users get to the heart of the matter, to the bloody mash at the center of the thing we hide in our words like Nature, Environment, Wilderness, Ecosystem" (106–107). This vibrant evocation of "the bloody mash pounding at the center of the thing" evokes both the intensity and the violence of emplaced existence. It echoes Rick Bass's exultation at breaking into the heart of the felled larch trees to find their "luxuriant amber-orange" centers, "like pumpkin meat" (41). Beyond any imaginative or intellectual relationship mediated by words, the physical contact necessary to those who work on the mountains yields a more profound understanding of them. The testimonies of these users are therefore essential threads in the dense textual weave of *Frog Mountain Blues*; they offer alternative discourses that complicate the other scripts studied so far. At the same time, the mountain lovers' stories are necessarily inadequate, since they try to put into words a connection that resists expression.

As opposed to the powerful, quasi-allegorical representation of the beleaguered mountains or the legendary mountains of the Indians and the whites, the accounts of these quotidian interactions appear both more restricted and more anecdotal. At the same time, the partial and inevitably imperfect expressions of the users' connection to their environment add the richness of human experience to the composite picture Bowden creates. The central figure in the array of past lovers is Buster Bailey, the old rancher for whom some of the sites in the mountains are named. Other figures are presented as rivals in affection, and together, they suggest the range of human activity on the Catalinas and the depth of the mountains' impression on users. Bowden collects the stories of the Lemmons, botanists who catalogued new species of plants and gave their name to one of the peaks; of Tony Zimmerman, a schoolteacher and then storekeeper who bought up land on the mountains and paradoxically loved them both for their wildness and their development potential; and of John Brinkley, the forest ranger, who lived on the mountain with his wife, Gerry, until despair over its degradation led to his suicide. Together these users and lovers give a composite and ambivalent impression; their stories show that one can be devoted to the mountain and disfigure it at the same time. Due to the changing history of use, the things the mountain dwellers remember have changed, even vanished, although, in their memories, "this part of the mountain . . . still throbs like a beating heart" (57). Their stories suggest that, contrary to the book's dedication, love is not enough and is not exclusive of a destructive streak.

The mountain dwellers' scripts serve as counterpart and foil to the writer's self-presentation. Although they know the place far more intimately, some of them represent ways of life that have become discredited in his eyes. At the same time, their testimonies permit Bowden to sketch himself with ironic detachment, reflected back through his interviewees' eyes. Their view of him relativizes and distances the bookish amateur and dilettante backpacker whose interests do not compare with the existential choices of his interviewees. Nonetheless, they also authenticate his broader vision of the mountain, insofar as it incorporates theirs. Both Gerry Brinkley and Buster Bailey collect newspaper clippings and other texts about the place they love, and Bowden cites their collections as well as putting them in perspective. He notes that in collecting "things he considers clues to the real West" (19), Bailey is "not squeamish about his sources of information" (154). At the end of the book, the writer returns to visit Bailey to ask him what should be done about the mountain. The discussion is represented as inconclusive and unsatisfying; there is no possibility of agreement: "I want to send the cows home; he wants his ranch back" (153). Both men want the mountains returned to a former state, only Bowden's ideal mountains are further removed in time from Bailey's. Still, the account of the conversation ends not in stalemate, but on a fragile, tragicomic note of hope. Bailey insists that Bowden read one of his latest *National Enquirer* clippings about a man awakened from a coma by the bark of his faithful dog. Closing with a final picture of the "slumbering" mountain, seen from Buster's dilapidated shack, Bowden hints that the land could be revived—"brought back from the dead" (154)—by the exhortations of its lovers. This scene resonates curiously with an elliptical earlier account of a visit to a dying woman's bedside. In that earlier scene, Bowden descends from the mountain "to dying rooms crackling with the sounds of high tech machinery" (113). The machines to which the patient is attached seem themselves destructive, recalling an earlier quotation from Aldo Leopold: "The engines wherewith he conquers these rocks and rills and templed hills are stronger than his understanding of what hills are, and more powerful than his vaunted love for them" (80). All the different lovers' texts and testimonies hang together in a perplexingly ambivalent script.

Interwoven in *Frog Mountain Blues*, the scripts on the beleaguered and beloved mountain humanize the place, yet without vaunting the merits of civilization. Love of place fosters attachment and destruction. From the moment the mountain falls into the hands of humans, it is condemned to upheaval and decay; it becomes inscribed, superscripted with human destinies, and its original nature becomes more and more unreadable. This is the feeling conveyed in a number of Dykinga's photographs, in particular the one taken at Oracle Junction in which numerous commercial signs in the forefront crowd out the very hazy mountain behind, and where an obviously plastic bighorn stands poised above the sign: "**WANTED** SUCCESSFUL 'HUNTERS'" (21). Balancing this impression of the land's complete submergence by the marks of civilization are two more personal scripts in which

Bowden circumscribes the mountain in the private sphere of his experience. These scripts safeguard the mountain's mystery and sacred potential, although they transform the Indians' revered space into an individual channel for escape and self-discovery.

A Mountain Born of a Swamp

Perhaps the most mysterious of the book's scripts is the one that continually spirals back into the writer's childhood to connect Frog Mountain to a number of other places in America. In creating these very personal connections in space, Bowden allows the mountain to contain a dreamer's world, quite the contrary of the user's world in that it fosters the quest for self-understanding and reconciliation rather than for profit. To lead readers to that nurturing place, Bowden guides them to a most unlikely spot that he portrays as a kind of mirror image of the mountain. Although a Wisconsin swamp might seem poles apart from an Arizona mountaintop, this is the leap that Bowden asks readers to make. The journey has a tutelary guide in the person of Aldo Leopold, who worked in the Forest Service in Arizona before settling down in the Wisconsin farm of *Sand County Almanac*. Nevertheless, Bowden's swamp is very different from Leopold's marshlands. The later writer's capacity to observe and connect with nature is far behind Leopold's. The swamp to which Bowden's father once led him is a site of perplexity and discomfort that is, nevertheless, fundamental in his relation with the mountain.

The maze-like, enveloping, and even imprisoning jungle of the swamp, secreting an atmosphere of aggression and oppression, strewn with scratchy brambles and other treacherous obstacles and teeming with mosquitoes, initiates the writer into the ungovernable wildness that is the source of his fascination with the Catalinas. Painful and grueling as it seems to young Bowden, that hike somehow determines his attachment to the mountain and his objectives in his explorations. It distinguishes wildness as something to struggle with because it is dangerous and entrapping but also something to engage with because it enfolds and defines human beings. This seems to be the source of the father's joy as he leads his son through the swamp, apparently oblivious to the child's discomfort. In Bowden's scripting of his relationship with the wild, that afternoon in the swamp leads back to a winter afternoon on his uncle's "ten acres of trees on a ridge above the Sag Canal" (51), where he followed the traces of a rabbit in the snow, and forward to the explorations of the Catalinas described in the book. The later hikes in the mountains almost always involve somber late afternoon or nighttime scenes; wintry, stormy, and hostile weather; heavy packs and cramped, uncomfortable sleeping arrangements. The writer affronts and cherishes this atmosphere of destructive and defining engulfment in space.

Though he was initially fascinated by what seemed to be a blank spot on a map, Bowden's exploration of the mountains reveals them to be anything but empty space. They are filled with both exterior stimuli and interior associations. Though they deliver freedom and solitude, they also produce the impression of confinement inside something that dominates and encircles, a sensation that Bowden transports through other wild spaces in America:

> I have never really gotten out of that swamp. The years pile up and move past and I remain twelve, mosquitoes screaming around my head, the raw gases rising from the ooze at my feet. I am lost in a place I do not seem to want to leave. As I wander across decades, time passes yet remains still. . . .
>
> Wherever I go, I stay in the swamp and that place has become a maze that crosses deserts and climbs mountains and paddles canoes down rivers safe from dams. I have never tasted a drug that approaches this tangle of land in power. (132)

This passage reveals a private mythology in which a bubble of rapture creates an enveloping, half-imaginary world that surrounds him in different places and entraps him like a maze. In the literature of place it is rare to find such a compellingly idiosyncratic account of an individual's personal relationship with the land.

The script of the mountain as swamp explains some of the more disjunctive passages in the text, where the central consciousness "knife[s] through time and distance" (133), leading readers away from the Catalinas through a mental labyrinth that connects such disparate places as a glacier in central Mexico, a snow-capped mountain in Utah, a forest on the edge of the Grand Canyon, a creosote flat on the Gila River, and an alpine meadow on Mount Rainier (133–134). This personal maze also leads to various figures from the writer's childhood, like the fisherwoman who seemed to him to be one with the "the pond and meadow and woods" (38) or the old man who initiated him into the delights of wild food picked from the forest (39). This idiosyncratic script leads away from the devastation of the mountain, the proximity of the sprawling town, and the nagging conscience of personal contradictions—"My life has no tidy consistency" (143). Besides allowing a form of personal coherence, connecting the mountain to the swamp shows the complex lines that traverse space, tracing a dense web of individual trajectories. Those connections lead away from the specific place that is the focus of the book, linking it to the whole American continent.

The Hiker's Mountain

To intensify his connection with the mountain and to discover the secret of its appeal, Bowden takes up a challenge: he sets himself the task of hiking all the trails in the Santa Catalinas, covering roughly two hundred miles of paths (146). Quickly, though, he realizes that while the distance is not very great, hiking it will not necessarily give him the knowledge that he seeks: "The mountain takes more time than I had originally thought" (146). The challenge is not to cover miles but to slow down enough to learn from and of the mountain, and that, Bowden admits, could be the task of a lifetime. The hiker's mountain is different from the one seen from the city or explored through the legends and stories it has generated; nevertheless, the motivation for this script is the same; its source is a desire to connect with an invisible force. Contact cannot be planned; it comes from outside: "I hunt for reports of this powerful country and they never come when I expect them or from sources I anticipate" (103). To recreate this unpredictable quality so that readers can follow in his footsteps, Bowden rarely situates his hikes in time or gives their exact spatial coordinates; his accounts are directionless and timeless tracings on the mountainside. His attempts at seizing the experience in language are avowedly and perhaps deliberately abortive. His quest can yield results only when he stops seeking: "And so I am by this stream in this canyon and I am determined to stay put, to let the mountain rub against me, to stop my boots from trudging toward some biological Jerusalem I can neither describe nor doubt" (119). Readers wait with the writer, hoping for the epiphany that is both promised and denied. The rare instants of connection coincide with a sense of self-loss that, paradoxically, also brings heightened awareness: "The mountain and I lose that distance and I am locked into the pulse of the thing. I shiver, watch and wait. I am no longer a visitor" (102).

In moments of closest contact with the mountain, words are of least avail. This avowal of the inadequacy of language generates the poetic metaphors that serve as alternatives to physical impressions that cannot be recreated. A passage describing random images seen on a hike leads to an expression of a sudden moment of communion. The text moves from an objective description of the scene—rocks, a tree, roots, moss, a hawk—to highly metaphorical language:

> All these bits and pieces were puzzles in some kind of aesthetic and I relished the view. But I was walled off.
>
> When the storm hit, the wall fell. There was not a living thing in the range that was outside the pulses I was feeling, and for a few hours we were all one, riding out the explosion of cold, moisture, wind, and the fists of the weather hitting the old craggy face of the peaks. (107)

The hiker's sense of his surroundings shifts from seeing them as an aesthetic puzzle that excludes him to experiencing them as an intensely tactile struggle in which combatants merge into one entity that beats with a common pulse. He moves from seeing the world as a collection of discrete objects to seeing it as vibrant matter whose pulse beats with his own.

In the effort to put the hiker's experience of the mountains in words, Bowden has recourse to certain topoi familiar from nature writing. At times, he adopts the discourse on empty space, though he subsequently deconstructs it. The "Frog Mountain" chapter begins with the statement "Nothing much happens here" (117). Bit by bit he effaces traces in the landscape: "I can see no sign of human beings but my own boot prints. I can hear no engines, make out no roads, glimpse no aircraft, and find no well trodden pathway" (117–118). These intimations of emptiness are achieved by "tricks of the eye" (118). Similar stratagems produce the empty landscapes of conventional nature photography, which differs markedly from the photographs chosen for the book. Gradually, the hiker begins to take notice of the sounds and sights of the canyon, with its constant interplay of water, trees, and insects. After the initial impression of something "ordinary," even "commonplace," the hiker "sink[s] into the feel of the ground" to experience the place as "unique" (122).

This distinctive space permits moments of discovery that inspire the topos of wonder. The sight of a band of coatis prompts a baroque metaphor that attempts to recreate the magic feeling of the sighting: "You walk out into your American woods and suddenly the branches part and there stands a unicorn" (30). This allusion to a mythical beast strains to capture the shock of the encounter. It is the prelude to a plea for the value of otherness: "They tell me I will never know the world they know. And this fact reassures me that there is more to life than I will ever imagine" (30). In spite of the contrivances of humanity, the mountain remains a space that allows contact with entities that inspire "our capacity for wonder" (159).

The hiker's baroque evocations of the mountain provide a counterpoint to the more explicit representations of his companion's photographs. The descriptions provide both the book's center of energy and the cause of its dispersion into a crazy-quilt montage. The desire to capture the mountain in words prompts the recourse to other voices, as well as the recurrent references in the descriptions of the hikes to a "we" instead of an "I," though it is a "we" that never produces dialogue. It accounts for the book's inconclusive, disorderly character, as well as Bowden's sympathy for Leopold's sprawling, unfinished, and unpublished book on the Southwest (79–81). The writer multiplies scripts and angles of vision because the mountain he is trying to circumscribe is finally unknowable. This is what the hiker discovers.

Looking back on his book in the afterword, Bowden admits the impossibility of his quest: "No one knows the mountain, and no one ever will. That is why I wrote a book about the range and why you read it" (159). Far from being an admission of failure, this statement affirms that Bowden is attempting a new kind of literature of place. Instead of posing as a knowing subject informing readers about an objectified and knowable territory, Bowden tries to suggest the appeal of a place that remains elusive in spite of the many discourses that try to evoke it. The scripts on the hiker's mountain and the mountain as swamp evoke the wellspring of its fascination for Bowden, while ensuring that the source remains obscure and partially concealed from readers. In spite of its attempts at opening onto other people and dealing with common interest issues, the book remains at heart a very private dialogue with a mountain. This, though, is its strength, for Bowden's personal scripts allow readers to experience the intensity of his passion for the place.

In conclusion, *Frog Mountain Blues* is a fragmented text, split into multiple strands: the legendary scripts impart magic to the book but also unreality; the anecdotal human scripts give it liveliness and authenticity but also erraticism and confusion; the personal scripts empower the book without fully elucidating the origin of that power. Bowden's book teeters on the edge of a contradiction between, on the one hand, a fascination with the traces of the mountain's existence in time, with all the complexity that implies, and, on the other hand, the fantasy of a pure virgin mountain whose existence the traces belie. Although in the afterword he opts for the latter, dreaming of the advent of an era of "penance" and "new virtue" (165), his book demonstrates that the sign of empty denies the complex multiplicity of stories gathered around Frog Mountain.

5

Suturing the Map of the Known Universe in Ellen Meloy's *The Last Cheater's Waltz*

Like Bowden's *Frog Mountain Blues*, Ellen Meloy's *The Last Cheater's Waltz* stages the writer's discovery of the ongoing human involvement in the geostory of a beloved landscape. The two writers embark on their discovery from different directions, however, and arrive at different conclusions. Whereas Bowden depicts himself as a visitor seeking to connect with Frog Mountain, Meloy's book describes her attempt to restore a disrupted union with her surroundings. Both books feature post-Transcendentalist, postmodern reassessments of the individual's relationship to the environment. The projection of the Self onto a deserted landscape that allows infinite expansion no longer works, for the idea of emptiness is an illusion. Meloy's book explores some of the reasons why, guiding readers through a personal struggle born of a crisis of culture and of representation. Moving beyond the circumscribed zone of a Self projected onto a blank space with no history, Meloy discovers in her surroundings the traces of continuous human activity. Her book stages the shift from the impossible dream of an unchanging, pristine desert to the reality of humanity's continuous relations in and with the land. This discovery necessitates a shift from the fantasy of a solitary waltz with a beloved place to the recognition that the desert is not faithful to her alone—it is a cheater. More than a rediscovery of a given locale, Meloy's exploration changes the engagement that she establishes with the land.

Contrary to conventional associations with the desert, the arid landscape of *The Last Cheater's Waltz* does not induce transcendence but rather intensifies enthusiasms and appetites: "It is a land of absolutes, of passion and indifference, lush textures and inscrutable tensions. Here violence can push beauty to the edge of a razor blade" (7). Far from being empty—a land of pure spirit—the desert nurtures ferocity and bears its superscriptions. The two extremes of beauty and violence that seem irreconcilable are born from the coupling of the desert and its inhabitants. Meloy takes on the challenge of stitching the two together; she does so by exploring and mapping her surroundings piece by piece and then suturing together the disparate fragments in her book. Her work of gathering and stitching demonstrates how art can begin to repair the disjunctions induced by the moderns' splitting of the world into zones of culture and nature.[1] Her discovery of her surroundings takes two complementary forms, as she explores both the sensory world and its manifold representations in cultural artifacts and texts. Of course the two experiences cannot really be considered separately, for representations not only reformulate but also sublimate and extend experience. Nevertheless, in creating an apparently random pattern of meanderings in space and mental perchings that cross vast stretches of time, the book's scripts emphasize, at least initially, dissociation rather than coherence. Readers must find the continuity in the fragments and perceive the complex design of a text that initially appears haphazard and heterogeneous.

Meloy's physical explorations of the area around her desert home can be grouped into two rather distinct kinds of quest conducted through numerous expeditions. On the one hand, there is the self-affirming pursuit of beauty, on the other, the self-threatening investigation of destructiveness. These journeys of discovery seem to map out two apparently irreconcilable domains: the writer scrutinizes both a familiar, private space where she tries to exist in harmony with her surroundings and a wider, more tumultuous region that encircles and presses in on the familiar one. The central issue the book stages is that of reconciling the two domains. Having relinquished the perfect fit between inside and outside that the illusion of empty space affords, the subject confronts the problem of establishing a relationship to place.

The Frustrated Longing for Aesthetic Fulfillment

The quest for aesthetic fulfillment begins with the writer's recognition that she has somehow become alienated from her surroundings. Although the word is not mentioned, the malaise she describes recalls the anomie of the desert mystics, except that Meloy experiences physical as well as mental alienation: "I could no longer concentrate or hold life's focus or keep a coherent thought in my head. I felt desensitized in a body that had a local, if not a regional reputation for sensory intensity" (4). Before the onset of the malaise, she had bonded with her chosen locale in a more sensuous variant of the Transcendentalist projection onto the landscape that has been the staple of nature writing since Thoreau. Looking back on her first experience of the Utah desert, she remembers thinking: "Here is a place, which given enough time, sun, and acquaintance, could come perilously close to transcendence" (199). In that form of literary appropriation, the land becomes a reflection of the writer's search for ego sublimation; in return, the elected landscape is unified and idealized through the writer's sensibility.[2] Yet in spite of obvious similarities, Meloy's quest is markedly different from her predecessors', first in the intensity of her personal investment, and second in the urgency that this form of identification acquires for the preservation of her mental health. There is in her cult of nature a fervor and a pathos that seem almost at cross-purposes with the serenity to which most nature writers normally aspire.

Looking back at the end of the book at her initial conception of the desert, the writer remembers a territory that seemed complete in itself and indispensable for her survival: "It is *all* there" (199). In her identification with that locale, she achieved (or enacted) the perfect fusion of Self and place. Her desert experience was a celebration of solitude: "Solitude, in fact, became for me an aesthetic sensation" (199). Free of human connections and quotidian responsibility, like the mystic, she accedes to illumination: "The spare desert stirred the most luxuriant imaginings; shadow and color bore meaning, light a deliriously languid ecstasy that felt like being touched. Often there would come to me mysteries more intriguing than any lucidity—how, for instance, in a place with few or no human beings, one could begin to see the worth of what it means to be human" (200). In such instants she is reduced to a thin membrane adhering to the surface of the world—in fact it is difficult for her to distinguish one from the other. In molding herself to the land, she becomes permeable to it, embracing it in a mystical marriage: "Here I could fit flesh to rock. The sole difference between me and the land was a membrane of skin" (6). Nevertheless, this Edenic state of grace has been lost. The book begins with the desert dweller's resolution to find a renewed connection with the land through aesthetic experience.

This quest for beauty propels Meloy on a journey to find claret cup cacti, plants that she relishes for what she facetiously describes as "sadomasochistic pleasure" (11). With their "gorgeous grenadine blossoms" (12) and "needle-sharp spines" (11), they promise to submerge the senses completely and to lure her back to her passionate commitment to the desert. The red blossoms and spines have the same combination of splendor and danger as the red canyons of Utah. She hopes that these emblematic flowers will help her break through the anomie that imprisons her. In contemplating them, she attempts to merge with the natural world: "I made myself into a very small bug, hovered over a bloodred cup, and, little bug heart pounding, dove in" (15). The lure of beauty allows for abrupt and unpredictable switches from the panoramic to the close-up lens, or from the soft focus to the hyper-realistic highlights characteristic of her aesthetic vision. Yet the moments of transcendental fusion are also distanced and choreographed, since they prepare for the second kind of quest. The prick of the cactus spines brings a comic return to reality and an abrupt end to her immersion in the aesthetic: "*Wait!* . . . I was only pretending to be a bug" (15). The sight of a road ends the "desert pastorale" (19) and orients the search in a new direction.

The scripts detailing Meloy's aesthetic longings debunk her youthful fantasy that solitary communing with nature can reveal the meaning of human existence. Her expeditions are aborted when she finds traces in the landscape that thwart her desire to reconnect through sensory experience alone. Having gone to the San Juan River to try to steep her senses in the immediacy of her surroundings, she finds herself distracted "from an otherwise mindless downriver drift" by nagging thoughts of history (94). Her beloved desert is not a faithful, monogamous partner, but a cheat that has danced with many others: "I felt betrayed. My lover, my pure and faithful desert, was cheating" (101).[3] The conventional nature writer's exclusive concentration on the nonhuman aspects of place imposes a one-sided relationship on the land designed for her sole pleasure. She creates the illusion of an exclusive bond with the desert by emptying it of its history. The dissolution of this imaginary marriage is one of the causes of the malaise that the book describes. Once the conviction of enjoying a passionate union with her surroundings is lost, the subject feels "either helplessly unmoored from my Self or hopelessly lost in the murk of Self. The problem, obviously, was that I could no longer make the distinction between the two" (3). In fact, the two are intimately connected in the desert lover's existential schema: projecting an exclusive, solitary union on a place lends consistency to the Self and, at the same time, exposes it, for when the connection no longer holds, the Self disintegrates or implodes.

The effort to regain the lost connection to the land is stymied by the writer's discovery of certain signs in her favorite haunts. Alerted by "the distinct sensation of a suppressed vibration in the landscape" (16), she looks beyond her immediate surroundings and discovers unexpected marks of human encroachment into her private desert. In the vicinity of the cactus plants she discovers "an unnatural talus" dotted with "mine shafts and waste piles" (16). This vision of the traces of the reality of humanity's exploitative relation to the land expels her from the illusory paradise of her "desert pastorale." The desert is not an empty wilderness, inhabited only by Indians. Through it runs "a carefully graded dirt road as elegantly broad as a Parisian boulevard, plunked down in the middle of wild, dust bitten, single-track Navajoland" (17). With the disruption of her personal, sensuous geography of harmony, the writer has to come to terms with a new geography of consequence that requires "the unnaturalist's eye" to decrypt its traces (177). She must expand the range of her vision from the private to the public sphere, moving from simplicity to complexity, from Eden to Armageddon. The innocent world of sensuality is part of a universe of ruthless competition and confrontation. With Meloy, readers confront the problem of making sense of the clash between competing scripts on the desert and finding a way to reconcile them.

The desecrated desert takes on a different coherence from that found in the sensualist's explorations. It is not open, as if yielding itself to the lover's gaze. It has been shaped by secrecy, efficiency, and exploitation. It brings time into what had seemed an eternal, unchanging landscape. In the scripts detailing her excursions into this newly discovered space-time, Meloy meticulously traces the network of connections that exists between the "alien pebbles" (21) extracted from the uranium mines near her Utah home and some of the more somber sites in American geography: the White Sands Missile Range, site of the first nuclear weapons test; the Los Alamos nuclear complex; and finally the Gasbuggy underground nuclear explosion site. Her explorations of the sites of the atomic age take the form of a detective investigation and finally, on the fiftieth anniversary of the Trinity test, of a pilgrimage. These two kinds of expedition combine the desire to know and the desire to ritualize that knowledge.

Her journeys to these sites and her examination of the traces left on the landscape are both systematic and imaginative; the combination of these two forms of investigation are particularly powerful in elucidating the various causes and consequences surrounding the fabrication of the first nuclear weapons. In visiting the different locations, she situates the desert landscapes of America's Four Corners in the history of global conflict, linking them to Nazi Germany and its émigré scientists, to the catastrophic outcome of the team's experiments at Hiroshima and Nagasaki, and to the U.S.S.R. and the era of Cold War nuclear deterrence. She is particularly attentive to the combination of ignorance, carelessness, and dissimulation that have congregated around the experimentations and to the mixture of sanctification and paranoid regulation that surrounds the site.

Connecting Emptiness with Strategic Death

Though apparently opposed, the scripts detailing the aesthetic quest and those exposing the desecrated desert converge on the question of empty space. Like the solitary desert lover, the defense agencies imagined the desert to be empty. This illusion authorized them to use it in any way they liked. We come to understand with the writer that the idea of emptiness creates not just desert solipsism but a more terrifying moral void that permits the realization of unimaginable horrors: "They inherited an ethos that says arid lands are wastelands, not merely marginal but submarginal, places where nothing rusts quickly and the land seems but a parched void. Here few people can be harmed by hardware that is intended for maximum harm. Everything is out of sight, yet nothing is hidden. Both the spectacle and the secrecy can become intoxicating" (32–33). The defense agencies' desert is a paradoxical site in which contradictions flourish: visibility and secrecy, beauty and destruction, eternity and annihilation. The nuclear tests take place on "orphan lands, . . . withdrawn from the public domain"

(32), and given over to military dominion. The victims of this devolution are numerous; on top of the populations of Hiroshima and Nagasaki, there are the human and nonhuman inhabitants of the purportedly empty desert lands of the Southwest. In a continual process of effacement that perpetuates the myth of emptiness, the victims of military policy are simply erased from history: "The sterilization of landscape allows its reinvention; only at zero can there be a beginning, a blank slate to fill, even if the story that fills it—an apocalypse—itself becomes nothing again, in an instant. Land considered barren and empty of life cannot be stripped of life" (29). Stories seem to be stillborn in lands designated as empty. It becomes the writer's mission to resuscitate them and render them readable for her culture.

Blanking out the land makes it available for unchecked creation and destruction. This is true for the weapons program, which Meloy ironically sums up as "fifty years of high-gear building and banging followed by untold years of debuilding and unbanging" (150). It is true also for wildlife management in the Four Corners. Imagining the southwestern deserts as empty of living things has inspired programs to "correct" the situation by introducing foreign species. Meloy relates the devastation wreaked on native plant and animal populations by the introduction of two sub-Saharan African species, the oryx (81–83) and the aoudad, or Barbary sheep, into the desert for the benefit of sport hunters (177). Through a trick of writerly anamorphosis, she connects these nonnative invaders to the weapons that proliferate in the desert. At the end of her tour of the White Sands Missile Range, she sights what seem to be "two ground-based weapons" (80). On focusing her binoculars, she "suffers a confusing lurch in geography" (81) when she finds they are the horns of an oryx.

In recounting these explorations of "the terrain of strategic death" (84), Meloy never resorts to overt indignation or protest but rather seems petrified in a kind of mesmerized contemplation whose only relief is laughter: "This deranged jungle of ironies coinhabits my skull like feathers and fireworks. My heart fills with stones. I am the mad aunt who laughs her head off at the funeral. There rises in me the most inappropriate hysteria in this most somber of places" (29). The hysteria comes from being caught herself in the contradictions of the desert. Her identification with the desert, as well as her personal history as an American baby boomer, binds her inextricably in a web of temporal and spatial connections. Her feelings are complex and deep rooted, but always placed on a personal and ontological basis. More than the desecration of a beloved space, the traces of strategic death in the desert pose a mortal threat to her own existence. In the punning expression that she employs, they confront her with "a self-canceling proposition" (84). The land is "beautifully terrible. It conflates the ultimate with the intimate, poises a strange equanimity between near-pristine lands and proving grounds for the extermination of life. . . . It evokes a conflict of psyche, a collision of dispassion and vulnerability, that may bear more veracity about our century's troublesome relationship to the western deserts than the most sublime nature photograph" (84). This realization does not deny the validity of the quest for beauty; instead, it demands that the naturalist expand her vision to take in the historical and political dimensions of space.

Accepting the Contradictions of Space-Time

Meloy's dual orientation in her explorations of space gives rise to an "incongruous geography" (50) of complexity and ambivalence. She is repeatedly shocked by the coexistence of destruction and vitality; in the military reserves, she even witnesses the signs of regeneration linked to the desert's seclusion from human interference. Contraries coexist in the "oddly harmonious anarchy" (50) that characterizes the Southwest. What particularly fixes her attention is the juxtaposition of the sublime and the monstrous: "Yet all manners of disturbing ironies surge forth—a desert as beautiful as it is terrible, its conflation of the scared and the profane, the tension of the pure and sacrosanct against the penultimate human domination" (61). The tension becomes unbearable and threatens to provoke "some kind of shameless and messy psychotic event" (62). Meloy's journeys of discovery demonstrate that aesthetic fulfillment is not enough to accomplish psychic reintegration. Instead, she has to open to the land's complexity through an enlargement of Self. To find her moorings again, she has to accept the lines of connection linking her home to the terrains of strategic death.

In *The Last Cheater's Waltz* Meloy takes a step that Bowden refuses in *Frog Mountain Blues*. Whereas he concludes by giving primacy to the connection with nature that he enjoys inside the restricted sphere of his sensations and wanting to efface the traces of other kinds of interaction, Meloy tries to accept responsibility for the land's history. This is an important mutation in the traditional literature of place. Her exploration of the infamous American military sites in the desert gives her a new understanding that alters her gaze. No longer the innocent sensualist, she now brings to the land "a perception tainted by ceremony, the imprint of human narrative on its stark contours of stone and shadow, as if such beauty must have to pay a somber penalty in sorrow" (68). This mournful declaration seems to acknowledge the writer's implication in the collective guilt that comes from her humanity and, more particularly, from her American nationality. Reconnecting with home means recognizing that every part of the land is implicated in a network of destruction: "At Trinity I had discovered that my own neighborhood might be wired to the vortex of apocalyptic horror. The land to which I devoted my most fervent loyalty ran a gossamer tightrope between beauty and violence" (100–101). Involuntarily implicated in the destruction, as the images of the wires and the tightrope suggest, she needs to find a new form of habitation that allows for contradiction. In other words, she has to assume her participation in the duality of American history; she has to acknowledge both the wilderness and the Trinity test site as "blood and home" (84). In spite of this new lucidity about the place she inhabits, Meloy remains linked to the older school of nature writing insofar as the devastating analysis that she proposes of the mechanics of destruction does not lead her to investigate sociopolitical causes, still less to militate politically or, unlike Bowden, to suggest alternative solutions. Her discovery of the defilement of the desert remains a private revolt and a private concern; she responds emotionally, expressing horror, grief, and fear at her discovery.

The plight of her home territory and by extension that of her country and the entire planet calls for a realization and conversion that individuals —herself first and foremost—must achieve within their consciences. Her painful exploration of the tainted desert aims to accomplish more than instruction or pilgrimage; it raises awareness in order to accomplish healing. The therapeutic dimension of the book comes across in the seriocomic scripting of her relation to place through her interactions with various animals that inhabit her neighborhood. These scripts weave a web of connections to the nonhuman that move the relation to place beyond aesthetics and into personal responsibility.

Moving toward Healing

The script that traces the writer's personal metamorphosis through her relationship with the other animals in her world could be called the lizard's saga, since it begins with Meloy's discovery of a side-blotched lizard drowned in her morning coffee. Not noticing that the reptile has taken shelter in her cup, she scalds it with boiling water, and when she goes to drink from her cup, she finds the floating lizard, "its belly the pale blue of heartbreak" (3). This unintentional act triggers the existential crisis in which the writer no longer connects with her surroundings, feeling either "unmoored" or "lost in the murk of Self" (3). Imprisoned within the limits of her consciousness, oblivious of the other lives around her, the writer is paradoxically also denied self-definition, since only by acknowledging the otherness of the external world can she affirm her existence as a subject. This is the vital lesson of Levinas's meditation on alterity in *Alterity and Transcendence*.[4] The lizard represents that which is most vital in herself—her ability to connect with the world. Its corpse serves as an icon of her alienation, an image of Self as Other and Other as Self. The reptile's rigor mortis and its heartbreak-blue color mirror the writer's "ever-creeping numbness of soul" (6).

Some kind of ceremony or ritual is needed to honor the lizard and to reconnect the writer with the world. The mixture of empathy, guilt, and sorrow that the death inspires prompts action: "To reinhabit my own body, I had to traverse, again and again, the desert's cruel and beautiful skin" (8). The remedy for spiritual paralysis is to reconnect with the land—made as alive and palpable as a lover through the metaphor that turns its surface into skin. In the ritual that ends the book's preface and defines the structure of its quests, Meloy takes out a map of the Colorado plateau, draws a small *O* around her home and a larger circle—the terrain to be explored—around it. She rests the lizard's corpse at the center—a sign of the Self to be resurrected and the Other to be recognized. The process of healing the rift between the Self and its surroundings takes place in a mood of malaise and neurasthenia, as if it involved changing skins. The resulting metamorphosis enables acceptance of a different form of emplacement in space. The haiku that is the book's epigraph suggests the radical nature of the transformation: "Since my house burned down, / I now own a better view / of the rising moon." What occurs is nothing less than a complete change of perspective. The solipsistic bubble that sheltered the writer from historical reality explodes with the lizard's death. To reinhabit herself, she must first venture out of herself.

The first step toward recovery involves the retracing of familiar paths. Meloy seeks out the claret cup cactus, a perfect emblem of the beloved desert in its "incarnation of the thin threshold between what the Zuni call the beautiful (*tso'ya*) and the dangerous (*attanni*)" (12). In this first effort to restore her sanity, she imagines herself becoming a desert creature and projecting herself fully into the flower's seductive and menacing embrace. The illusion is quickly broken—"I was only pretending to be a bug" (15)—and other animals (a lizard, two ravens, and perhaps a toad) remind her of her distinctive status. The lizard's gaze conveys a cautionary message: "*Homo sapiens* are oblivious to their imminent demise as a species" (16). In order to reconnect, the writer must first discover the extent of the difference that separates her as a human being from the other desert species. A new path appears, metaphorically as well as literally, as she sights the mysterious road that will lead her to take stock of the extent of human deviation.

The second phase of the journey takes the writer to the White Sands test site, where she measures the extent of her alienation by "approaching home from the outside in" (27). In a fitting development of the lizard's saga, the writer enters the moment of the first atomic explosion by relating the fate of the spadefoot toads that "unburied themselves" on the morning of the first atomic explosion (25), waking up from a period of dormancy with the arrival of a monsoon that momentarily delayed the test. The amphibians' biological imperative inspires an ironic mixing of roles and metaphors. The toads, who were certainly vaporized by the blast, "writ themselves into history" while the "scientists spawned the primary death anxiety of the rest of all time" (26). The atomic age gives birth to strange new hybrids like the spawning scientists who produce an element (plutonium) that feels warm to the touch, "like a live rabbit" (27). In this sinister atomic site, males give birth, metal comes alive, and living things die. The sacrifice of animals for science arouses an emotion that the writer punningly names "animal anxieties" (48). The evocation of the nonhuman animals that are victims of nuclear experimentation (toads, mice, monkeys, beagles) weighs against the description of the wild menagerie that thrives thanks to the limited human impact on the military site. Yet some of these animal inhabitants—the oryx—are seen as menacing aliens, emblematic of the unnatural doings in the missile site. The writer's imagination strains against such inconsistencies, and her language works to conjure up and to highlight the uneasy contradictions.

When her mind balks, Meloy seeks to reconcile herself physically with the wounds that the atomic tests have opened up in the earth. At the black lava obelisk marking the site of the first explosion, she seeks understanding through contact, ready "to lie down on the seam that joins" the landscape to the memory of the terrible genesis (36). She attributes the intensity of her emotion to "separation anxiety" (36). Marking a site of rupture, the obelisk compels a double grief: both the Self and the place are bereft: "Both of us—woman and land—are orphaned" (36). This unexplained riddle points to the need for a period of mourning for the loss of the bond that formerly existed between the writer and the desert and also for a process of readjustment between them.

The discovery of these incongruities in the desert confirms her "estrangement from Place" (112) and prompts a retreat to the quest's starting point. Meloy returns to the center of her personal map: "I changed direction. I looked under the lizard's belly. I tried to find Home" (101). In what might seem a flight from the unpleasant truths discovered at the missile base, Meloy seeks refuge in her own plot of desert, participating in the construction of a home (97–147). In some ways this episode revisits the American story of settling the West. Meloy and her husband begin by stringing a barbed-wire fence around their eight acres, demarcating a private territory cut off from the outside world. Nonetheless, rather than fencing in the land in order to extract the wealth it can provide, Meloy's plan is to reclaim it from the cattle that have laid it waste. Inaugurating the St. Thomas Aquinas Cactus and Succulent Society (111), she gives free rein to "botanical anarchy" (112). The choice of the society's patron saint is not explained, but perhaps it derives from his link with natural theology, his detection of God in the workings of nature. Thoreau is the unnamed patron who oversees the "slut's Walden Pond" (111) that Meloy seeks to create. The boundary of the fence places Meloy's home at the center of an ecological restoration project and inaugurates what Daniel T. Spencer would call an "*ethics of praxis*."[5] In inviting desert species to share her home Meloy takes the first step toward mending the split between humanity and nature that had enabled the projection of emptiness and invited devastation.[6] It is also a way to atone for the damage inadvertently done to the lizard and thereby to begin healing the Self. Meloy decides to "earn" her place on the earth (142) by making it welcoming for plants and animals. One of the ways she works to restore the land is by making it propitious for the return of spadefoot toads. If these amphibians were to return in spite of the nuclear horrors she has discovered, she senses that everything would be "right with the world" (144). In spite of its promise, this pastoral interlude comes to an abrupt end upon the discovery of a yellow rock—"right there under the lizard's belly" (145)—that she identifies as carnotite, the raw material for producing plutonium.

This discovery connects home with the terrain of strategic death, sending the writer back to the periphery of the known universe to further investigate the military complex, this time in Los Alamos, where she tours the museum and, at the same time, spirals back to memories of growing up in America in the atomic age. Once again, Meloy confronts a disquieting mix of fertility and devastation. Her naturalist's eye picks out the wildlife on the "pine-cloaked mesa" (151), while she meditates on the radioactive corpses of laboratory animals "buried in hot dumps set among off-limits compounds" (151). Her quest continues northward to Carson National Forest, site of the Gasbuggy tests in which Los Alamos scientists tried to reconvert atomic explosions for peacetime use in the ironically named Plowshare Program. They succeeded in turning places they saw as "empty" into environmental danger spots. Once again, Meloy discovers a paradoxical space, a toxic burial site where elk wander freely: "To a lesser degree yet bearing the same irony as the White Sands Missile Range, this place mixes a marginal 'wild' with massive human impact" (176–177). In a replication of the earlier journey, Meloy discovers another desert space in which wildlife proliferates alongside the ultimate symbols of human destructiveness. This time, because of the sun's heat, the words on the commemorative plaque at the Gasbuggy site are imprinted *backward* on her derriere, "like a branding iron" (169). Though marked by the experience, she literally begins to put it behind her, which signals the final step in her reconciliation with place.

In the final chapter in the book, Meloy faces a dilemma: to abandon the home she feels has cheated her, or to reconcile herself with its impurity.

Her faith in the desert seems to be at its lowest point. Having tried to deepen her knowledge of home, she is propelled not toward "resurrection but a collapse of faith. Was I on the verge of an apostasy of place?" (189). The start of the chapter shows her preparing her escape from a shelter that has seemingly turned into an apocalyptic nightmare. The animal world seems to be in chaos, with hummingbirds becoming entrapped in the mesh of her screened shelter, coyotes howling and fighting all night, and lizards raining down on her by day. The house seems to have become a trap and the violence at the edges of her familiar territory seems to have come home with a vengeance. The squabble between coyotes over a rabbit is the trigger for her escape. The morning after the struggle, when she finds the remnants of the rabbit, she has to factor violence and destruction into her private world. In an expression of solidarity with the victim, she comically puts on the dead rabbit's ears. Then, in a final gesture before leaving, she rescues a lizard that has been buried in the sand by a passing truck. This recovery of the lizard hints at the reconciliation to come, but before it can be accomplished Meloy needs to identify the suspicious yellow substance found on her property. In an episode of comic anticlimax, the rock turns out to be simply a piece of yellow-painted asphalt from the highway; the way is clear for a reconfirmation of faith, but first the writer passes through a final night of doubt.

As if to corroborate the destructive streak in human nature, Meloy goes looking for a pre-Columbian burial site that attests to humanity's homicidal tendencies. Instead, she gets lost, opening the way to a new discovery (201). Camping on a rock ledge she encounters a kit fox: "On tall, spindly legs, this one trotted resolutely by as if it were late for church. Where the kit fox brushed past me, my skin burned. The rest of my body became like smoke. *Don't go out there,* I thought with a laugh as I dropped down to hands and knees and crawled across the sand and into my bed" (209). With its blend of reverence and humor, this scene suggests that in spite of her anxiety, she has reconnected with the more-than-human world.

Paradoxically, though, the last step in the writer's reaffirmation of the world and her reinhabitation of her body occurs at a moment of refusal. Balking at the signs of the twentieth century's alarming history discovered on the desert's skin, she remarks in the pages of her notebook that she has decided "to fling the Map of the Known Universe off a sheer, thousand-foot-high cliff" (211). Throughout *The Last Cheater's Waltz*, the act of transferring the traces of her discoveries into the notebook has been the writer's way of being, in every sense, drawn into the world. The discarding of the map is thus a refusal of the historical truths uncovered on her journeys and a rejection of her "duplicitous lover," the desert. However, the moment of doubt only sets the subsequent reaffirmation into a more theatrical scenario. In a chaotic scene, which combines the song of piñon jays and the lightning flashes of a sudden monsoon, she changes her mind, retrieving the Map and deciding to "to suture the folios into a whole" (216). In stitching the Map together (presumably into the book itself), the writer makes the contradictions "all fit beneath the belly of a lizard" (216). The cure for her malaise is to return home with a new understanding and commitment: "There was but a single way to exist here, to make my way through this land with grace: take it into myself and rediscover it on my own breath" (217). This vow to sing the world into existence like the Australian Aborigines surely constitutes another metatextual reference to Meloy's own book. As if to confirm the rightness of this decision, the epilogue recounts the return of the spadefoot toads to the site of her desert home. The series of encounters with desert animals confirms her connection to the land. They are totemic beings demanding the responsibility that comes with kinship.

The Map of the Known Universe, centering on the lizard and showing all its subsequent avatars in other desert animals, holds together the book's two opposing experiential quests. The search for aesthetic fulfillment in the desert reveals the violence that is inseparable from the natural beauty but has been pushed to unnatural extremes in sites placed under the sign of empty. Although in the terrain of strategic death the writer discovers traces of the apotheosis of human destructiveness, she also finds, in the desert and in herself, the capacity for regeneration. If her problem as a lover of the desert is to understand how humanity violates wild places, her task as a writer is to find the language that expresses that contradiction. To this end, Meloy assembles various patterns of inscriptions that parallel and concretize her movements in space. Like most of the texts in the new literature of place, the book stitches together different scripts that contrast and converse with one another, allowing readers to trace their own paths across the resulting map of the land.

Investigating Ways of Knowing

The Last Cheater's Waltz gathers written traces emanating from, on the one hand, the universe of knowledge—the facts and theories privileged by society at large—and, on the other, the known universe—experience filtered though the artist's individual perception. In venturing into public spaces such as missile sites and museums, Meloy enters the world of officialdom where objectifying discourses are employed in very specific ways. This universe of knowledge contrasts with the artist's private universe, where a highly individual and original sensibility filters the information coming from the outside. Rather than privileging solely the latter form of knowledge, Meloy conscientiously explores the former. At one moment she describes herself sitting down in a lawn chair to read "not soporific Thoreau or sinuous Rilke but *The Los Alamos Primer* and a treatise on particle physics that promised once and for all to unravel the cosmic onion" (136). This scene of reading encapsulates the mixture of detached humor and exactitude with which she pursues intellectual understanding. At the same time, the image of "unravel[ing] the cosmic onion" also suggests her opinion on the dangers of abstraction. In fact, her book makes a distinction between highly theoretical sciences, physics in particular, and the life sciences or earth sciences that help her get a grip on her surroundings.

The abstract sciences reconstruct the world in intellectual terms and thereby detach human beings from its tangible realities. Going beyond the readily verifiable understanding obtained by the senses, the nuclear physicists reduce the world's working to mathematical formulas. For Meloy this degree of abstraction is both alienating and dangerous, or dangerous because alienating:

> Somewhere out there intelligent people are reducing the birth of the universe to an equation. Those laws seduce us with their purity and precision, physicist Alan Lightman wrote in *Dance for Two*; scientific knowledge provides a reassuring degree of certainty. "Even Heisenberg's quantum Uncertainty Principle, which proclaimed that the future cannot be determined from the past, gave a mathematical formula for containing uncertainties, like a soundproof room built around someone who is screaming." (95)

Reassured by the purity and perfection of their science, the atomic physicists were able to produce the deadliest of weapons. Somehow their ignorance of the desert biotope complements their detachment from the consequences of their experiments. Abstraction distances the world, making it available for the worst kinds of excess: "The mind hides on the wrong side of words" (45). At White Sands, the technical language creates a "neutralizing distance from the fact that much of what graduates from these testing grounds is designed to obliterate mammalian life" (46). Through her investigation of the historical sites of atomic research, Meloy thus arrives at conclusions similar to those of Bruno Latour about anthropological investigations of Western culture. The conceptual split between mind and matter licenses the moderns to manipulate the material world. Their insistence on the separation between the social and the natural permits them to carry out experiments that give rise to ever-proliferating hybrids.[7]

At White Sands and Los Alamos, the same projective tendency that emptied out American space removes the physical world from material consequences. In fact, Meloy makes a revealing connection between these tendencies when she notes in the epilogue that "physicists who study the smallest of particles call the spaces between them a *desert*. On his charts one physicist illustrates this emptiness with drawings of little saguaro cacti" (223). Here we see that Meloy's choice of claret cup cacti as the object of her initial quest is not innocent. For her, as opposed to the unnamed physicist, cacti are not symbols of nothingness.

By juxtaposing the science of abstraction to the more congenial life and earth sciences, Meloy denounces the rift in human understanding that permits environmental catastrophe: "The great abstraction of nature—physics and the tools that enabled it—lay across a gnawing chasm from our most tangible experience of nature: the land. Yet here again, on this grand mesa, the two had coupled intimately" (165). Complementing the excursions into the abstract discourses of physics and military jargon, she guides readers toward a fuller knowledge of the land by adopting the discourses of biology or geology. Although very different from her lyrical raptures, these more factual passages harmonize with them by demonstrating the intricacy and fullness of the land. Though personalized by her penchant for remarking on absurd and grotesque details, Meloy's impressive knowledge of the organic and inorganic elements in the biotope is normative in that she critiques the implantation of nonnative species like the oryx or aoudad. The displays of factual knowledge can be contrasted to the moods of cartoonish light relief and burlesque playacting that surface throughout the book and produce the paradoxical blend of self-distancing and self-dramatization that suggests an acute sensibility. The writer's more individual form of understanding comes across in a series of private inscriptions—her personal stenography of the world—imprinted on the desert.

Meloy's Sensuous Mapping of Her Known Universe

Interwoven with the official scientific discourse on the real, we discover the sensuous materiality of the world as filtered through Meloy's exuberant receptivity. Describing herself mockingly as a "congenital sensualist" (46), she steeps her description of the environment in compellingly concrete detail. Her focus on the physical does result in the sometimes comical mention of her body parts in incongruous places in the text. Her description of the visit to Los Alamos, for example, begins with the announcement that "the nuclear weapons laboratory was quite concerned about my breasts" (149). The point of this opening sally is to acknowledge that the discoveries of the nuclear physicists have relevance for civilian applications, in this case, medical imaging. These varied stylistic traits constitute the characteristic Meloy Weltanschauung—representing a bodily inhabited and body-permeable landscape.

In Meloy's deployment of multiple scripts to recreate the experience of place, the text follows a general metonymic principle in which things connect to each other. Thus the claret cup cacti stand by themselves but also stand for the desert itself. Moreover, the writer stands in for readers, inviting us to experience the world as she does: "You want to but should not fall facedown into the lush halo of nectar inside each cup-shaped flower and wallow there" (11). The writer's language conveys her passionate attachment to beauty and demands readers' adherence. Her description of the claret cup cacti, for example, aims at seduction: "A mound of claret cups in full bloom throws its glory against the russet desert in brazen harlotry. Theirs is a wild and transient beauty of sweet, precise torture" (11–12). Metaphors lend physicality to Meloy's descriptions; here, the force of the claret cups' attraction is rendered through the verb "throws." The voluptuous encounter of sweetness and violence that she attributes to the plant comes across not only in the lexicon, but also in the sonority of the phrases, with the long vowels and diphthongs (mound, bloom, throws, glory) contrasting with the ensuing sibilant consonants (against, russet, desert, brazen). The words beg to be spoken out loud, so that, with the writer, readers can "rediscover the world on [their] own breath" (217).

As an extension and also a figure of the personal world that she invites readers to share, Meloy fashions the "Map of the Known Universe" (8), a pictorial representation of her surroundings that acts as an interface between herself and the world, an objective correlative of home that she plays with and that acts as a defensive protective shell. In sketching the contours of her world, she seeks an antidote to her soul's malaise; she tries to construct a private universe in limited interaction with the outside world: "A map, it is said, organizes wonder. When I created mine, I had hoped to instill more deeply the desert aesthetic that year after year reflexively seduces me. From the most quotidian, instinctive details of my environment—light, seasons, creatures, textures, moods—I would draw a revelatory oasis, passion turned into something holy" (100). In its initial conception, then, Meloy's map has a limitative and consolatory function. However, insofar as it serves as an incitation to exploration, the act of drawing the map leads her in a completely different direction, revealing the existence of alien presences: "Even though I had cast it over home terrain, it netted unsouled shapes and cruel angularities. I was convinced that foreign armies occupied the Known Universe" (100). The discovery of these "invaders" threatens the writer's integrity, for the map is supposed to be "a map of my own body" (136). Like a skin irritated by a foreign agent, "the Map . . . *itched*" (100). This discovery marks the failure of the Transcendentalist identification of Self and universe. The map's itching signals a new stage in the metamorphosis of the writer's consciousness. At this point, Meloy's cartography assumes a therapeutic role in allowing a diagnosis of the deep roots of her malaise. The map's circumscription of the world enables Meloy to keep her divagations under control, even as she enlarges the scope of her understanding. Through her periodic recapitulations of the icons traced on the map (83, 142, 213, 216), she is able to observe the progress that is imperceptible in her actual encounters and explorations in the field. She perceives more than she expresses through her sometimes-catatonic reactions. Finally, she uses the map in order to position herself inside her mental confusion. In placing an *O* at the site of her home, she situates the start of her quest and at the same time makes humorous reference to the various "ground zeroes" that she will uncover in the known universe. The lines she draws connecting these peripheral hot spots to her home materialize the web of connections that existence in space implies.

As her explorations discover more and more information about the past, the map becomes a kind of midden, both a heterogeneous deposit like the Anasazi burial site that she seeks on her final expedition, and a medley that brings together the indispensable raw material of events and things for the creation of her book. These medleys or middens figure prominently at regular intervals in the book, when, in the course of her peregrinations, she encounters accidental and heterogeneous gatherings that combine confusion and concretization. They might initially be considered as antiscripts, because instead of connecting they seem to jumble things together. Nonetheless, their miscellaneousness furthers the quest to find a place in the universe. Insofar as they constitute a hodgepodge world in which difference survives without impinging too much on others and without too much risk to its own specificity, these middens are talismans against self-destruction. As Meloy lists some of the items found at the Basketmaker burial site that had been excavated near her land (131–132), she finds a link to her own sense of home. Meditating on the discovery of the bones of a Canada goose atop those of a man, she thinks of how the geese that still fly over her home "daily bring [her] serenity by their mere presence [and] announce [her] place . . . in the family of things" (132).[8] These pre-Columbian middens also link up with the town dump where Meloy and her neighbors inspect the discarded remnants of individual lives, sometimes retrieving them and giving them new life, creating a collective community of trash (120–122). Moreover, they connect to the point bars on the river where miscellaneous debris collects, exposing a motley blend of organic and inorganic detritus that brings together human and nonhuman existence. Los Alamos also has its post–Cold War midden in the form of "The Black Hole," a warehouse of salvaged surplus scientific equipment that, in contrast to the other miscellaneous collections Meloy describes, strikes her as profoundly alienating. Still, this sinister collection attests to the materiality of the scientists' work, despite their preference for abstraction, and it offers tangible, historical traces of their work of destruction.

These middens suggest the prototypical format of the book, supplying some of its glorious profusion, while lacking the order and the connectedness that the writer offers. In the end, instead of throwing away her map, consigning it to a midden, Meloy decides to amend it by stitching it together (216). The resulting creation is a montage of various styles, places, perspectives, moods, and modes of address. *The Last Cheater's Waltz* offers a new construction of place through juxtaposition. Like the waltz of its title, it brings contraries together in "a precarious union of delirium and control" (212). It creates a reflection on space made of confusion, discovery, and acceptance, rather than intellectual cogitation. Meloy's work combines the heterogeneous montage that Bowden favors with underlying strata of coherence that inhere in dispersed but highly suggestive metaphoric motifs that readers can rearrange in acts of interpretation. The book does not simply reflect complexity like Bowden's; it gives it a new definition. In fact both the loosely gathered assemblages and the intuitive cohesions are complementary aspects of the book's stylistic imprint.

The Last Cheater's Waltz is a hybrid of mind and land, a mental landscape that registers an enlarged and enhanced form of knowing that breaks through the limits of traditional nature writing. It represents a new mode of inhabitation that characterizes the contemporary literature of place. The major breakthrough in Meloy's text is the discarding of the sensual appropriation of nature that she stages dramatically at the outset and its replacement by a more responsible inhabitation of her elected environment. Her book is a valediction to the dream of a pristine universe. Her beloved desert is not empty, nor wholly wild. It is neither exclusively a place of exile nor a privileged site of self-enhancement. The Known Universe encircling her home makes it a complex site: "Home is both the mass and the space, the red-boned rock and the places where one tries to shape belief around mystery" (223). Home has become "the heartland of consequence" (224), a place where one can and must reconcile private and public obligations. Although she witnesses other forms of engagement like the man who throws blood on the obelisk at Trinity (222), Meloy favors responsibility for her emplacement rather than revolt. If this form of engagement remains personal and isolated, it does not lack commitment. On the contrary, the writer vows "to live here as if there is no other place and it must last forever" (224), a pledge that would change the world if everyone adopted it.

In the books discussed in Part II the writers undergo a transformation in their attitudes toward the land. They move from seeing favored places as empty spaces for personal expansion toward understanding how they sustain complex networks of humans, animals, and things with their own histories and trajectories. After the initial blankness attributed to the land, place attains a state of quasi personhood in these books; it is troped as wife (Bass), friend (Bowden), and lover (Meloy). While that new status gestures toward according places rights in the "parliament of things,"[9] the attachment the writers form to their homes remains intensely personal. It is a love relationship with an anthropomorphized site. These projections acknowledge its sustaining role and also, to a degree, its distinctness, but the writers' intense personal attachments are not necessarily transferable. In spite of the opportunities for participation that their scripting techniques offer to readers, their rapport with place remains somewhat exclusive. We can witness Meloy waltzing with the desert, but can we join in the dance?

The writers featured in Part III are less passionately possessive in their commitment to the places they explore. From the outset they are skeptical about attributions of emptiness; their inquiries aim at finding new ways of viewing the American territory. They refuse the cultural division between the civilized and the wild, the inhabited and the uninhabited, in which so-called empty places have served as repositories of civilization's refuse or refuges against its encroachments. In this new perspective, the land is neither a sanctuary for an exceptional people, nor the repository of transcendent values. Instead, in a radical change in attitude, the American territory is considered as a co-creation of place, people, and things. The land is no longer a value in itself, bad or good, malefic or transcendent; it is no longer considered in isolation as an alternative to society; rather, it becomes a kind of litmus test revealing the nature of the human and social engagements invested in it. It is considered in terms of the way it is occupied. In that perspective, if the land appears bad, it is due only to bad usage and not to its intrinsic worthlessness or its malefic intention, as some immigrants ruefully came to believe. By the same token, inhabitants cannot sustain a romantic connection with the land; if their relationship is to endure, romance must give way to a bond of mutual suitability and acceptance. With the books chosen for Part III, the scope of the new literature of place widens from the coupling of individuals with beloved places to the relationship of the nation to its territory.[10]

These changes in the perception of space open up the range of possible sites of reflection in the literature of place. Writers no longer select places exclusively for their beauty and isolation. They refuse to see humanity as "only a visitor" in segments of the American territory. They renounce the nature writer's task of capturing "wildness" in prose so as to refresh readers' appreciation of the fullness and the rightness of things prior to their defilement by society. There is no place that is not marked by the traces of human interaction. Even the regions that seem the most remote and that are placed under the sign of empty participate fully in the nation's social, political, and economic life. In choosing to write about place in this new way, these writers acknowledge the role that perception plays in policies governing the territory. These books seek to change the way readers think about place in America.

III.

Retracing Paths and Reassessing Emplacement

The Peopled Shape of the Land in Jonathan Raban's *Bad Land*

In the new literature of place, emptiness is not represented as an objective quality found in the land, but as a subjective projection imposed on it. This alternative vision is suggested in Jonathan Raban's title, *Bad Land: An American Romance,* which places two different projections in ironic opposition. The subtitle, *An American Romance,* evokes the 1944 King Vidor film relating a clichéd version of the American dream in which a penniless Czech immigrant succeeds through hard work. The extended metaphor in the book's opening pages comparing the Montana prairie to an ocean and the writer's car to a vessel reinforces this intertextual connection. Raban's use of the conventional trope of the prairie as ocean recalls the film's opening scene of a boat bearing its load of hopeful immigrants to Ellis Island. In employing the metaphor, Raban inscribes his peregrinations in the tradition of discovery narratives. He casts himself as the European adventurer arriving in the New World. The title, *Bad Land,* seems at first to undercut the archetypal myth of the American Dream by opposing a realistic vision to a romantic one. Nonetheless, it would be truer to the book's revisionary thrust to interpret both the title and the subtitle as ironic. The land—in this case, the plains of eastern Montana—cannot be bad in itself but only in the eyes of those who have invested their hopes in it and who expect to derive a profit from it. Moreover, only those who project improbable dreams onto their chosen destination can assimilate immigration with romance. With this ironic opening flourish Raban situates himself within the unromantic, postlapsarian perspective that characterizes all the books treated in Part III.

Bad Land presents a revised history of the West that rewrites the legend of the frontier in a number of ways. It focuses on the wave of homesteaders that moved west in the early twentieth century, well after that movement had supposedly ended. It shows the complexities and the ramifications of a system based on the erroneous supposition that America offers an empty surface on which to shape dreams of the good life. Based on this illusion, the immigrants' fate was more or less programmed and their failure almost predictable. In a bitter remark that underscores the irony in the book's title, Raban represents their story as more typically American than the Horatio Alger success stories that helped inspire their acts: "These people came over, went broke, quit their homes, and moved on elsewhere? So? This is America, where everyone has the right to fail—it's in the Constitution" (354). Nevertheless, his telling of the story is sympathetic, and he understands the pain involved: "Yet the homesteading experience was more than just another episode in the history of failure in America. It scorched people too fiercely to be shrugged off" (355). Several episodes related in the book give an idea of the trauma experienced by the homesteaders in being driven to abandon the land in which they had invested so much of themselves. Like other historical traumas, this one deserves to be remembered. It holds valuable lessons for a culture that is all too prone to amnesia.

Raban explores the graveyard of the homesteaders' dreams to discover the workings of a system. To pursue that inquiry, he brings together field notes detailing his explorations and glosses on texts relating to the installation of the Montana immigrants. In the book's textual montage, passages from Percy Wollaston's memoir of his family's homesteading experience intersect with information concerning such diverse subjects as the Land Ordinance system, school textbooks, farm machinery, and popular American fiction. Given the prominence accorded to Wollaston's memoir, one could almost say that Raban's explorations are a continuation of that earlier text;[1] nevertheless, Raban's book aims beyond the reiteration of past experience.

Raban's imaginative exploration of the homesteading system in eastern Montana demonstrates that the statements we formulate and the acts we perform in relation to our surroundings not only reveal our engagement with the land but also commit us to a certain manner of conducting ourselves, thus expressing a definite ethical position. Comprehension of the land is not just a matter of conceptualizing it; it is always an interaction engaging the land and the self. For this reason, besides representing the settlers' relationship to their land, Raban also commits both himself and, vicariously, his readers to an exploration of the Montana homesteads.

The primary purpose of *Bad Land* is neither to describe the land nor to narrate the adventures of the early settlers, but rather to evoke a set of expectations and relations. To that end Raban shifts the book's focus between present and past, alternating scripts that deal with historical events with descriptions of contemporary encounters related in anecdotes and interviews. For example, the visit to Ismay's "Joe, Montana" parade and the visits to the ranch at branding time demonstrate the way people's relationships with the land have developed. Alongside these contemporary scenes are passages that progressively relate the former inhabitants' relation with the land, stage by stage, from the immigrants' dreams, to their journey westward, to the fencing of the land, and so on. Sometimes past and present converge; for example, the repeated visits to the Wollaston estate with one of the descendants contribute to extending the traumatic failures of the homesteading system into the present.

Different rhetorical strategies help to implicate readers. For example, Raban frequently uses the pronoun "you" to connect the immigrants to himself and his readers: "You couldn't get your bearings. . . . It was scary country in which to take a stroll. You felt lost in it before you started" (57). With Raban, we espouse the immigrants' ways of thinking; we follow them as they progress through the different stages in their itinerary. Thanks to the scripts that return to past events, we follow the Wollaston family from their origins in England to their first installation in Minnesota, their transcontinental voyage, their building of the family home in Montana, their initial success, and, finally, their devastating failure as accumulated climatic catastrophes cause the downfall of their farm. In giving these detailed imaginative re-creations of the past, Raban demonstrates that the homesteaders' failure is not properly speaking a tragedy. There is not really "a Prince of Darkness pulling the strings" (255), nor does individual hubris bring on the disastrous situation; there is simply a misfit between the system, the land, and some of the homesteaders. Some manage to adapt to the brutality of the climate and develop their resilience, while others rely too heavily on the false promises made by the railroad companies and the banks. The romance with the land leads either to marriage or to disillusion and separation, but for all the homesteaders, it begins under the sign of empty.

The book's multiple scripts address the illusion of emptiness in three related ways. First, *Bad Land* gathers some of the fictions that have been projected onto a space conceived of as empty. Then, in the hopes of being able to get at the roots of the cultural practice of geohistorical erasure, the book probes the issue of seeing. Finally, to strip away all illusions of emptiness, Raban portrays the present-day residents of the Montana plains and shows how the place has shaped its people while being fashioned by them.

Fictions Written on a Blanked-Out Space

In order to give more emphasis to his analysis of the homesteading system, Raban sets aside the history of the prairie before the building of the Milwaukee Road line. The slaughter of the buffalo, the eviction and confinement of the Plains Indians in reservations, and the installation of the first ranchers at the end of the nineteenth century are barely evoked, for the imprint they have left on the land has almost completely faded in Raban's eyes (9). When the homesteaders arrived, the tracks made by the buffalo, the Indians, the cattle drovers, the army, and the railroad companies "added up to no more than a few hairline scratches on the prairie" (58). The indistinctness of these marks is one of the causes of the newcomers' initial disorientation on the vast plains. The faint tracks also prefigure the fate of the homesteaders, since the trace of their own "civilization . . . was fading rapidly off the land" when Raban arrives to contemplate it (8). The ranchers, politically defeated and overrun by the unwelcome flood of homesteaders, merely bided their time and waited for their rivals to fail before they reclaimed the plains (134).

The emphasis on the traces marking the land is important, since, as we have seen in preceding chapters, the myth of emptiness is sustained through cultural amnesia. When the new inhabitants arrived in eastern Montana in the early twentieth century, the details of previous occupations had already been blanked out by the forward-looking American culture. The Plains Indians had been relegated to ethnological relics evoked in a peculiar homework exercise proposed by the village school, inserted without comment at the end of chapter 5 of Raban's book. The first question of the test asks: "Who were in this country when the white men first came?" (188). The use of the past tense in each of the nine questions about the Indians implies that they no longer inhabit eastern Montana, although the Cheyenne, Assiniboine, and Sioux still live on reservations there.[2] Dedicated to shaping America's future, the early schoolbooks neatly disposed of the country's first inhabitants, whose "strange" beliefs and practices—the word "strange" appears in three of the nine questions—are clearly meant to seem out of step with the twentieth century.

What seems to have motivated Raban's concentration on the homesteaders, besides the persistence of the traces that they have left and the desire to preserve in writing the human stories that the land is slowly effacing, is the fact that their arrival was the result of a concerted system—a scenario imposed on the land and enacted by the immigrants—that Raban ironically describes as an American Romance. For the late-twentieth-century immigrant that Raban has become, the homesteaders' stories reveal something vital about American life. Their experiences have much to teach about what motivates people to pull up roots and resettle, about the way social institutions govern people's actions in spite of the American attachment to ideals of liberty and independence, and about the way people and institutions interact to inhabit the vast territory of the United States of America.

The social and political machinery surrounding the Enlarged Homestead Act of 1909 could have been put in place only thanks to the by-now-familiar mythology of emptiness: "It was the old story, of the prairie as a blank page" (280). Onto this blank page, the scientists, politicians, railroad companies, and the immigrants themselves projected their dreams and desires. In almost total disregard of the specificity of the land and of the history of human implantation on it, the Enlarged Homestead Act tried to reproduce Jefferson's ideal of the independent farmstead in the dry plains region.[3]

One of the prime movers behind the homesteading rush in eastern Montana was the Milwaukee Road rail company. As a tribute to the unrealistic nature of the settlement scheme, Raban begins to address its role in the chapter entitled "Fictions." He does not insist so much on the railroad's economic hegemony and its consequent political clout as on the arbitrary nature of its practices in its dealings with the land. The company's route was planned with an eye to an imagined future rather than with any interest in what was already in place. First the railroad was built, then towns were sketched out at regular intervals along the line, and the customers were expected to follow. In Raban's eyes, the railroad tried to play God: "Its creations were as arbitrary as those described in Genesis. The company said, Let there be a city: and there was a city" (21). Subsequently, the railroad magnates played Adam's role, assigning to the newly created towns names that reflected the whimsy of the moment, rather than any degree of attention to the topography of the land or to the names that already existed: "The West was still thought of as a great blank page on which almost anything might yet be inscribed. Its history could be erased, its future redrafted, on the strength of a bad breakfast or a passing fancy" (22–23). These newly imagined towns then became the sites of "architectural fictions" (23), as speculators created trompe l'oeil facades to attract investment. In this fabricated landscape, place became a commercial proposition open to promotional drives and marketing.

The Enlarged Homestead Act of 1909 was complicit in this commodification of space. It prepared the immigrants to conceptualize the land as merchandise that they had to prove up before they could own and dispose of it at will. Although in theory homesteading was meant to foster the permanent settlement of the land, in practice it worked somewhat differently. To begin with, the territory to be converted into homesteads was mapped out on the great national grid by the federal Land Office. The grid system was a rational means of expropriation; it dealt with the territory in the abstract, "squar[ing] up the West like a sheet of graph paper" (59). Abstraction was a way of occulting the human history of the land; it posited an "undiscovered, unsettled North America" that was "still the domain of unknown 'savages'" (58). In reality, once the occupants—first the Indians, then the ranchers—had been disposed of, the locators (often ex-surveyors) moved in to make a profit from finding the homesteaders' claims on the unfamiliar, unreadable expanse of the prairie.

The homesteaders were lured to the region by several arguments. First there was the cheap land promised by the Homestead Act, but that would not have been enough in itself to lure people to a place that was known as "the Great American Desert" (24). The railroad invested in a massive promotional campaign, paying writers and illustrators to paint "a picture of free, rich farmland, a picture so vivid, so fully furnished with attractive details, that readers would commit their families and their life savings, sight unseen, to a landscape in a book" (25). Thanks to the promotional material, the immigrants did not so much buy land as subscribe to a fiction: "The copywriters (who had probably never set eyes on the prairie) and the art editors created a paper country, as illusory as the land of Cockaigne" (309–310). The eastern promoters did not represent the land as Raban, or for that matter, the homesteaders, first saw it; instead they presented idealized farms and a cornucopia of produce. On the front cover of a widely distributed promotional book, an iconic image of the agricultural variant of the American Dream showed "a fresh-faced young man steering a plow drawn by two horses. As the virgin earth peeled away from the blade of the plow, it turned into a breaking wave of gold coins" (28). This obvious wish fulfillment fantasy might have been easily dismissed, except that its suggestive influence was reinforced by the testimony of scientific experts. Potential immigrants were assailed by the persuasive skill of both modern advertising and modern science. The railroad company recommended consulting a book by Hardy Campbell, who was touted as "the noted farming expert and inventor of the Campbell System of scientific farming for semi-arid lands" (34). Like the promotional material, Campbell's book promised wealth, but it based its claim on the experimentally proven "power of capillary attraction" (37) and the special tools designed by Campbell. Added to this was the persuasive force of Professor Agassiz's 1867 prediction that rain would follow the plow due to "the disturbance of electrical currents caused by the building of the railroads and the settlement of the country" (31). Even though this electromagnetic theory of rainfall "had been discredited in serious scientific circles" long before the pamphlets were published (154), it promised what the immigrants wanted to hear. Neither the advertisers nor the pseudoscientists paid attention to the reality of the land; instead, they created a spurious image that corresponded to the immigrants' former residences or to various imaginary ideal locations. Together they offered a recipe for failure by predicating the settlers' hopes for the land on falsity and artifice. Of course, these propagandist drives were reinforced by the potential immigrants' desire to believe in them. Their gullibility and their impoverished circumstances in Europe or in the East predestined them to become victims of these official lies, in what seemed to them "a miraculous conjunction between the real world and the world of private daydreams" (47).

Raban's analysis does not indulge in indignation or anathema but patiently teases out all the elements in the construction of a fiction that fosters a double despoliation of the land: first, in erasing its local geographic specificity and substituting verdant pipe dreams, and second, in creating settlements that were doomed to fail. This double denial gives a dual sense to the notion of empty: first it erases the reality of eastern Montana for the purpose of profit and then provokes the inevitable abandonment of the land and the emptied wrecks of the settlers' homes. Both have to do not so much with the physical nature of the land but with the failure of a relation, a failure to come to terms with the intrinsic characteristics of a given place.

Insofar as it was founded on erroneous beliefs and false images, the homesteading system in eastern Montana imposed an exterior mercantile conception on the land; it fostered the idea of a readily accessible territory dividable into appropriable units. The system predicated a covetous and speculating subject, detached from the land and prepared to extract as much as possible from it. This is the message conveyed in the image of the plowman turning up gold coins from the furrows of his land. The homestead scheme suggested that "the equity was in the ground itself . . . and in the plowman's own hard work" (196). Lured by this deceptive message, the normally frugal and cautious immigrants became willing pawns in the hands of the banking system and the administrative agencies from which the whole system originated. Self-sufficiency placed the homesteaders at a safe distance from the hazards of the American economy; quickly, however, indebtedness put them in the power of the government and the banking system (205). The homesteaders' stories show how short-lived the practice of commodifying the land was. When the farms ceased to produce and the loans could not be paid, the borrowers lost everything and the banks failed to recuperate their investments.

Most, but not all, of the present-day residents have learned to avoid the lures of get-rich-quick schemes, as Raban shows in reporting the commercial fiasco of the mercantile "Joe, Montana" day. The scheme to rename the town of Ismay with the first name of a football quarterback in the final stage of his career is an example of everything that is wrong in people's attitude toward the land. Raban recounts how a radio station in Kansas City, the final stop in the quarterback's career, decided to persuade a small Montana town to change its name as a publicity stunt: "Ismay bought the pitch and changed its name" (113). Like the earlier immigrants lured by dreams of plowing up gold, the twenty-eight-member Nemitz family imagines that their activities will create a new gold rush for the town. With dry understatement Raban describes watching a videotape of a news report on the scheme in the family trailer. The reporters who flocked to the town to report the event are obviously poking fun at the remote Montana town and its inhabitants. A year later, the town is apparently no longer newsworthy. The media pass over the event, and the townspeople's elaborate preparations for the parade produce an ironically anticlimactic result. The whole episode illustrates the problem of seeing the land as empty and reinscribable; that way of thinking produces a spurious relationship that inevitably ends in disappointment.

Seeing beyond the Illusion of Empty

In order to conceive of a more sustainable way of life on the Montana prairies, one must first remove the perceptual block created with the idea of empty land. Raban does this by centering a collection of scripts on the problem of seeing. The reader's education in how to view the prairies will emerge from the writer's own lessons in perception. From the opening lines of the book, Raban mocks his own culturally conditioned perspective. Throughout, he casts himself in the role of the outsider, the "urban tourist" (4) unable to identify the crops growing in the irrigated fields, and so, initially, capable of seeing only "hillocky emptiness" (4) in the plains. A series of interrelated scripts deal with his education in perceiving the place.

In encountering a place for the first time, we are culturally conditioned to occupy the role of outsiders, and we impose learned criteria on what we find. We may experience satisfaction or, when the landscape fails to meet our criteria, we may reject it, as Robert Louis Stevenson does in viewing the American plains and dismissing them with the rhetorical question: "What livelihood can repay a human creature for a life spent in this huge sameness?" (62). Whether it is praised as sublime, or dismissed as "nothing" (62) or "empty" (63), the reality of the land becomes submerged under a slew of assumptions and aspirations that can be realized only in the viewer's subjective gaze. Unlike the ardent appreciators of chosen sites who guide readers in the books studied in Part II, Raban approaches the Montana plains as a transient and an alien. Still, this outsider's position gives him the advantage of experiencing the land in a way that he can approximate to that of the homesteaders. He attributes to them his own "similitudinous cast of mind. Everything *here* is seen in terms of how things are done *there*" (27). Like the homesteaders, Raban finds that his vision is split between the western plains and a familiar place of origin. He is a foreigner groping for the means to make the unknown place take shape in language. Initially Raban's Montana is a construction based on his prior experience. Like James Fenimore Cooper in *The Prairie*, Raban conveys the strangeness of the western prairies to eastern eyes by likening them to the sea: "The ocean was hardly more solitary than this empty country, where in forty miles or so I hadn't seen another vehicle" (3). When another vehicle approaches at last and the driver stops to talk, he is compared to one of the sea captains in *Moby-Dick*, bringing his boat alongside for a "gam" (6). Through the extended metaphor, Homeric in its elaboration in the opening pages and recurring regularly throughout the book, Raban draws attention to the artificiality of the description and to the challenge that the prairies pose to representation.

The first step in the education in seeing the plains is to remove the obstacle created by European ideas of landscape. To conceive of the land as a scene, as a conventional travel writer or landscape artist does, is to imply that everything is organized around a privileged viewer and that it exists for his or her own private benefit as a form of spectacle whose value lies in its entertainment or aesthetic potential.[4] Since landscape is a culturally defined commodity, the plains were initially passed by as a subject for painting. Raban discusses the difficulty experienced by the painter Albert Bierstadt, "a compulsive workaholic" who sketched the plains during a trip to the Rockies but failed to produce much more than "a pile of mostly formless daubs" (65). Turning to the more successful photographs of Iowa-born L. A. Huffman, Raban shows how vision is culturally shaped. Huffman is better able to find interest in the flat plains: "He was bred to the 360-degree view . . . comfortably at home in these landscapes" (88). This discussion of the problem of representation in "Pictures" points up the spuriousness of questions about the intrinsic aesthetic merits of the land. When the beauty of a particular terrain is put forward as an argument for paying it special attention, it is not just a locale that is being designated but also a form of interaction (or noninteraction) between a person and a place. Descriptions of the land thus reveal the degree of the describer's commitment to a place.

The features of the Montana plains are initially indistinguishable for newcomers. Eastern Montana residents have "the wrinkled long-distance gaze [of] solo yachtsmen" (5), whereas the British-born author suffers from "congenital tunnel vision" (70). His cultural conditioning blinds him to the land's specific geography: "Bred to looking at landscape as if it were a picture, to the posted scenic viewpoint, I was responding to the prairie like a shut-in taking his first walk across a blinding city square" (70). This humorously self-deprecating characterization may seem surprisingly counterproductive in the literature of place, where readers expect to be led by an authoritative guide. In fact, Raban's self-portrayal as alien émigré is vital in debunking the false impression of emptiness that has been attached to the American plains. The writer invites readers to learn to see along with him; he represents himself not as an expert but as a greenhorn who needs to acquire a new vocabulary of place.

Like the immigrants who have preceded him, Raban needs to convey an idea of the land to the people back home who have never seen it, and his initial efforts are woefully inadequate. For his wife, who remains behind in Seattle, "Baker, Montana, was an unplace" (68), and his descriptions do not render it any more tangible: "It's flat and colorless. That's about all. . . . Oatmeal. Lumpy oatmeal. That's my only image" (69). His snapshots are no more revealing, since the scale of the plains defies efforts to capture them: "The view through the lens fell hopelessly far short of what I could see with my naked eyes" (70). His failure to produce an adequate image sends him on the trail of his predecessors, not only the literary ones, but also the landscape painters and photographers that he treats in the chapter entitled "Pictures." His primary teacher in the art of photography is Evelyn Cameron, a British émigré who preceded him almost a century earlier. Her prints capture "the ambiguous and disquieting character of western space" (72). Through her judicious positioning of people and objects in the frame of her pictures, Cameron manages to convey the treeless immensity of the plains. Instead of seeking familiar impressions of the sublime or the picturesque, she creates original and unsettling images of human interaction with the land that Raban attempts to emulate in writing. Cameron teaches Raban to perceive the odd mismatch between the newcomers to the land and their surroundings: "Nearly all her people looked as if their presence in eastern Montana came as a bewildering surprise to them, and they were photographed in surroundings that were either much too big, like the open prairie, or much too small, like the dog-kennel interiors of their claim shacks" (72). In describing these photographs Raban displays his developing skill at writing about the unfamiliar land. Ekphrasis becomes both a form of apprenticeship and a means of demonstrating literary mastery.

Cameron's ironic vision of the incongruity of western settlements mirrors Raban's, and the judgment he makes on her point of view could easily describe his own: "Evelyn brings to the prairie a British, middle-class sense of scale and proportion, and her photographs are often statements of visual incredulity at what she sees. Looking at the picture of the homesteading couple, you know that these people and their houses are making Evelyn laugh, and the laugh (which is not unkindly) is still here, preserved in a gelatin plate" (91). Raban's ironic laughter can be heard too when he describes the town of Terry with its "too-wide street" and its "too-low buildings" that make him feel like "Gulliver in Brob-dingnag and in Lilliput all at once" (73). The horizon is so vast that the simple meeting of two people on the same road creates an ephemeral impression of emplacement: "It was so empty that two strangers could feel they had a common bond simply because they were encircled by the same horizon" (6). The Montana prairie demands that homesteaders, writers, and artists establish a new relationship with place. Rather than offering pastoral contentment or inspiring lyrical effusion, it confronts humans with their limits, their isolation and relative insignificance: "You're very big and very little all at once—and being both, are neither" (68). Humans are no longer protective or appreciative of their surroundings but rather exposed and vulnerable, lacking definition.

Raban offers much more than an informative complement to the narration; at all times readers have the impression of sharing the intimacy of a fascinating and humorous companion. A good example of the way he knits a relationship between himself, the immigrants, and the readers is found in the chapter on Montana weather. After a series of mild winters and clement springs, "the winter cold gave the settlers their first taste of the pitiless and extreme character of the climate" (208). Raban compares the winter's violence to "a boot in the face" (209), but metaphor is not enough to convey the way the Arctic temperatures punished the newcomers. Raban recounts his own experience of returning on foot from a Missoula restaurant to his hotel less than a mile away during a cold spell one January. He takes several pages to tell his story, mapping his progress block by block and focusing on both the physical torture and the psychological terrors—he relives the doomed Scott expedition in his imagination. The reenactment and the expression of his shocked initiation into the rigors of the Montana winter are more important than the anticlimactic outcome of arriving in the warm bar of the hotel. His brief research trip serves to highlight the difference between the comfortable lives of the middle-class writer and his readers and the difficulties that the homesteaders endured.

A People Shaped by the Land

It may seem paradoxical, but in the arid Montana plains landscape, which, because it is sparsely populated, habitually evokes the word "empty," human habitation and human history become all the more significant. In Cameron's photographs human figures and their possessions provide reference points and scale. Similarly, human experience gives focus to Raban's exploration of the land. Although at first he speaks of emptiness, he subsequently describes the ranches that map the land, endowing it with the names of former residents (7). Then he notices the "little hilltop graveyards" (8) that dot the land, the remains of the homesteaders that once inhabited it. Though the landscape is not empty, it had once been more crowded, and Raban gives as much importance to the settlers who are gone as to those that remain. In fact, the overriding impression he wants to convey is of the land as "a graveyard, . . . strewn with relics of the dead" (8). The book is an attempt to fathom the experience of those departed immigrants "before its imprint [becomes] as faint as that of the Plains Indians' teepee rings or the shallow grooves worn by the single-file herds of buffalo" (9). Particularly poignant are the traces that underline absences, the objects destroyed because the memories they evoke are too painful—the Wollastons' burned family album (105), the silver cup thrown into the river (269)—and the "large sad space" in Percy Wollaston's narrative that corresponds to the drought years (237). Somehow, the relics of the homesteaders' lives both reinforce and contradict the impression of emptiness. They offer clues to solving the conundrum posed by the land and promise some understanding of how humans succeed or fail in finding a place in the immensity of the plains.

The attitude toward place in *Bad Land* is very different from that encountered so far. There is no trace whatsoever of the musings of the solitary nature enthusiast. There are no private moments of communion with the land, no lyrical effusions or jeremiads; instead, the writer endeavors to investigate, to understand, and to empathize with the plight of the departed immigrants. Raban is not in the least concerned with preserving pristine places from the deleterious influence of society; instead, he wants to understand why people have built homes on the plains only to desert them. His orientation is historical and sociological, but his main concern is the nature of the bond between humans and their surroundings, a fundamental question that he matches with his personal anxiety about settling in a new land: "An emigrant myself, trying to find my own place in the landscape and history of the West, I took the ruins personally" (11). The difficulty of claiming a home is a concern that permeates the text, as suggested in the disturbing question concluding the book: "Anybody home?" (358).

Raban attempts to reimagine, reenact, and relive the individual and collective experiences of immigrants confronted with unfamiliar terrain and extreme weather conditions. He studies texts and images, collects oral interviews, and follows in the footsteps of the homesteaders. He enlarges the scope of the issue of habitation from the individual's perspective to that of the group. The questions of settling the territory, making a living, and forming a society are not the subjects of anathema, but rather vital human challenges addressed to the land and in urgent need of resolution.

The abstract manipulations of imposing a grid and naming arbitrarily selected towns were the culture's way of proclaiming its belief that humans alone shape the land. The homesteaders' experience shows the contrary to be true: "They'd come to the land and tried to shape it according to their imported ideas of science, progress, community, landscape. Now the land began to shape them. Its message to the people was blunt: live here and you will live barely and in isolation. It shook itself free of the litter of surplus buildings, the fence posts and barbed wire with which the Lilliputian homesteaders had tried to pin it down" (260). Raban not only anthropomorphizes the land in this Swiftian image, giving it a voice and agency, he also adjusts the scale to give a better idea of humanity's relative puniness on the plains. Nonetheless, in several places, he underlines the process of mutual cocreation that occurred between the homesteaders and their land: "In 1909 and 1910, they had found an empty space. They'd made a place of it. Today the open prairie is cobwebbed with paths that go from house to house, except that the houses themselves went west long ago; and each path is the line of an old friendship, a dependency, a working partnership" (258). In this statement, "empty space" describes a land devoid of human relations. By contrast, the imprints made by the settlers express not only their relations with each other, but also the connection they forged with the land: "They had come for keeps, and saw themselves as married, for richer and poorer, to their plots of dust and scoriacious rock" (258). The homesteaders saw themselves as wedded to the soil in a union in which both parties had to sacrifice a portion of their individual freedom in exchange for mutual support. As opposed to those who left because they were crushed by the harsh climate and the system, those who stayed shaped their lives to suit the region. Even their bodies came to take on the aspect of the land. Raban's somewhat exaggerated depiction of a group of ranchers emphasizes this point: "One way in which people became *a* people here was simple weathering: after sixty years of exposure to this climate, almost everyone's face looked like the badlands—brown, eroded, mapped with branching creek beds and coulees" (281). Not only do people begin to resemble one another like members of a distinct race or nation ("*a* people"); they also blend in with the land, taking on its characteristics and becoming *its* people, as weathered as the surface of the terrain they inhabit.

The necessity of establishing an enduring relationship between humanity and the land is the most decisive argument that the new writers of place have to propose in response to twentieth-century grievances about the disappearance of "empty" spaces. The land does not exist independently of its human or other-than-human occupants; on the contrary, inhabitation inevitably shapes it. No land is intrinsically good or bad; it is always the reflection of sustainable or improper usage.

The question that particularly fascinates Raban as a newly arrived immigrant is how people manage to find their place in their adopted land. He is looking for histories similar to his own, of people that "caught a shadowy glimpse of a new life, and flung [themselves] at it" (12). He sees in the story of the homesteaders' westward movement "someone else's cast-off history that would fit my case" (12). In a nation peopled mainly by immigrants, the homesteaders' history is of course a widely shared story. Raban makes it vivid by tingeing his evocation of the various western types with a distinctively Dickensian humor; he has a taste for the grotesque and eccentric. Besides the Wollaston dynasty that he follows along the railroad to the state of Washington, he describes other families that represent the wide range of "honyocker" types. There is the Worsell homestead, "a blot on the neighborhood" (109), run by a less sinister, Cockney version of Pap Finn. The father's fecklessness leads, unsurprisingly, to the son's final bitterness and destitution, suggesting how the isolation and independence of the homesteading life could allow a certain relaxation in human ties and even a certain degeneracy. Another homesteading family type is the Zehms clan of Seventh-day Adventists. Their apocalyptic convictions allow them to stay on the land when conditions deteriorate because they see their hardships as the fulfillment of biblical prophecy. There is a certain fit between these ardent millennialists and the land they settle in: "Its sheer bald exposure opened it up to the vengeful gaze of the Almighty. Its fantastic weather left man in no doubt as to his littleness and vulnerability" (231). Even though they finally abandoned their homestead, the Wollaston family also offers an example of adaptability and resilience. After reluctantly moving on, they create a new bond with the land elsewhere. In the house they build in Thompson Falls, which Raban visits at the end of the book, Ned and Dora Wollaston manage to survive mainly thanks to the produce from their garden and the fish and game from the land (331). This "Rocky Mountain Eden" (330) brings the couple's travels to an end; in Raban's view they have found "as safe a berth as one could hope for the young Minnesotan with a compass-rose tattoo on the back of his hand" (332). For Raban, the land and the independence it demands of its inhabitants tend to foster extremes of human behavior; thus he is not surprised to find "surly misanthropic loners" (140), antisocial terrorists like Timothy McVeigh (334) and Ted Kaczynski (335), or reclusive sects like the Waco Branch Davidians (229). Finally, Raban's amused but sincere admiration goes to the Householder family, who had the moral resources to surmount adversity and adapt: "The ranch exuded an air of thrift and rectitude" (234). They resisted the temptation to take on large debts, sticking with their horses in the years the neighbors mechanized (232). They feel that the land has been good but know it can also be cruel (234).

Another question that Raban considers in *Bad Land* concerns the type of society that the homesteaders create from an oddly assorted mix of people of different creeds and national origins. That society is not easy to recognize for someone using European models as his standard. Raban quotes E. V. Smalley's assertion that "in no civilized country . . . have the cultivators of the soil adapted their home life so badly to the conditions of nature as have the people of our great Northwestern prairies" (138). Indeed the communities of former homesteaders look "bleakly centerless" to an outsider (139). Nevertheless, Raban shows how independent families spontaneously invent a kind of democracy founded on the defense of their individual rights. Evoking their varied communal activities, Raban gives an idea of its genesis and manifestations. One of the tasks around which the community coheres is the important work of building fences. This might be seen as the western equivalent of "Mending Wall," except that it is more elaborate and inventive. To underline their importance, Raban gives the title "Fences" to one of his chapters. First of all, the homesteaders' fences, following the straight lines marked out by the Land Ordinance surveyors, were an assertion of human dominance, "a statement of the belief that this unruly land could be subdued. Rectangles rule" (134). The barbed wire that the homesteaders used belongs, in Raban's mind, "to the iconography of war" (136); he recalls the "'fence wars' of the 1880s in Texas and elsewhere" (134). Nevertheless, there were no fence wars in eastern Montana; the ranchers simply waited for the homesteaders to fail on the dry terrain. Instead of being a factor of dispute, the barbed-wire fences became, paradoxically, a way of bringing the community together. Their cohesion began with the journey to the Cedars, one of the few areas where wood could be found. Raban finds the trace of that social unity in the forking paths leading from the different homestead sites and converging in the same direction. In cutting the posts and stringing barbed wire along a common boundary, the homesteaders made contact with each other. This activity was "a fine way of bridging their different languages and social classes" (136). The fences also gave the new neighbors a means of communication, knitting together a rudimentary telephone system: "the barbed wire phone service" (137). In the local museum of another town, Raban even discovers a barbed-wire collection. In describing his "rapt scrutiny" of the pieces on display (312), he humorously pays homage to the virtues of that crude fencing material as both a barrier and a link between neighbors.

A second expression of the homesteaders' brand of spontaneous democracy is the school situated astride several properties, built by the busy farmers and run by young, single men and women with no more than a high school diploma. The school was a sign that the community had put down roots and was planning for its future. It was also "a political nursery" (162), for the community had to elect a school board and had to interact with county and state education agencies. Raban's description of these prairie schoolhouses is characteristically tongue-in-cheek, but he compares them favorably to their European counterparts (167). The school had the difficult task of bringing together its motley immigrant pupils and inculcating them with a new, secular ideology of independence, self-reliance, and good citizenship. Founded on the confidence that the immigrants had in their land and built with the proceeds of their first successful crops, the school was the center of community life on the prairie. It served as gathering place for discussions and potluck meals, and it knit the community together.

The little schoolhouse stands empty when he visits, and Raban gives a rather melancholy description of his exploration of the abandoned building. By contrast, in his evocation of the frenetic energy of branding time, he depicts an activity that binds together the modern-day ranching community. Although he is clearly an outsider, unused to the early hour at which the event begins and sensitive to the calves' suffering, he recognizes that he is witnessing an important event, "a splendid fête champêtre" (273), in which local families come together for work and enjoyment. In the shared work of herding, roping, branding, and castration, every rancher commits himself to the service of all the others in the neighborhood, thus promoting "a rooted and stable rural community" (272). In Raban's analysis, the huge, scattered ranches are better suited to the prairie than the juxtaposed half sections of the homesteaders: "After the great humbling of the Dirty Thirties, people learned to conform themselves to the nature of the place. The land allowed just so much habitation and farming and no more" (272). The surviving homesteaders and ranchers have made peace with each other and with the land, intermarrying and joining their properties to remap their community.

Raban approves a distinctive form of emplacement or inhabitation that is indigenous to America. In observing those who left and those who remained on the Montana plains, he discovers two types of American. On the one hand, he recognizes that those who moved on seem to conform to a recognizable stereotype: "The West is a realm of chronic impermanence. . . . People got what they needed from the land and moved on, like grazing cows" (257). On the other hand, in observing the families who made it through the bad times, Raban discovers a new form of attachment to the land founded on mutual recognition and also a form of atonement: "The homesteaders now understood, at last, how dry the land really was, and how it needed to be gentled back to health. . . . This land might not be much, but it was theirs; and its weakliness made them cherish it the more. They had abused it. Now they would atone for that abuse. The homesteaders who survived into the 1920s found that their attachment to the land had grown beyond reason, as love does" (256–257). The trials undergone offer a lesson in homespun realism that refutes the false promises of an ideal or a system. The homesteaders find something more valuable than the dream that lured them—a responsible relation to their land.

Ironically, the authentic form of prairie habitation resulting from the people's interaction with their environment is recuperated in specious images projected in twentieth-century developments in rural tourism. A way of life forged in adversity through the community's triumphs in adaptation and empiricism is once again, as in the heyday of homesteading propaganda, repackaged as a romantically appealing existence, "a living fragment of western history" (263), a vision iconized by Grant Wood's *American Gothic* (262). Urban tourism has created a new relation to the land and superimposed it on the reality of the famers' lives, changing the settlers into museum exhibits and the tourists into spectators. Raban treats the Buffalo Commons idea with similar irony, taking it as an example of outsiders' absence of sensitivity to the hardships involved in the settlers' adjustment to the prairies. In Raban's view, Buffalo Commons, a project conceived by two New Jersey researchers, Frank and Deborah Popper,[5] involves turning back the clock to "reinvent the old frontier here" (280). The Poppers want to dispossess the ranchers who have successfully adapted and forged deep attachments to the land and to convert the whole region into a giant national park where buffalo roam as in the days before the arrival of the railroads. He inserts the project in the same ideological frame as that of the railroad magnates who were partly responsible for eliminating the buffalo: "sketching a fantastic future for the land, with an Olympian disregard for what was actually here" (281). As romantically appealing and ecologically intriguing as it may be, for Raban this latest project for the Great Plains conforms to the emptying relation that produced mendacious images like the Great American Desert or the Wild West.

Raban replaces the "American Romance" of claiming empty space with an assertion of the illusion of emptiness and of the land's power to shape human history. Coming toward the end of his painstaking re-creation of the inhabitants' struggle to adapt to the land, to put down roots, the Buffalo Commons proposal strikes him as indecent: "To the ranching families, it was a *place* . . . with all the shape and particularity of home" (281). Raban has learned that perceiving the land as empty opens it to all kinds of aberrations and tragedies: "To outsiders, this land still looked like *space*, and could as easily be a weapons test site, or a safari park" (281). This allusion to the cultural practice of projecting dreamscapes onto so-called empty lands could easily be applied to the next book to be studied, Rebecca Solnit's *Savage Dreams*.

After following in the footsteps of the homesteaders, Raban reaches the end of his voyage having shifted from the superficial impressions of an "urban tourist" to a more informed perception. The plains do not reveal their secrets right away: "Imprinted with these ghostly social usages, the land, which looks so bare when one first sees it, ignorantly, from a car window, continues to have a peopled shape, a residual body of meaning of a kind that mere space cannot yield" (258). Instead of emptiness, Raban finally sees "a peopled shape" that is not defined by the absence of humanity but, on the contrary, by the multiplicity of tenuous human marks that only an eye informed of their existence can perceive. The land, in turn, has shaped the inhabitants, making them adapt to it or leave it. To understand it as such, the writer has to take lessons in what to look for and how to see. Finally, *Bad Land: An American Romance* is not the conventional Western adventure story set against a backdrop of wild, uninhabited land ironically evoked in its title. It is instead a field guide to a peopled place.

7

Unsettling Oppositions in Rebecca Solnit's *Savage Dreams*

In *Savage Dreams: A Journey into the Landscape Wars of the American West*, Rebecca Solnit juxtaposes two places that haunt the American imagination—Yosemite National Park and the Nevada Test Site—and draws surprising connections between them. In the course of being claimed as parts of the national territory, the two sites that are the book's focus were both placed under the sign of empty. Investigating their past and present occupation, Solnit writes these purportedly timeless, uninhabited spaces back into the network of national geohistory. Place becomes a field for the observation of phenomena that exceed by far the local and personal. In the acknowledgments that preface the book, Solnit describes her orientation: "This is a book about trying to come to terms with what it means to be living in the American West, learning as much from encounters with landscapes and people as from readings" (x). Here Solnit admits what other writers have demonstrated in practice: in the quest to grasp the complexity of space-time, the land alone is not an adequate source of information; its enigmas require recourse to books and to other people as well. Living in the region is not enough; "to come to terms with what it means" Solnit has to seek the traces of previous interactions inscribed in documents and on the territory.

Her book marks a definitive rupture with traditional nature writing, since it focuses not on the exceptional character of these sites, nor on the author's personal involvement in them, although both these aspects are touched on, but rather on the relations between people and the territory they occupy. The book widens the scope of inquiry to encompass the communities inhabiting these emblematic sites along with their stories and aspirations, the "savage dreams" referred to in the book's title. Far from the luminous transparency that the Transcendentalists attribute to their surroundings, a projection that resurges at times in the moments of epiphany recorded in the books studied in Part II, Solnit finds in the sites she explores an opacity that conceals accumulated strata of history needing to be uncovered, examined, and connected.

The scope of the observation poses a serious challenge to the writer. On the one hand, in mapping the complexity of the spatiotemporal networks crisscrossing these two western sites, she jeopardizes the book's coherence. On the other hand, in selecting and centering spatiotemporal events, she risks oversimplifying them. Solnit's solution to these problems is to open her book to a multitude of voices and texts, building a multilayered text composed of personal reflections, notes, interviews, and documents; and at the same time, to make these disparate scripts cohere by weaving together recurrent themes and motifs.

Dust and Water: Hidden Connections

Savage Dreams relates the quest to uncover the realities beneath the layers of forgetfulness, indifference, falsification, and myth that surround the American West. To pursue this objective, Solnit investigates two sites that represent extreme cases of what are collectively recognized as empty spaces: a military test site and a national park. In linking these two places, rather than exploring just one site of election or predilection like most practitioners of the literature of place, Solnit demonstrates her interest in investigating the collective mentality more than her own personal responses. Projected onto these two very different sites, the sign of empty is not an expression of either transcendent or negative values, but a fabrication that masks social, political, and collective aspirations or "dreams." The designation "empty" is the expression of a national hubris that is declined in two opposite but related forms: on the one hand, the Nevada Test Site represents the execrated site of Armageddon where the United States has set off humanity's most destructive weapons; on the other, Yosemite stands for the sacred space of a simulated return to Eden, an American showplace.

Apparently poles apart, these sites turn out to be linked by many factors; perhaps the most important one is that their significance is obscured from the public gaze. In the case of the Nevada Test Site, its remoteness from densely populated regions and the inhospitable nature of its biotope make it the ideal site for military operations: "a blank on many maps, a forgotten landscape, off limits to the public and swallowed up in a state which itself seemed to be overlooked by the rest of the country" (7). Yosemite National Park is also strangely secret. Even though it is open to the public and visited by millions, its disclosures turn out to be deceptive. In displaying "plaques, maps, and road signs everywhere directing visitors to the principal sites" (223), the park deflects the visitor's gaze from its human history. The scant traces of that history that can be found contribute to the process of mystification at work in the park's presentation of itself to the public. In the main park museum, "only the aeons of nature exist" (278), while the more marginally situated Indian Museum seems like "a monument to an extinct way of life" (274–275). The latter museum deceives the viewer into imagining that the descendants of the original inhabitants of Yosemite have vanished. This is a carefully staged illusion, as Solnit discovers: "Among all the glass cases and pedestals was a living woman in period costume, seated on a platform demonstrating traditional crafts" (224). "Framed as though she were caught in the past like an insect in amber, a relic of something lost rather than a viable way of life" (275), the woman could be an ironic representation of the park itself.[1] In a telling scene, Solnit describes the shock of seeing the figure in the diorama of nineteenth-century Ahwahneechee life in Yosemite suddenly move, "as though she were a ghost or one of the objects had come to life" (224). This could be compared to the effect Solnit achieves in *Savage Dreams*, for she restores spatiotemporal vitality to places that had been immobilized in the public consciousness thanks to the attribution of emptiness.

Both places have been fixed in the illusion of timelessness through their allegorical associations with biblical sites. Yosemite is a self-conscious simulacrum of Eden, a small remnant of the virgin paradise discovered by whites and subsequently destroyed by them. The Nevada Test Site resembles the opposite imaginary site in the Judeo-Christian cosmos, Armageddon, the location of the last battle that announces the end of time. Solnit's investigation will unsettle these paralyzing identifications, showing how the two poles connect and commingle: "It seems strange now that I found this country's national Eden so full of disturbing surprises and its Armageddon so comparatively pleasant, at least for its wide skies and gallant resistance community" (367). Evidently, these sites of illusion need exploration, investigation, and rediscovery.

In placing the Nevada desert and Yosemite side by side as a literary diptych and then commuting between them, Solnit emphasizes both the specificities of the two places and, more generally, certain constant features that characterize the occupation of space in America. The fabrication of emptiness transforms lived-in space into a commodity that can be exploited and manipulated at will, whether as a tourist attraction, a mine site, a weapons test zone, or a dumping ground. In reducing places to basic elements and drawing a parallel between the sanctified purity of "water" and the devastated barrenness of "dust," both situated under the sign of empty, Solnit suggests the denaturing logic of this commodifying process.

Of course, the two places diverge radically in the national imagination. Yosemite National Park is revered for its purity and beauty while the Nevada desert is one of America's forgotten, neglected, and devastated areas. Their social impact is poles apart. Generally thought of as remote and worthless, the Nevada Test Site is centrifugal; the radioactivity and nuclear waste it concentrates has the potential to affect vast numbers of people. Yosemite, in contrast, is a centripetal place: it is a magnet for hordes of Americans seeking the spiritual fulfillment promised by Muir or quite simply looking for the much-photographed landmarks of American scenery. Yosemite has been emptied out through the forced eviction of its inhabitants; the Nevada Test Site was declared barren and rendered so by the accumulation of destructive materials. The former seems like Eden, the latter like Armageddon; nevertheless, their opposition through these biblical allusions also suggests their convergence. Since both representations appeal to mythic extremities—the return to innocence or the arrival of retributive final destruction—they both evince a neglect of the intermediary stages, the in-between of existence. This is precisely the zone that interests Solnit since the allegorizing vein in American culture has historically left it out.

In Yosemite and the Nevada desert Solnit discovers a similar process of displacing and nullifying a previous culture. These places are empty by decree no matter what the reality of their habitation. Instead of getting to know the indigenous peoples of the American West, the Anglo-American invaders invented a New World and "manufactured" an empty landscape

(311). For Solnit, the West was made empty through the work of "painters, photographers, writers, namers and gunslingers equally" (311). As she suggests through this list grouping painters and writers with gunslingers, representation is a superficially innocuous means of doing violence. Even the gentle John Muir is implicated when he says of his campsite near Lake Tenaya: "No foot seems to have neared it" (220). This statement discounts the history of the land and its human inhabitants. Solnit recovers that history from Bunnell's account of the Indian War of 1851, which describes how the invading whites renamed a lake for the chief they had just defeated. At first, Tenaya fails to understand, since the lake "already has a name" (219). Then the chief's face shows distress, for "he thought the naming of the lake no equivalent for his loss of territory" (219–220). Indeed, the renaming marks a double dispossession, since both Chief Tenaya and the lake (Py-we-ack) lose their names and this act of expropriation ruptures their long relationship. Names become funeral monuments that paradoxically both commemorate and erase: "Like the Tomb of the Unknown Soldier, many of the names across the country are monuments to what has been forgotten" (313–314). By renaming a place one considers that the names that existed before are irrelevant, that the culture that they evoke can be safely erased, and that places can become blank surfaces on which the signs of another culture can be imprinted.

The construction of emptiness inevitably entails a process of dissimulation. Since the sign of empty conceals strategies of control, the writer becomes an opponent of those strategies in order to reveal the "hidden wars" against the land.[2] She joins the protesters at the Nevada Test Site in forcing the secret institutional violence into the open: "Unlike criminals, nonviolent direct activists take action publicly with readiness to deal with the consequences of their acts" (10). They offer their frail human bodies, "pathetically vulnerable objects to put between the landscape and the military" (12). In participating in the demonstrations, writing about her actions, and relating the stories of other protests, Solnit exposes what the military has done in land that has been placed off-limits. In Yosemite, by contrast, control is exerted as much through suggestion as restraint. A complex orchestration of the visible puts on show "the official version of Nature" (229): "There were plaques, maps and road signs everywhere directing visitors to the principal sights. Tour buses and a peculiar roofless train of the kind used in zoos provided an even more regulated experience" (223). In turning the indigenous people's homeland into landscape, much is "left out of the picture" (222); the land's hypervisibility hides Yosemite's human history. Turning the park into the apparently pristine landscape admired by tourists required a great deal of violent erasure. Well after the battles that defeated Chief Tenaya, attacks on the indigenous residents continued. Interestingly, the military initially handled the newly created park.[3] In 1906 the army burned the Indian village on Yosemite Creek (287). In 1929 the park superintendent ordered the burning of the village in Indian Canyon and the construction of a new village on a different site, this time restricted to descendants of the early inhabitants (287–288). Finally, in 1969 this village was destroyed (288). This history of destruction is hidden by the park's emphasis on the apparently timeless beauty of the place: "Nothing could seem further apart than the battlefields and this paradisal valley, but it too had been a battlefield" (236). Thus Solnit searches for what is beyond "The Rainbow" that her first chapter on Yosemite highlights. Beauty conceals violence "like a halo around a secret" (227). In retrieving Yosemite's invisible stories and unveiling its secrets, Solnit links the national park and the test site in an ongoing war against the land and its Indian inhabitants.

Solnit further shows that even the obvious contrast between Yosemite and the Nevada Test Site actually connects them. The purity of the former and the pollution of the latter make them complementary places on the nation's map: "The national parks counterbalance and perhaps legitimize the national sacrifice areas" (246). In this rationale, the water of Yosemite symbolically purifies the radioactive dust of the missile site and washes away the nation's environmental sins. The national parks assuage the national conscience, compensating for the land desecrated by extraction industries like logging and mining. In fact, Solnit points out that Yosemite was created as "a specific refuge from the frenzied earth-moving of mining. It serves as a world of recreation in contrast to the world of work, a compensation. To say that Yosemite is Eden is to say that everywhere else is not. 'This place shall we set aside and protect' implies 'all other places shall we open up and use'" (246). In this perspective, it is not simply a coincidence that many of the people "who shaped Yosemite's fate in the fourteen years after the Mariposa Battalion marched in were involved with gold mining" (245). Their appreciation of Yosemite's natural beauties did not prevent them from ravaging other sites. Preserving one place was a way of atoning for the ruthless exploitation of many others. Solnit's critique of the mind-set that underlies the creation of the national parks resonates with the objections Cronon makes to the American veneration of pristine, uninhabited lands and the way in which "wilderness tends to privilege some parts of nature at the expense of others."[4]

Like Cronon, Solnit objects to Bill McKibben's vision of the relationship between humanity and the environment in *The End of Nature*. For McKibben nature is, or should be, "something independent of man" (294).[5] He clings to the moderns' view that "nature is separate from us" (295).[6] He mourns the time "when the Grand Canyon was a blank spot on the map" (295). In placing her critique of McKibben's elegy to a paradise—which was "uninhabited and untouched" before the Europeans arrived (295)—immediately after her chapter on the drive to exterminate the Indians from Yosemite, Solnit reveals the force of ideology underlying the idea of emptiness; it has effectively erased the land's history. She also argues for the utter impossibility of empty places: "If nature is only itself before it's touched, if it's a place where we don't belong, then we can only experience it as it's disappearing, and our presence alone is enough to make it something else" (295–296). In following the logic of the binary split between humanity and nature to its absurd conclusions, she shows its fallaciousness. Indeed, the split between nature and humanity is a holdover from pre-twentieth-century science; Heisenberg's uncertainty principle teaches that such a division is impossible; the observer modifies the thing observed.[7] Moreover, the history of Yosemite demonstrates that the land that seemed "virgin" and untouched in European eyes was actually shaped by centuries of interaction with its human inhabitants: "The land [w]as not wilderness but something far more complex, and interdependent with its human population" (305). There is no separate nature, no place distinct from human history; instead, space is always the co-creation of humans and others in interaction with their habitats.

Solnit's analysis is devastating and her conclusion trenchant: in ignoring the connections between geography and history, Americans have lost their sense of place (323). The popular vision of American history as a constant advance is false; Solnit rewrites that story as "a retreat from the past, from memory, and from responsibility" (377). She calls for an end to the myth of Eden and of Adamic innocence. Indeed, the quote she borrows from

James Baldwin as an epigraph to *Savage Dreams* sums up what is wrong with America's ignorance of its history: "It is the innocence which constitutes the crime." In this way, she links up the moral conflicts that shaped American history, suggesting how easily injustice can be perpetuated by forgetfulness.

Walking toward Knowledge

As a corrective to Americans' collective amnesia and to a land "strangely innocent of its own history" (211), she makes recommendations that are at the same time tentative and provocative, modest and original. They involve both intellectual and physical involvement: "I would be back, on my own terms and my own feet" (211). She links up past and present, reconnects time and space, and joins up the scripted fragments of her book by walking through the land and reporting her findings. Readers follow her footsteps through the Nevada desert and Yosemite, and in tracing the map of her journeys we too move toward a better understanding of the land.

First of all, a new kind of knowledge is needed: "To know a place, like friend or lover, is for it to become familiar; to know it better is for it to become strange again. Not novel in the easy way of the new, but strange in a deep, disturbing way that does not dissipate, an unsettling revelation of what should have always been known, a revelation that implicates its belated discoverers" (341). Superficially this declaration seems to be at cross-purposes with the whole thrust of a book devoted to gathering information and testimonies in order to reach a better understanding of place. It suggests, though, that the deepest form of knowledge is not easily acquired or exchanged; it is not a commodity but a way of becoming. It requires personal commitment ("a revelation that implicates its belated discoverers") and remains incomplete (the "strangeness" of place "does not dissipate"). *Savage Dreams* aims to encourage the hermeneutic rediscovery of America or perhaps quite simply the discovery, for Europeans mistook the Indians' home for an empty continent. Stepping into an unfamiliar landscape, they mistook "somebody else's mother" for "a virgin bride" (222). Intellectual knowing predicates but does not replace personal involvement. Thus it appears that the book is propaedeutic to a new form of learning that is always ongoing. As Solnit says in *A Field Guide to Getting Lost*, "The things we want are transformative, and we don't know or only think we know what is on the other side of that transformation. Love, wisdom, grace, inspiration—how do you go about finding these things that are in some ways about extending the boundaries of the self into unknown territory, about becoming someone else?"[8] Significantly, the metaphor she uses for the self is spatial, as if to recognize that personal transformation involves contact and interaction with something outside the self. Knowing place in the way she recommends involves transforming both personal and national identity.

Another implication of this new way of knowing place is that the process of becoming is never complete; the American self engages in perpetual co-construction with the territory. This insight applies to both the conquerors and the conquered. In imagining the Indians as "a doomed and dying race" (276), the dominant culture denies their ability to improvise and to integrate change. Solnit's portraits of contemporary Native Americans show the ideological distortion in the image of the vanishing Indian. Both the first people and the new arrivals have been constantly adapting in a dynamic relationship to the land. Though she fears the newcomers "may destroy the land before we learn to live with it," Solnit finds "the process of improvisation . . . exhilarating" (182). She sees American culture "as a series of inadequate adjustments, settlings that have never yet ended the unsettled nature of the culture, and the abandonment of settlements" (183). The idea is distinctly postmodern in that it accepts an ongoing process of mutation that finds in its failure to achieve completion its own energy and justification; a constant process of deterritorialization, in Deleuze and Guattari's terms,[9] that excludes all forms of bounded territories and creates its own area of dispersion. It fits the restless pattern of discovery mapped out in the book and the vindication of rambling as a means of inquiry.

Savage Dreams is an eye-opener, an examination of the complexity of the land and a reminder of the vagaries of history—a history of a new type, "not only the history of human actions, of causes, but the history of effects, of ecological damage" (47). Conceiving of history in that way is a vital antidote to the chronic forgetfulness that characterizes the American nation:

> Histories of conquest are stories of disjuncture, and the great curse of Euro-American history is its shallowness, its failure to take root in a place so different from its place of origin. There are other countries which have absorbed their conquerors, but the States can't absorb an immigrant population which can't remember where it is or who preceded it to the place. It is

> conquerors and invaders, not the conquered or invaded, who have lost their roots, their ties, their sense of place. Amnesia is one potent means of overcoming the traumatic dislocation of the conqueror: Rather than lacking a personal past in a particular place, the amnesiac lacks the past. (323)

Memory functions best when it can be invested in tangible objects or places.[10] David Abram argues that for indigenous peoples in particular, events belong to places so that remembering and relating them situate people in the land.[11] This vital connection is missing for Euro-Americans, and although their culture generally celebrates the independent unattached agent, Solnit sees that type of person as incomplete, deprived of essential connections to time and place. Though the absence of roots might allow new beginnings and thereby foster inventiveness, it is also restrictive: "The inability to remember the past becomes the inability to imagine the future, and it is not surprising that a country with a ten- or hundred-year past can't make wise decisions about the long-term future" (324). Recovering the history of a place becomes a prospective as well as retrospective activity. Understanding how and why landscapes have changed can suggest how changes might affect the future of the land. Solnit's approach to history is thus ethical more than political. It aims at defining forms of occupation that are more responsible than those that have so far prevailed in the West.

Solnit offers her book, with its stories of protest marches and its rambles through history, as a new map for America, indicating new orientations. Whereas the amnesiacs turn away from difficulties, the protesters deliberately confront them: "To walk toward the problem is an act of responsibility, an act of return, and an act of memory" (377). Recovering an absent past in which place and time connect requires the creation of a text that is different from a conventional history. Within its immediately apparent diptych structure, *Savage Dreams* assembles fragments in what may initially seem to be a random, crazy-quilt style. Nevertheless, the book links cultural memory to the body and the land by assembling scripts that produce intersections, coincidences, and convergences. Through multiple textual recursions Solnit creates patterns that accord with the hidden complexity of the American past. One of the central motifs connecting the scripts is rambling.

Repeatedly, Solnit both describes the walks she takes in the Nevada Test Site or Yosemite and connects the act of walking to the construction of the book. "A sentence, or a story, is a kind of path" (108), she announces at the beginning of a chapter in which she brings together such topics as Thoreau's "rambling essay," "Walking" (108); the concepts of Arcadia and Utopia; and the history of nuclear physics. "Rambling" becomes a way both to explore a place and to present ideas. In *Wanderlust: A History of Walking*, she makes the cryptic observation, "Walking is a subject that is always straying,"[12] punningly suggesting that the walker, the act of walking, and the topic itself digress at the same time and in the same terms. Digression, or rather roaming—exploring the world for some unforeseen but not unreal purpose—appears to be a favored intellectual discipline. Solnit shuns the straight line of calculated intention, the demonstration's forward thrust, or the chain of causes and consequences; she is all for the enveloping, meandering, and inclusive approach. The paths she follows may seem erratic or convoluted, but they progress, although the progression may follow a meandering, circular pattern like the labyrinths laid into medieval cathedral floors. Thus, at the end of the book, we find a statement that both mirrors the earlier one quoted above and opens it up: "A road is itself a kind of sentence or story. A real place, it's also a metaphor for time, for future becoming present and then past, for passage" (366). In this rewriting of the American topos of the road, movement is not an escape from time but a way of connecting time and place. As such, movement is also resistance: "It is a refusal to merely flee, forget, and survive" (377). In retracing through writing the paths she has followed, Solnit transforms her walking into a cultural form that serves to perpetuate memory.

If Solnit favors rambling between genres and disciplines, it is because the straight line inevitably falls into the groove of ideology. At one point in *Savage Dreams*, she provocatively states, "I have trouble with the abstract and the concrete" (23). This self-mocking comment on her involvement in the antinuclear demonstrations at the Nevada Test Site perplexes readers so as to orient them in new directions. Clearly, Solnit favors the empirical and the experiential, the tentative and the meditative over concepts, theories, systems, and other such ready-made structures, but she also admits that discovering accurate, detailed facts about a place requires the commitment of mind and body. Driving through Nevada after exploring Yosemite, she refers to that manner of traveling as simply "'filling in the map,' since it isn't a way to know any place, only a way to see how the terrain metamorphoses between known places" (371). This comment illuminates her modes both of traveling and writing, since she constantly peregrinates through ideas as well as space before settling on the revealing features of a discourse or a place. She refuses to accept ready-made views of the land without testing them out for herself. After finally being allowed an official tour of the Nevada Test Site and hearing the carefully scripted official version of the place, she remarks: "It was the journey that gave the landscape meaning for me, not this arrival. I would be back, on my own terms and my own feet" (211). Her progression through landscape and through text is processual rather than demonstrative, inquisitive rather than conclusive; she relies on chance adventures, transitional states, the serendipity of whim rather than the propriety of other people's interpretations or her assumptions. She excludes no trail, but she also privileges none in particular.

Weaving a Spiderweb of Stories

As a figure of her meditative ramblings, she adopts the trope of a spiderweb: "A spiderweb of stories spreads out from any place, but it takes time to follow the strands" (24). She returns to the same image near the end of the book: "If a story is a kind of path, as I have said before, then a group of stories makes up a spider's web of paths, a map" (320). She thus conceives of her book as a structure placing her elected places—"crucible and touchstone" in the case of Yosemite (221), "sacrifice" and "scapegoat" in the case of the Nevada desert (58)—at the center of various concentric circles. Leading to these hubs, she sees "lines of convergence" (24, 25) that expand the stories condensed and concealed in these high-density spatial cores. Some of the major lines of convergence that she follows are the mutating stories of the Indian Wars, which have their own coherence and irregularities, which connect to both the Nevada Test Site and Yosemite National Park, and which endure into the present. She finds convergences and correspondences in the confusion of actors and elements coming into contact in the American West: "land, war technology, apocalypse, Thoreauvian civil disobedience, bureaucratic obscurity, and Indians, part of the great gory mess of how we will occupy this country, whose questions are as unsettling as its land is unsettled" (30). Rather than following the strict logic of historical processes and turning this tangle into a straight line, Solnit's approach consists in weaving a web of correspondences around events and people in order to express intersections, recurring patterns, and convergences.

The book's "spiderweb of stories" might be unsatisfying as a way to convey the density of place were it not for the wealth of narrative and cinematic techniques that Solnit deploys to energize her construction. In order to counter the national amnesia that obscures place by representing it as empty, she resorts to a plurality of sources and perspectives. Oral accounts figure prominently in the evocation of the Nevada Test Site, since the stories they tell are mostly absent from official accounts. Neither the protests, nor the explosions, nor their destructive aftermaths receive much news coverage (27–28). Thus, she tells the story of the Sheahan family, who had mined in Nevada for four generations and stayed on their land during the testing. An incendiary bomb blew up their mill, the parents died of cancer, and the Air Force finally put their property off-limits to create "a buffer zone, a zone of invisibility" (35), to shroud Nellis Air Force Base. This story of conflict and resistance resonates with that of the Dann sisters, Western Shoshone ranchers whose struggle to continue living on their lands reaches back to the previous century. Solnit actually participates in this story when representatives from the Bureau of Land Management come to confiscate the sisters' cattle, and she thereby joins in the Indian Wars, taking the sisters' side against the government. Her involvement in the struggle to protect the land and its people from nuclear dangers thus intersects with the longer war for the West and thereby connects the history of the Nevada desert to that of Yosemite Valley. The two places have a long history of continuous occupation that is denied by official accounts. Solnit describes some of the legal wrangling by means of which the Shoshone and the Ahwahneechee try to maintain their claims to their land. Oral stories and firsthand experiences are placed alongside the narratives of early witnesses and actors in the history of the American West. She places Lafayette Bunnell's self-aggrandizing story of discovering Yosemite next to the account that the Belgian miner Jean-Nicolas Perlot sent home to his family. Whereas Bunnell describes the Indians as savage and doomed to disappear, Perlot depicts them as abiding by their own laws and customs and thoroughly at home in their valley. In accumulating all the different stories that emanate from the same places, the text moves forward and backward in time and space, weaving a complex tapestry that refutes the simplistic stereotypes about the American West.

Solnit's way of treating history is necessary, because, although they are false, the cultural clichés gathered under the sign of empty have deleterious effects: "If the vanishing Indian and the virgin wilderness are the characters and landscape of the popular imagination, then they occupy the crucial place for political decisions and cultural representations, whatever their presence or absence in the real landscape" (309). The writer counters the popular images with her own representations, using the writerly equivalent of close-ups and wide-angle perspectives to overprint the familiar snapshots with less widely known alternative views. For example, she describes the photography of Richard Misrach, whose images of the American West show the bomb craters and dead animals that are usually hidden from public view: "These lush documents of political catastrophe point out that politics has invaded the landscape, that the landscape is now a victim of history" (47). In addition to describing Misrach's work, Solnit gathers other memorable images of the atomic sublime, for example, a sight witnessed by Dan Sheahan: "a herd of horses that wandered east onto the Sheahan lands with their eyes burnt out, left empty sockets by a blast" (34). Like stories, images are set in counterpoint. For example, she describes petroglyphs etched on the rocks in a canyon: "beautiful complexes of rusty pattern on the pale face of the rock, strange figures and lines and jagged bolts and circles" (89). These signs of the former inhabitants' relationship with the land are juxtaposed to a bomb crater nearby: "a shallow basin about a hundred feet across where the earth had dropped, and the bushes growing in it were slightly paler than the bushes anywhere else" (90). These ironically juxtaposed marks on the land are "traces of human presence" (90) whose significance Solnit invites readers to contemplate.

One of the most innovative principles in Solnit's textual strategy is to situate rather than dramatize, to relativize rather than demonstrate. She has devised her web of texts in order to show that reality does not give rise to fixed, monolithic truths but to relative, pluralistic, and shifting configurations of events that allow readers to construct their own interpretations. This is particularly evident in her treatment of history, for she rejects both the rigid application of the laws of causality and the recourse to the American myth of history as constant renewal, the dream of being able to start afresh. Her evocation of the birth of the atomic age, the Cold War, and the arms race is implacable. Nevertheless, she shows that at all stages other options were possible, other bifurcations and outcomes conceivable, and that it was only the obstinacy and madness of a few decision makers that fostered the accumulation of deadly weapons and permitted countless nuclear explosions.

Solnit treats the story of the development of nuclear weapons in the chapter intriguingly entitled “Lise Meitner’s Walking Shoes.” In this chapter rambling is more than a figure of speech or a mode of investigation; it is a thematic thread that allows her to gather together in new ways the dispersed details of scientific history. In describing the walks that brought together key scientists and created the conditions for new insights, she emphasizes the accidental, meandering courses events take. In writing this history she focuses on key encounters and conversations that led to sudden epiphanies. In her account, the truly important discoveries came not from the technicians at work in government-directed laboratories, but from intellectuals contemplating the nature of the universe as they strolled and conversed. Thus she presents Max Planck’s discovery of quantum physics as it was recounted to his son on a walk in the Grunewald forest in 1900. Then she describes Neils Bohr and Werner Heisenberg hiking together in Germany twenty-two years later, when “between them, they established a basis for quantum physics” (123). Shortly after, in 1926, Solnit recounts how, as Heisenberg walked late at night in Copenhagen’s Fælledparken, he mulled over the question that was to lead to his uncertainty principle. The following year Robert Atkinson and Fritz Houtermans were on a walking tour together: “As they strolled together through the German countryside they began to speculate on the nearly inexhaustible energy of the stars, and of the sun that shone on them” (125). Finally, as Lise Meitner hiked through the snow with her nephew Otto Frisch, the two were discussing the meaning of a colleague’s recent findings when it dawned on them that he had accomplished what was supposed to be impossible: “Hahn had split the atom” (127). In juxtaposing these different scenes of revelation, Solnit emphasizes both the haphazard course of events and the nonprogrammatic nature of creativity. Seen in retrospect and in perspective, history is not a question of necessity or design but of a spectrum of opportunities, coincidences, and choices.

In relating the history of the atom bomb through a series of discussions in natural surroundings, Solnit makes the case for the humanism of these peripatetic scientists and the pacifying influence of walking: “It seems that walking maintained their sense of human scale and thus of humanity even while they speculated on the activities of stars and subatomic particles. Their epiphanies and confidences in the landscape suggest the way they thought of themselves as innocents involved in a beautiful and morally neutral practice. They had shattered other worldviews, though, and their own was about to be shattered" (125–126). In Solnit's version of history, the Arcadian innocence of these pioneering scientists was destroyed by the arrogant ambitiousness of the men who followed them. At Los Alamos, the technocrats took the place of the philosophers: "Physics turned from philosophy to war technology" (136). In the associative logic of Solnit's web of scripted connections, the pioneering physicists connect to the marching protesters more than to the Cold War military complex to which they unintentionally gave birth: "And so if the great early physicists were walking toward the Test Site without realizing it, perhaps a few of them were marching across the cattle guard before us, not landing in the government jets" (144). Solnit gives a nuanced account of the past that leaves room for uncertainty and speculation, as seen in the "if" and "perhaps" that modulate her judgment here.

Writing from the Periphery

Perhaps it is this capacity to analyze the multiple dimensions of a situation and to appreciate its nuances that situates Solnit slightly on the margin of the antinuclear protests. She depicts herself as "a shorebird," someone who looks on from the edge, reluctant to take the plunge into the "flooded river" of a political crisis (93). Rather than being a position of weakness, this marginal stance allows Solnit to serve as a convincing witness. Significantly, posted as a lookout on the Danns' ranch when the "war" for the occupation of the land reaches a climax, she watches through a periscope, soaking comfortably in a hot spring, and then views the confrontation on video later in the day (193). Her detachment often takes the form of good-humored caricature, aimed at herself as well as her fellow protesters. For example, she describes her action of crossing the cattle guard into the military site as being comparable to taking part in "one of those Communist Chinese ballets of the 1970s, in which ballerinas in tutus with machine guns enacted a decorous interpretation of revolutionary history" (72). Protesters and guards alike play out their roles, accepting the pattern of trespass, arrest, and subsequent release. Though they are engaged in a struggle against the authorities, the protesters' actions fall short of heroism or revolution. The activists are a comically heterogeneous and mismatched assortment, sometimes motivated by naive ideals; Solnit even admits her frequent embarrassment at being associated with them (118). Describing one political meeting "with an old French priest, an under-age half-Shoshone, a rustic German, a wannabe demagogue from Vegas, a working-class young woman with a bad attitude, and only one other child of middle-class white American privilege" (199), she sees the occasion as "slapstick" (200). Nonetheless, she appreciates the ambience of camaraderie and friendship with these people pursuing a common cause.

In a kind of postscript discussing her sources she apologizes for failing to give "a clear exposition of the beliefs, strategies, and history of the contemporary direct-action antinuclear movement" (388). Yet in refraining from being either a spokesperson or a historian for the movement, she maintains her liberty to roam. The forms of activism she describes at the Nevada Test Site show participants involved in a loosely constituted grassroots rebellion against the duplicity and monstrosity of what is taking place there rather than adhering to a coherent political position or program. Her position in Yosemite is even more clearly that of an observer. Indeed, she begins the chapter entitled "Spectators" with the declaration: "I came back to Yosemite again and again, but nothing ever happened to me there. It was a place where nothing was supposed to happen" (228). Though she discovers similar issues of dispossession, violence, and injustice there, she feels they called for "a different kind of response" (228) from the one she gave in Nevada. Still, in both places, her response to situations in which "politics has invaded the landscape" (47) is to explore the mentalities that have produced the situation rather than to seek confrontation. Positioned at "the border territories between disciplines,"[13] she occupies the ideal site to observe the complex webs created by human interaction with the land. Over and above ideology, her position is simple but fervent; she militates against hypocrisy and injustice in whatever form, time, and place, but especially where she can trace its ramifications to her own existence.

Even though *Savage Dreams* affirms the value of collective protest and connectedness, it also illustrates the persuasive force of the writer's peripheral position. Solnit's physical and intellectual motility prove valuable in facilitating her work of gathering some of the "stories-so-far" that help define the realities of particular places. As relayed in *Savage Dreams*, America's geohistory is made up of patterns of interacting and interconnected individual stories presented in aggregate rather than as some coherent, unified whole that elides the specifics of particular places. Instead of offering complete understanding, the different ideas, systems, and concepts that have been proposed to explain events and to characterize places contribute to their complexity by playing a part in their unfolding in space-time.

The observer's peripheral position is the contrary of the experts' imposition of overarching master narratives or tropes onto U.S. history. Looking behind the attributions of aesthetic beauty or desolation that make Yosemite and the Nevada desert available for exploitation, Solnit gives credence to the experiences and lifestyles of individual residents or "uninhabitants" (154), to use the ironic self-description of one of the people she encounters. In the same way that they can designate land as empty, institutions such as the Atomic Energy Commission (151–155) or the Smithsonian Institution (292–293) have the capacity to blank out the existence of troublesome individuals. By telling the stories of these individuals, Solnit renders them audible and visible. Thus she opens her book to the verbatim testimony of Janet Gordon from Utah, one of the "downwinders" from the Nevada Test Site who watched her brother die "by inches" from pancreatic cancer after being exposed to radiation from the testing (152). She reports the experience of Jay Johnson, a Yosemite Park forester and a descendant of the indigenous inhabitants of the valley, who discovered on a visit to the Smithsonian that his people, the Ahwahneechee, were no longer supposed to exist. Solnit points out the multiple ironies of his situation, for "he has managed, with the interruption of Indian boarding school and military service, to stay in the valley his whole life, where he takes care of the trees and the trails. But he is due to retire, at which time he too will be evicted from his home in the valley, unless things change" (290). Against the unconcern of the modern-day bureaucrats and officials who dismiss the claims of these "uninhabitants" of "empty" places, Solnit restores dignity and substance to the people in her stories, while generally allowing their persecutors to remain nameless and faceless.

Though she tells other people's stories, Solnit also represents her own personal investment in unraveling the complexity of the American occupation of the West. She confesses to having experienced a detachment from the land similar to that she attributes to the early invaders. Like them she measured the country of her birth according to standards inherited from Europe: "I realized that I'd spent my adult life living in the West as though it were an outpost of Europe, that I had always looked at it as a flawed copy of the original, and like the first white emigrants, longed for ruins, stories, and marks of my own ancestry, had lived in the West facing east" (88). The cultural myopia she acknowledges here is by now familiar; it derives from the projection of alien models onto the American soil. With this confession of her own ignorance, Solnit shapes a narrating persona with whom readers can easily identify. Rather than posing as an authority, the writer modestly admits to having only a peripheral knowledge of her subject. With her, we embark on a quest for understanding. With her, we piece together the multiple scripts issuing from the land she explores.

Viewing America through the distorting prism of European art, Solnit concedes that she was blinded to its specificity, and consequently she forfeited the possibility of understanding her own country: "It was like crying for food at a banquet, and like trying to navigate the Sierra with a map of the Sussex Downs" (88). She allows that prior to writing her book, she had been unaware of the continuing war being waged against America's land and its indigenous people: "I'd been living in a war zone my whole life without noticing the wars, since they didn't match any of the categories in which I'd been instructed" (88). When she fails to receive a scholarship to study the history of landscape at Oxford, she welcomes the opportunity to look more closely at the American scene. Rather than tracing her culture back to its European source, she turns her attention to "the ways that it had mutated, invaded, hybridized, mixed with the vastly different ecology and cultures of the West, and shaped and warped the vision of those making land policy and living on the land out here" (89). Once again, she raises de Crevecoeur's question, "What is an American?" but unlike him, she does not find the answer in the attainment of the European immigrants' dreams of owning independent farms. Setting aside such settlement myths, she studies two sites in the American West to find how the immigrants have interacted with the land and its human and other-than-human residents and to understand what aspirations have inspired that occupation.

Inhabiting America

The final chapter of *Savage Dreams* joins up the two places explored in a single journey, when Solnit drives through Yosemite on her way to participate in the activities improvised around Columbus Day at the Nevada Test Site. There she joins first a session in a sweat lodge (381) and then, quite paradoxically for a book about place, a moonlit walk up to an unseen and finally unattained marker on a hill (383), and finally a circle dance that gathers together the heterogeneous community of protesters. In relating these events she takes a certain distance from the outsider's role that she has scripted for herself in the course of the book. Her rambles through space-time are a prelude to the deeper connection that she affirms in the final words of her book: "I was already home" (385). She hints at a new way to lay claim to America. Rather than emptying the land in order to discover and define it, she embraces it by weaving a web of connections linking past and present and demonstrating the relationships between places and people.

Solnit's rambling connects self to place, creating a space that both liberates and circumscribes her. The numerous depictions of the western scenery that she gives in her text render it from the perspective of a body in motion. This angle of vision eschews the commodifying gesture of framing the landscape in the manner of a painting. All the picture-making viewpoints and devices found in the national parks are, in her opinion, ways of separating the viewer from the landscape: "We look across a distance at something that is not ourselves and does not include us" (263). Instead of giving a vision of something picturesque or sublime that is known as nature, her writing imprints her individual sensibility upon the land and, at the same time, demonstrates the changeability of her surroundings and the relativity of her perspective. Walking along the Merced River, she remarks, "Something surprised me every few minutes" (248). In turn she surprises readers with a description of a scene whose elements are themselves in motion: "The river bent, the valley turned a little more due west and a last ray of sun stretched toward me, a stand of trees gave way to a meadow, a space between the trees opened up a view of a sheer wall or the deep V of the west end turning rosy" (248). In contrast to Emerson's "transparent eye" that reflects *and* absorbs reality, the walking subject is absorbed into this landscape. She performs a complex dance with the other-than-human elements of her environment.

In Yosemite, the walker and the land engage in a game of "hide and seek" (248). The desert is more open and revealed to the person moving through it, so movement is the way to connect with it.

A rather different effect is created in Solnit's description of James Savage's gravesite, which seems to offer a suggestive critique of his more violent mode of inhabiting America. The former soldier's rapacious attitude to the land and its indigenous people is somehow reflected in the drowned forest that emerges from the reservoir beneath his tomb: "These trees drowned in place were uncanny, terrifying. Their branches lifted up like imploring hands, their immobility was a curse where land and water themselves so often changed place. They had died of fidelity in an unfaithful landscape and then been buried and unburied, like something in a horror movie" (363). The "buried and unburied" trees recall Savage's triple burial, as successive projects demanded his relocation. In this suggestive description, the trees seem to mirror the man, and yet they are also his victims and mourners. They are far more revealing of the complexity of his story—and, by extension, of the story of the American West—than the simple white obelisk placed on the hill.

To counter the illusion and dangers of the identification of iconic American places as empty in their desolation or in their virgin perfection, Solnit advocates seeing the American landscape as a "unfinished project" (182). The land and its inhabitants interact in a process of constant creation and permanent renewal that fosters, if not necessarily improvement, at least change and constant improvisation. This is the quality that Solnit seems to recognize, for better or for worse, as the constant characteristic in the American occupation of space.

In living as in writing, Solnit favors adaptability, flexibility, and constant creativity: "The one thing the American landscape promises is that the future will be nothing like the present. I like being part of an unfinished project, however disastrous it has been to date. Improvising something better is an exhilarating challenge, and this is why I am happy to be another unsettled Euro-American rather than someone as well grounded as the Western Shoshone" (182–183). Aware of her own contradictions, since she critiques the Utopianism of Thoreau and Cole, she finds herself "endorsing Thomas Cole's notion . . . of the meaning of the American landscape lying in its future rather than its past, as Europe's does" (183). In the course of the book she comes to terms with the fact that Americans have failed to settle their land in the European manner, finding "something secretly comforting in the incongruity" of "the tawdry and the sublime, out west" (182). That incongruity, that "friction between people and land" (182), turns out to be one of the things that is peculiarly American. The temporariness of the buildings and the tastelessness of the kitsch objects placed in sublime landscapes are hallmarks of a peculiarly American vernacular.

As opposed to the writers of place studied in Part II, Solnit begins from a certain indifference to or isolation in the places that she visits. At the same time, in contrast to those who are bent on conserving an ideal state of nature, she progressively adjusts to the American West as she finds it. Moreover, the open spaces of Nevada and the rivers of Yosemite gather significance because of her quest. Progressively, she becomes more involved in place. She comes to realize that in spite of "all the English novels and French poems . . . I'd been a cowgirl growing up . . . and in those days my daydreams fit my territory. I realized I had been a Westerner all along" (88). What had been missing was an understanding of the connection between her everyday life and the land: "For almost a decade I lived in a city where it never snowed without realizing that every drop from my faucets was snowmelt, sucked out of a valley of legendary beauty that had been drowned by a dam" (88). As a resident of San Francisco, she draws her water from the Hetch Hetchy dam; thus, her body is intimately connected to the Yosemite Valley, even though she is only a visitor there. In a more sinister way, the nuclear fallout from the Nevada Test Site potentially touches the lives of all Americans. It is a concern for her as a woman, since it contaminates mothers' milk and the bones of their children (97). Surprisingly, though, she becomes more attached to the arid Nevada landscape than to the lush beauty of Yosemite. She misses the expansive sky after learning "a new grammar of scale between self and surroundings" (202). In words reminiscent of Robert Frost's poem "The Gift Outright,"[14] she muses: "The land of Crescent valley owns me now, in some sense. For the month after my last long trip there in 1992 I dreamed about it almost nightly. The dreams were not significant for anything but the repetition of that landscape over and over again in my mind, as though it had taken possession of me" (202). Unlike Frost, Solnit denies that a people can own the land. Her attitude has more in common with Native American thought: "No one ever took the land. It's still here, it never went anywhere, only the people come and go" (189). In the course of the book, though, she describes the process of becoming one of the land's people.

One of the primary aims of *Savage Dreams* is to stave off the national amnesia and thereby create a foundation for new, more responsible forms of emplacement. Nonetheless, Solnit keeps the options for that emplacement fairly open. Though she protests past injustice, she does not advocate national repentance, only the honoring of past commitments and the egalitarian application of democratic rights. Although she respects the choices of the people whose cause she defends, she does not advocate emulating them. The Euro-American protesters who support the contemporary Shoshone inhabitants of the desert are not interested in adopting their way of life. Indeed, Solnit points out the irony of environmentalists defending cattle ranchers and reports her brother's joke about his plans to protest against the way the Shoshone sisters use the desert if ever the fight to secure their land rights is won (173). In spite of her respect for the past, Solnit does not believe it can be recaptured. The ancient petroglyphs found in the Nevada canyon are for her "keys to a door that had been destroyed" (89); whatever they might signify about how to relate to the land is now "out of the reach even of our imaginations" (89). The key to the present is to continue the debate over the right ways to inhabit the land until an equitable solution is reached. Emptying the territory of its residents preempts that democratic process.

In the course of the book, Solnit discovers that her own way of inhabiting the West does not imply settlement. She is against fixity and inertia in all its forms. Besides being a way to discover, think, and write, rambling turns out to be her way of connecting with place. Rather than staying in place and erecting boundaries, she advocates a nomadic relation to the land: "Walking claims land not by circumscribing it or fencing it off as property but by moving across it in a line that however long or short connects it to the larger journey of one's life, the surrounding roads and trails, that makes it part of the web of experience, confirmed by every foot that touches the earth" (20). In the history of the American West, claiming land has usually meant asserting ownership over territory that is quite unfamiliar to the claimant. Solnit redefines the term so that claiming stands instead for the forging of an intimate connection with place. This new form of claiming is not an assertion of ownership, but the acknowledgment of an existential bond. With "every foot that touches the earth" the subject confirms her attachment to the land.

This personal attachment to the land comes across in the strange but revealing metaphor she employs to describe her new relation to Crescent Valley: "It was as though my sense of place had absorbed that terrain so profoundly it crowded out all others and lingered on long after I'd left, a phantom limb of location" (203). There is an ambiguity in the final appositive phrase, for it seems to refer both to the terrain and to the author. The land inhabits her as a "phantom limb," an unreal extension of herself. At the same time, she has left part of herself in the land and she misses it like the traumatic memory of a lost limb. The metaphor thus suggests the way in which the subject is both attached to and dispersed in the land without pretending to own it. More than that, it suggests that the two are mutually constitutive in an entangled relationship that could be identified as "space-time-matter-in-the making."[15]

Becoming American means expanding to take in the wide space of the West. The book's large scope takes in not only the sites Solnit visits but also the roads that link them and the many stories that connect time and space. Appropriately, *Savage Dreams* ends with the image of the circle dance linking Indians and whites in a "counterquincentennial" Columbus Day celebration (384). The dance represents an alternative to conquest, a pledge of harmonious coexistence in the land. As she drives back to San Francisco she reflects: "This time I was just going back, because I was already home" (385). Even though she is returning to the California city, she no longer feels a stranger in the Nevada desert; she can claim it as home, for the concept has been aggrandized to the size of the American West.

Savage Dreams investigates the hidden history of places conceived of as empty in order to reveal the genesis of the construction of emptiness. If we follow the writer's rambles, our definition of place evolves from a fixed point on a map to a relationship, even a co-creation, involving the land and its people, a definition that engages our responsibility to the places in which we live. The attribution of emptiness shifts from something that could apply to place to become instead a perception that humans impose on the land. The wild dreams of sanctity or destructiveness that they project onto the land are the signs of their dissociation from it. Paradoxically, as

Solnit's personal example makes clear, the desire for self-identification in space that inspires traditional nature writers persists in the new literature of place, but in her revisiting of the impulse, it becomes a quest that requires constant motion rather than definite emplacement. To avoid replicating the errors of the past requires taking into account human history as well as place in the shaping of identity. At the end of the book, the wide circle that is "home" balances locale, social commitment, and personal awareness in a precarious, temporary, and shifting web of connections.

8

Robert Sullivan's Reverse Commute in *The Meadowlands*

The book chosen to conclude this study of recent revisitings of sites that have been placed under the sign of empty may seem surprising, since the area it explores is situated on America's East Coast, in one of the first states to be colonized by Europeans. According to nineteenth-century representations of the settlement of the continent, this eastern site should be a shining example of progress, while the twentieth century would assume it to be a place where industrialization has blotted out the natural environment. Nonetheless, as Robert Sullivan shows, the Meadowlands have resisted efforts at domestication. In *The Meadowlands: Wilderness Adventures at the Edge of a City*, Sullivan guides readers through a place that is probably one of the least visited and most consistently desecrated areas in the New York City region. It is perhaps the least celebrated of any of the sites described so far. The Meadowlands have been subjected to numerous projects aiming to convert the swamplands into a site that can serve human ends; however, they have continually resisted attempts to render them useful. At the same time, more durably than any other place, they illustrate the ecological violence that has been done to lands that are deemed empty. Sullivan's original contribution to the literature of place lies both in the attention he pays to this neglected region and in the comic vein with which he describes his swampland adventures. At times the book is a pastiche of canonical texts that chronicle America's discovery or extol its wild places. Nevertheless, despite the humor that arises from the incongruity of situating the New Jersey Meadowlands within the hallowed lineage of writings about celebrated

American places, Sullivan's book raises serious ecological questions. In his seriocomic form of scripting, incompatible discourses jostle one another to produce an ironic commentary on the occupation of the land in the United States.

A Discovery of America in Reverse

In the book's incipit, Sullivan employs the familiar place-writing topos of presenting the images that unfold before the eyes of a subject moving through the land. By means of a rather unusual slippage from the first person singular to the first person plural, readers are invited to share the view that greets the traveler entering the Meadowlands. We are thus immediately required to collaborate in the writer's conspiracy against the moderns' bifurcation of the social and the natural.[1] One does not need to be familiar with local geographical prejudices to appreciate the irony of Sullivan's account of the bus ride from the Port Authority Bus Terminal through the Lincoln Tunnel to the territory beyond Bergen Hill, for the irony arises from the writer's play with language. In scripting his explorations of the Meadowlands as a voyage of discovery, Sullivan summons readers' experience of texts from the extensive American tradition of place writing and asks us to note the strange new hybrid of the wild and the industrial that he is grafting. This new association produces a strangely heterogeneous aesthetic experience:

> And then, in just a few minutes, as we drop down the other side of Bergen Hill and cruise into a low, flat land of lush grays and greens and pockets of rust and more and more circles of concrete, the bus seems to genuflect at the landscape before us. When the sky is clear, the water in the far-off creeks and rivers shines through the reeds like a sheet of aluminum foil that has been crumpled and then spread out again. When the sky is gray, the clouds mingle with the smokestacks' clouds of steam and smoke so that it is difficult to tell which is which. (13–14)

The scene he conjures up is both seductive and shocking, for he borrows the tropes of nature writing to describe this blasted landscape. Indeed, his aim is to undo the split between natural and artificial elements by questioning "which is which." Aesthetically pleasing vegetal tones—"lush grays and greens"—merge with the industrial palate of rust and concrete. The polysyndetic coordination of these elements suggests a lyrical vein that is undercut by the juxtaposition of incompatible elements. The mention of circles gives a Transcendentalist cast to the scene that is immediately mocked by the fact that they are "circles of concrete." The reverent attitude of the genuflecting bus conforms perfectly to this mock naturalist vein of writing, recalling, for example, Barry Lopez's habit of paying homage to an exceptional sight.[2] The comparison of the rivers to aluminum foil echoes Hopkins's poem "God's Grandeur," quoted in the epigraph to *The Meadowlands*. While the nineteenth-century poet's incongruous metaphorical evocation of "foil" and "oil" jolts readers into a renewed appreciation of the beauty of creation, Sullivan's descriptions remind us of the unholy mixedness of contemporary peri-urban landscapes.

In venturing into a place long reputed to be "one of the most disgusting areas in America" (107), Sullivan launches an adventurous project of discovery that explicitly invokes accounts of Lewis and Clark's exploration of the West as well as Thoreau's descriptions of eastern sites, in particular Walden Pond, texts cherished by a long line of American writers of place. The "*Walden* Swamp" chapter of *The Meadowlands* makes these connections explicit, while emphasizing the comic disparity between the latter-day adventure and its famous precedents. The adventurer discovers that there is only one way he can explore the swamp: "You pretty much have to take some kind of a boat, which was what I started to think I ought to do. I began to consider taking a trip to Walden Swamp and then spending some time out there and maybe even contemplating nature and civilization just like Thoreau, or someone like that" (75). The demotic phrasing of this passage has a distancing and debunking effect that smacks of burlesque. Then the adventurer's difficult quest to obtain a canoe in the Meadowlands makes his exploit appear ludicrous: "Lewis and Clark . . . would already have had access to a canoe" (76). The itemized shopping list of the equipment purchased at the Campmor store (77) imitates both Clark's "Memorandum of Articles in Readiness for the Voyage"[3] and Thoreau's list of expenses in the "Economy" chapter of Walden.[4] Sullivan also claims that his canoeing companion, Dave, is related to Meriwether Lewis (78). When, after venturing dangerously near a toxic cleanup site and feeling more and more lost, the two men are rescued by a security guard named Ed, Sullivan states, "Ed was our Sacagawea" (91). Sullivan's evocation of these hallowed texts may seem pure pastiche and his book may appear to be simply a lighthearted spoof of the American adventure story; however, the humor is a vehicle for a more serious inquiry into cultural assumptions about place.

First of all, the parodic style of Sullivan's book distances readers from the gratifying roles of vicarious adventurers and nature lovers that the literature of place conventionally offers them. If anything definite surfaces from Sullivan's debunking, it is that the spirit and determination of America's famous explorers are unsuitable for tackling the difficulties facing the intrepid souls who venture into the Meadowlands. The New Jersey wilderness presents less heroic but more perplexing challenges. Modern pioneers must battle mosquitoes resistant to all efforts to eliminate them and brave the contamination, fires, and explosions caused by industrial hazards. Only the crazy desperadoes of the swamps—the occasional fishermen or canoeists—routinely ignore them.

The combined evocation of the colorful early explorers and the Thoreau that everybody idolizes (although not the one that Sullivan wants us to rediscover in *The Thoreau You Don't Know*[5]) suggests other parodic intentions. The contrast between America's hallowed natural sites and the polluted Meadowlands highlights the way in which westward expansion led to the abandonment of responsibility for the lands left behind in the East. Thus Sullivan's ironic discovery script demonstrates the consequences of the spatial division that Cronon critiques in "The Trouble with Wilderness," published just three years before *The Meadowlands.* In turning our attention eastward, Sullivan asks us to confront the evidence of the history of ecological exploitation on the American continent: "I am creeping slowly back into the East, back to America's *first* West—making a reverse commute to the already explored land that has become, through negligence, through exploitation, and through its own chaotic persistence, explorable again" (14–15). The "reverse commute" suggests a new direction in thinking about the American territory. Sullivan's exploration of the Meadowlands is an act of writerly reclamation that has ecological weight in spite of the author's self-derisive attitude.

His exploration of the place is not only a voyage in space but also a return in time through the archives documenting the Meadowlands' history. Sullivan braids the account of his own discoveries together with those of earlier explorers. The temporal perspective afforded through this strategy points out the contrast between the area as it once was and as it has been altered by two centuries of use. Passages of lyrical effusion about the region discovered by early visitors clash with descriptions of its present desolation, as in the opening lines of the ironically entitled chapter "An Achievement of the Future": "Once, there were actual meadows in the Meadowlands, decorated with wildflowers the way they are today littered with bits of paper and plastic and truck tire shards. In the spring of 1819, John Torrey, the father of American botany, toured the Jersey meadows and reported patches of white, yellow, and purple violets" (35). There follows a long list of the varied flora that botanists found in the Meadowlands, but the list is punctuated with the record of the 1910 oil spill that wiped out the wild rice growing there. The lyricism of the evocations of past abundance only redoubles the irony of the observations on its present state.

Sullivan unearths an 1899 article by Charles J. McGillycuddy that reveals the attitude toward marshland lying at the root of the changes: "Within three miles of the New York City Hall is a tract of wasteland, seventy-two square miles in extent. Its reclamation and utilization is an achievement of the near future which will provide an object lesson to every community in the United States" (McGillycuddy, quoted by Sullivan 48–49). For McGillycuddy, the marshlands are an invitation to development, a wasted space that presents a challenge to the ingenuity of the nation. Sullivan heads the chapter from *The Meadowlands* in which this quote appears with the title of McGillycuddy's article, "An Achievement of the Future." Recontextualized in this way, McGillycuddy's optimistic late-nineteenth-century progressivism takes on a hollow resonance, since Sullivan goes on to list a number of projects advanced over the centuries for draining and developing the Meadowlands. Far from being a testament to progress, this list records the failure of American enterprise and the indomitable resilience of the swamp. As a last resort, the "wasteland" has been used as a dumping ground for the debris and waste of civilization. Despite the disdain with which they have been treated, the Meadowlands have evinced a "chaotic persistence" (15) in resisting the misguided schemes to render them useful to the nation. Nonetheless, in situating them, albeit ironically, in the tradition of American writing about place, Sullivan implies that the values that the nation has cherished, as well as the vices that it has hidden, are revealed in one of its most enduring dumps.

When our literary guide to the Meadowlands asks us, provocatively, to think of the place as both "an undesignated national park" and as "a more classic tourist designation, like Paris" (57), he is not simply being flippant. The Meadowlands bring together both extremes; the enduring wild is overprinted with the signs of urban life. The place is just as much an emblem of the nation as the national parks and the great cities. Cronon has argued that the policy of isolating places from the rest of the country for conservation in the institutions of national parks or wilderness sanctuaries leaves the rest of the territory open to systematic despoliation.[6] The guided tour of the unloved swamp that Sullivan gives readers could readily have taken on the tone of an ecological jeremiad, but the readership for such tirades would probably be restricted to the already converted. The writer resorts to humor as a way of unsettling commonly held views and of offering a fresh look at an area that most Americans would choose not to contemplate.

The modesty and good-natured optimism of the author's persona allow readers to participate in his adventure vicariously and to follow him into the most repugnant toxic waste piles. The chameleonic authorial voice mixes mild provocation, naïveté, burlesque, and objectivity; the narrator's attitude remains elusive, ungraspable, difficult to pinpoint. Sullivan adopts a series of roles that he plays with mock seriousness. He is the Thoreau of Walden Swamp and the Lewis and Clark of New Jersey. He is also the Whitman of the marshlands, "sing[ing] the Meadowlands" (20), adopting the anaphoric style of *Leaves of Grass* to apostrophize them (203) and to "marvel" at their contradictions (18–20). At the same time, he plays the part of a kinky garbage lover or a pursuer of trivia like the collection of all the translations of *Gone with the Wind* in the Kearney Library. He is the self-styled "dot on the Meadowlands' exclamation point" (20), an insignificant but determining accessory to the place that he wants to showcase.

Through his multiple voices and sundry adventures, Sullivan critiques the cultural orthodoxy about place. The adulation for beauty spots and the revulsion inspired by contaminated places are attitudes that are so deeply rooted as to be beneath the level of consciousness; they are taken for granted. Sullivan destabilizes these ingrained convictions in order to change them through infiltration and deconstruction. The attitudes that have created the polluted swamps are not condemned in their energy but in their orientation. In resorting to parody, the book defuses these attitudes from the inside, seemingly embracing them in order to reorient them toward more constructive perspectives. The humor contains empathy as well as ridicule for the behavior that the author wants to change.

An American Reality Check

The problem with places like the Meadowlands is that their existence is ignored or denied by most Americans. This blanking-out mechanism applied to sites placed under the sign of empty should by now be familiar. Even the hotels and motels that fringe its western edge "try to pretend the Meadowlands are not there" (58). As our guide to this occulted place, Sullivan insists on his responsibility to look at it carefully and to tell us what he sees. Perhaps the first guest at the Days Inn in East Rutherford to ask for a room with a view (58), Sullivan catalogues the disturbing sights that he sees around the hotel. The Days Inn adjoins a toxic waste site where workers in protective clothing busy themselves with a task that one of them swears is "nothing, really" (60). In contrast to this pattern of denial, Sullivan offers an American reality check. The scripts detailing his explorations take readers from "one unattractive attraction to the next" (60) to detail the surprises and the horrors.

The Meadowlands escape national attention in part because of the persistence of the illusory conception of nature as a transcendent value distinct from the places in which humans live and to which they must journey in order to renew themselves. For this reason East Coast residents taking off from Newark airport follow the traditional westward migratory pattern "to travel and explore" (14). This urge to leave in search of virgin territory is one of the causes of the deterioration of places like the New Jersey swampland. The Meadowlands cannot pretend to attain the American ideal of pristine wilderness: the place is neither unadulterated nor unsullied, neither outside history nor empty of human traces, neither immutable nor timeless. Yet, like the "virgin" spaces that the contemporary nature seekers yearn to find in the West, the Meadowlands have been named empty. Sullivan humorously links the nation's eastern and western extremities: "All over the Meadowlands there is uninterrupted panorama. It's Big Sky Country East" (61). The ironic parallel drawn between the two spaces has its foundations in American cultural practice. After all, the "wild" West was once considered a dumping ground for society's outlaws. Later its "emptiness" offered a promise of land for settlers to cultivate. Whereas the western territories were described as uninhabited in order to facilitate the nation's expansion and its appropriation of indigenous people's dwelling places, the swamplands were pronounced barren and unreclaimable in order to serve as a depository for civilization's waste products. The sign of empty always functions in a similar way—it produces a mental image of the territory that favors designs upon it—but the aims differ. It has served to clear the land for settlement, to set it aside for recreation, or to ready it to swallow the nefarious by-products of industrialization. The new value assigned to emptiness in the twentieth century, the one attached to the national parks and wilderness reserves and celebrated in traditional nature writing, offers a panacea for the ills of industrial life. Sullivan's account reveals how these extremes meet up somehow in the Meadowlands; they have the distinction of having been "the largest garbage dump in the world" (93) and of paradoxically remaining undeveloped. In the words of a newspaper article reporting a train accident there: "Though only three miles west of Manhattan, the site was strangely remote, a wintry marsh of scrub and frozen ponds" (25).

The Meadowlands continue to serve as a blank slate upon which people project the wildest plans. Of course, the place is not a void: it contains the city's rejects and garbage as well as resilient forms of wildlife. Paradoxically, its placement under the sign of empty makes it replete with the most active ferment for regeneration. It is a place of destruction and creativity, of creativity associated with destruction: "People were always trying to invent new uses for the Meadowlands; most people felt *anything* was better than what was there" (48). In this italicized "anything," Sullivan encapsulates the unsettling mix of zest and resourcefulness that goes hand in hand with the ecological irresponsibility.

As opposed to the wild places honored by the Wilderness Act, the Meadowlands are anarchic, chaotic, and degraded, but also indomitable. Denied the purity that promises transcendence, the Meadowlands evince the earthy quality of resilience; they have been able to withstand the worst outrages. Sullivan lauds this persistence in his closing apostrophe to the place: "And how is it that you will somehow manage to be spoiled but unspoiled, trod upon and bulldozed, remediated and reclaimed, dumped in and sprayed all over but somehow never spent?" (204). Thanks to the land's "chaotic persistence" (15), vitality is everywhere under one form or another.

Pulsing with exuberant energy and full of a magmatic current of transformation, the swamp is a place of encounters and social mixing. Unlike the solitary confrontation with the wild usually described in nature writing, Sullivan's adventures always point to the convergence of human and more-than-human activity. He discovers a variety of stories embedded in the place, from the romantic to the sensational. He also encounters a variety of engaging characters like the intrepid mosquito hunters of the "Skeeters" chapter, the indefatigable treasure hunter of the "Treasure" chapter, and the "two local Meadowlands celebrities" of the chapter named for them, "The Trapper and the Fisherman" (185). These last two denizens of the place they designate "an urban wilderness" (195) are firmly convinced of the swamp's capacity to bring forth life. Because of this resilience, the Meadowlands offer hope for renewal. Though Don Smith, the naturalist "trapper" employed by the Hackensack Meadowlands Development Commission, admits that the place will never be returned to the state in which it existed before the arrival of Europeans (199), he points to the progress made in improving wildlife habitat. For him, the work of rehabilitating this degraded but still vital place is as important as that of preserving the more prestigious national sites typically chosen as wilderness areas and national parks.

By revealing the Meadowlands in all their complexity, Sullivan embraces the new attitude to place that replaces the myth of empty land and the harmful split between developed and virgin spaces. For the explorer who has the patience to excavate, the Meadowlands offer a condensed and abridged introduction to American culture, in the shape not of an orderly narrative but of a disheveled trash pile of history. Whereas the wilderness ethic tends to efface previous histories and impose the myth of timeless, immemorial nature, Sullivan's swampland investigation presents a multilayered geohistorical space. The chapter entitled "Digging" proffers an appropriate metatextual image of Sullivan's archaeology of modern America. There he recounts a number of exploratory searches, notably for the remains of Jimmy Hoffa, who disappeared in 1975, and for the rubble of Pennsylvania Station, demolished in 1964: "When I dig in the Meadowlands, I do so in an attempt to rouse some of these people, places or things from their sleep in the swamp" (143). The swamp is the repository of the nation's repressed memories and Sullivan works to bring what has been forgotten to the reader's consciousness.

Scripting America's Hybridity

Sullivan's burlesque exploration has a serious intent; he offers a new vision of America issued from a place that is readily accessible and yet deliberately ignored. So far this survey of the new literature of place has complexified the vision of sites placed under the sign of empty; the books examined reveal the inseparability of history and geography, culture and nature. Nevertheless, at times some of them still evince the longing to restore wild places to their pre-Columbian state. Although, as Ladino has shown, this nostalgia for an imagined past can mobilize people for environmental causes,[7] it can also deflect attention from the places where most people actually live. The works studied so far focus on sites relatively far away from the most densely populated areas of the United States, and in these choices linger traces of the cultural habit of opposing the urban and the wild. Even though the writers blur this duality, they do not utterly efface it. In *The Meadowlands* Sullivan reveals it to be illusory. The American continent is not a dichotomous space; rather it is a heterogeneous, interrelated, and systemic entity. Sullivan gives a breakthrough literary illustration of the conclusions reached by scholars in various fields, notably those gathered by Cronon in *Uncommon Ground*. Instead of holding to the culturally fabricated dualisms, he exults in the complex hybrids produced in the modern era. Instead of wavering between two opposed and presupposed entities, Sullivan explores phenomena that exist and mutate in interaction. His evocation of the swamplands adjoining the New York conurbation illustrates the rich aggregates formed through human and other-than-human cohabitation. The resulting hybridity is evoked through four correlated phenomena: complementarity, creativity, organicity, and transformation.

Sullivan repeatedly emphasizes the oddly harmonious scenes produced by the superposition of New York City's skyline onto the swamp. In the trapper's oxymoronic phrase, the Meadowlands are an "urban wilderness" (195). They are the only place where one can see herons take flight against a backdrop of the Manhattan skyline (18). Rather than dissociating the two spaces, Sullivan insists on their complementarity. The book's subtitle, *Wilderness Ad-*

ventures on the Edge of a City, reminds us of the importance of the border zone, the site where city and swamp interact. There is a continuity between the city and its dumping ground hinted at in a sight spotted from Walden Swamp: "At one point, midtown lined up with a view of an old Coca-Cola sign, and the coincidence seemed of astrological significance" (87). The foregrounding of the Coca-Cola sign stresses the city's consumer culture and links the plastic soda bottles floating in the canal to its commercial activities. The activities of the city have their repercussions in the Meadowlands: consumption in New York creates garbage dumps in the Meadowlands (93–106); commerce incites piracy (132); urban crime demands a space for Mafia executions (142). The subterranean continuity between the ostensible commerce and the dealings of the Mafia and other unofficial actuators of American society is suggested in the legends surrounding the body of Jimmy Hoffa and the numerous reports of lurid deaths that have taken place in the Meadowlands or corpses that have ended up there. The swamp is the territorial equivalent of the unconscious of modern life.

Precisely because the Meadowlands are judged to hold nothing of value, they offer a space of creativity, an inexhaustible spur to human inventiveness. Like other areas placed under the sign of empty, the swamp has been a site of projection, a target of the wildest schemes and dreams of instant riches, as the title of a 1970s pamphlet, *Turning Swamps into Dollars*, suggests (50). This phrase recalls the deceptive advertising aimed at immigrants to the Montana plains. Like the plains, the Meadowlands have resisted development schemes. However, in the symbiotic relationship that New York City conducts with the marshlands at its edge, construction and destruction go hand in hand, as the example of the Pennsylvania Station demolition illustrates. America's constant renewal of itself has its corollary. Sullivan's exploratory work to trace the station's remains shows this with humorous indirection. Like an archaeologist on a dig, he painstakingly hunts for relics of the disappeared station and treasures a possible fragment when what is really in question is, of course, the wanton destruction of the imposing Roman-style edifice that the station used to be. Even more shocking is the complete effacement of all traces of its existence in people's memories. The "Digging" chapter ends with Sullivan having photographs of his find notarized by a woman who "had never heard of Penn Station" (163). He quotes without comment, as the last word of the chapter, her laconic "Oh" in response to his explanation.

More than an exercise in remembrance, the book demands that readers reconstruct the successive phases of creation and destruction that history has occulted. To help us do so, Sullivan relates an impossible dream of turning "the bottom of the Meadowlands to the top and restor[ing] what was thrown into the muck back to its pristine predumped condition." This "de-wasteland-iz[ing]" of the Meadowlands would miraculously resurrect all the buried strata (141). This dream could be seen as a last attempt to preserve the old duality of pristine nature coexisting with the march of progress, except that it is clearly a perfect impossibility. It is a childish fantasy, just like an earlier exercise he describes: "If you make a fake telescope with your hands and block out the backyards on the top of the cliff and you concentrate on the little leafy trees instead of the garbage dumps behind you, then you can imagine you're in a tropical place" (41). These are environmentally less costly forms of escapism than the western flights out of Newark airport. They are also imaginative reminders of the consequences of American progress. Creativity should not be evaluated simply in terms of achievement; the accumulation of failed attempts and surplus refuse should also be factored in. Nevertheless, this conclusion is not explicitly stated; it is only implied by ironic suggestion.

There is an organic relation—Sullivan speaks of "synergy" (43)—between the city and its environs, a sort of economic regulation of town and country, city and swamp. The term "economy" should not be understood simply as the production and exchange of goods but also as a global organization involving ideas, things, animals, and people. The pig farms that the mayor of Secaucus boasts about amply demonstrate this organicity. The pigs that fed the city were themselves once fed by New York's detritus: "So we were *recycling!* And we were recycling long before anyone else was," the mayor exclaims (28). A relation of interdependence exists between Manhattan's pulsating energy and the earthier activities on the other side of the river in New Jersey.

Another emblematic illustration of the organic connection of formerly dichotomized places can be found in the description of the dumps in the chapter humorously entitled "The Valley of the Garbage Hills." This chapter reveals the economy of consumption that is at the core of modern societies. Economy is no longer perceived solely as the production of goods to satisfy human needs but also as the production of waste that is the antagonist of production, a production in negative. The balance between the two is troped in the depiction of garbage hills that match the high-rises of the city: "There are whole suites of organisms in each hill as if each hill were a bacterial high-rise" (96). There is even the evocation of shadow hills inside the visible ones (96). They are made of water and they deliver leachates that contaminate the whole system. Another graphic illustration of the reciprocal process at work between the swamps and the cities is the practice of baling garbage in cubes, which simulates the production of goods and de facto creates the conditions for a flourishing activity involving heterogeneous participants: "It was like a little planned garbage community. . . . Giant tractors were setting the compacted trash cubes into the hill as seagulls cheered them on" (101). Sullivan deliberately omits human agency from this description of the "planned . . . community" formed by the concentration of New York's garbage, the dump site's tractors, and the seagulls drawn to the piles of refuse.

This new organic world of vibrant matter is pulsating with energy and in constant transformation.[8] It is one of the neglected dynamos of modern American society. Things are not only organically related; they are also crushed and transmogrified in a never-ending process of renewal and reinvention. America's is a changeable reality in which what we perceive is only a fragment of what there is—the shadow hills, for example—or what there was—like the missing portion of Snake Hill that has left what residents see as "a rotten tooth" (26). Magmatic mutation prevails in the Meadowlands. The physical power of the swamp buckles and finally sinks the roads that humans build there. This vision of a metamorphic Heraclitan universe displaces and regenerates the more rigid dualistic conception of nature and culture as separate spheres.

Associated with this new conception of the American space is the advent of a new aesthetic based on humor, indirection, and baroque excess. This mixed style is vital to the scripting of hybridity, since Sullivan is not so much chronicling a new reality but embracing a new way of accessing reality. The book's manner of address functions similarly to the way in which Sullivan sees Thoreau's writing working, as "an implement that clears away the topsoil—some good, some tired—and offers a view of the root."[9] Humor is the cue that alerts us to contradictions or fissures in discourse, signaling gaps in the tissue of representations. For example, through a witty reference to the commercialization of soothing sounds from nature, he captures the hybridity of his chosen site: "Altogether, the chorus is a kind of wild industrial New Jersey sound track, which unlike the environmental sounds of the Eastern forests and Pacific Coast whale migration routes, is not available on cassette or CD" (15). This amusing description of New Jersey sounds not only emphasizes the mixedness of the auditory experience, it also points to the work of filtering habitually carried out by cultural agents. In an oblique manner, Sullivan alerts readers to the occulted realities of their world. At the same time, he reorients interest in new directions, perhaps toward new solutions.

Sullivan's indirection also takes the form of quoting his interlocutors' words without comment, allowing their frequently ironic significance to filter through the context in which he has set them. These pregnant statements often appear at the end of a chapter, leaving the reader to catch their resonance. The "Valley of the Garbage Hills" chapter ends with a vignette of the dump owner, Anthony Malanka, complaining over the burnt sausage he has been served for lunch: "What is this, a turd?" (106). In the course of the book, readers have discovered the intimate connection between restaurants and refuse, and pork and manure, so the rhetorical question has a double-edged irony. Don Smith is given the last word in the chapter "The Trapper and the Fisherman," and it resonates with everything that goes before, so that his efforts to restore the Meadowlands sound suspiciously like other schemes for transforming them: "But we're working on something else that might work in there instead" (201). Bearing in mind how many other projects have been undone by the transformative power of the swamp, his efforts seem both valiant and quixotic.

The baroque is a key element of this new aesthetic. The pulsating energized combination of contradictory elements that generates new perceptions is suggested in the epigraphs to the book. Hopkins's paean to the regenerative force that redeems the weary world in "God's Grandeur" is immediately undercut by the prosaic counsel proffered by the New Jersey animal control officer, Al McClure: "If you dig out here, you sure as heck are going to find something." Sullivan's prose zigzags between these two extremes, occasionally rising to lyric beauty and then falling to demotic familiarity. Most of the time, though, his writing works on a double plane, since the lyrical embellishes the abject, while the commonplace presents the extraordinary. Readers are constantly kept off balance and forced to reflect on what appears to be an unconventional mismatch between style and subject. Rather than rhapsodizing on the egret he spots in Walden Swamp, Sullivan describes it in terms borrowed from the setting: "its long curved white neck the shape of a highway off-ramp, its white feathers the color of Styrofoam" (80). Similarly, rather than lamenting the presence of refuse floating in the water, he invests it with aquatic vitality: "The waterlogged cigarette butts were bloated and curled as if impersonating shrimp" (80). The blending of organic and inorganic substances violates the distinctions on which the moderns' worldview is based, confronting us with the realities that it fails to take into account. This style could be called grotesque,[10] except that its consistent employment to chronicle a familiar place eventually deprives it of its shock value.[11] Rather than the sense of anxiety or revulsion produced by the grotesque, Sullivan's descriptions produce a shock of recognition. The mixing of genres and categories forces us to recognize that the natural and the human-made are not separate. They blend together inextricably in the swamp. His baroque vision works rather like a gestalt image where figure and ground are balanced, inviting viewers to see double rather than to filter out one aspect of the picture.

Through employing a new ecopoetics of entanglement that combines humor, indirection, and baroque excess, Sullivan rehabilitates the incongruous, the impure, and the abject, returning the repressed knowledge of the Meadowlands to public consciousness. His book is not simply a comic response to a national embarrassment; it is also an act of faith that aims to foster a new understanding of the national territory. *The Meadowlands* asks us to see the places that have remained shrouded because the moderns' aesthetics of purity ignores all the hybrids produced by human activity.[12] Just as Sullivan's account of his exploration guides readers through the labyrinthine canals of the Meadowlands, his scripting of hybridity invites our minds to take new paths. He draws new mental maps that respond to the complex events taking place in space-time.

A Question Addressed to America

Sullivan provides "a challenging new model for how we ought to pay attention,"[13] a new lucidity concerning the American territory. This new vision does not promote more trustworthy or efficient means of controlling our environment. After taking the long historical view, the author is bound to be skeptical about attempts to control the swamp. His caution appears in the evocation of the ecological debate and reclamation plans in connection with the Meadowlands.

Much as he is sensitive to the reclamation programs that have been proposed, Sullivan is aware of the challenge that the swamp's wayward resilience poses to human dreams of domination. More than an interventionist, utilitarian, operative attitude, what is needed is a change of mind. The technocratic approach prevents individuals from being personally implicated; it also tries to solve the ecological crisis by manufacturing new, often unpredictable, hybrids rather than working on the behaviors resulting from deeply embedded mentalities. Sullivan's critique of human intervention in the environment is evident from his tongue-in-cheek appraisal of John Smith, "the prophet for a mosquito-free New Jersey" (109), and the failure of his attempts to eradicate the resilient insects. Sullivan points out that Smith's elaborate system of ditches may have dealt with the saltwater mosquito problem, but that it "actually *increased* the number of freshwater mosquitoes in the Meadowlands" (114). The problem persists, as shown in Sullivan's mock-heroic account of the mosquito control warriors in the present-day Meadowlands. Human efforts to tamper with the swamp seem misguided, futile, or irresponsible, especially since dualistic thinking blinds the specialists to the complexity of the ecosystem.

Even the best efforts to understand the intricate ecology of the place yield limited results, as we see in the debate Sullivan stages between two fervent Meadowlands guides, the trapper and the fisherman, a confrontation that remains inconclusive. One of the protagonists would like to see the swamp reclaimed as an urban wilderness with ecotours, a garbage museum, and even weddings, while the other is satisfied with making a living organizing boat tours around the marshlands. Both adopt a pragmatic attitude and are using the Meadowlands as a field of observation and experiment. Sullivan chooses to strike at the roots of the system that produced the mess by inquiring into the frameworks that produced it.

This is the implication of the final chapter, entitled "Point-No-Point" after the southernmost site of the exploration. In a closing apostrophe to the Meadowlands, Sullivan gives a litany of the errors that Americans have made and will perhaps continue to make in placing this stretch of their territory under the sign of empty:

> What new industries will one day rise up from your waste-laced soils and smear your already smeared landscape and write on you once more, progress's palimpsest, technology's Etch-A-Sketch? How many people will look at you some day and write up a memo or organize a commission or hire someone to write a prospectus and say that you could be something else, something more, something much better with new and improved features for everyone to enjoy, even the kids? (203)

The rhetorical questions remind us of the repeated errors of ignoring the lessons of the past and failing to take into account the specific realities of the land that a consideration of its history reveals. What is needed is not a new project, but a new way of thinking about America, a mentality makeover.

The need for a conceptual revolution is only suggested, never explicitly stated; that would defeat the purpose of the book. Sullivan is not preaching but prodding, stimulating reflection, encouraging the acceptance of past and present complexity, even when it may appear unseemly and even grotesque. His strength as a writer is to pose questions, and in that he follows the Thoreau that he asks us to rediscover with him: "Thoreau doesn't offer answers. His is the analysis that leads to the questions."[14] Still, *The Meadowlands* points toward a new way of seeing the history of Americans' engagement with the territory. Clearly, progress does not entail the replacement of the wild by the civilized. The failed results of that persistent dream of the Puritans and the pioneers are found in the Meadowlands. Nor does it lie in escaping to the West by taking off from Newark airport. Progress would mean accepting the Meadowlands as they are and proceeding from there, for the land, blighted as it seems, still offers hope. As Sullivan says in his study of Thoreau: "I was getting the feeling more and more that in the city I might find nature in a lot more places than I might have looked for it before, that *wild*ness was more important than wilderness, that wildness was everywhere, if I looked for it."[15] The evidence of the persistence of "wildness . . . everywhere," including in urban places, undoes the split that founded the nation's policies for its territory. On consideration, the unloved marshlands are emblematic of the anarchic processes at the core of life that involve creation and destruction, innovation, loss, and survival. Sullivan's book invites us to take into account the interrelatedness of apparent opposites and to come to a better awareness of the consequences of our actions. Like Thoreau he uses humor and paradox to provoke a clearer understanding of where we live and how we live.

Conclusion

The Void Calls; Earth Calls Back

In 1969, the year of the first manned moon landing, Loren Eiseley gave a series of lectures at the University of Washington that were subsequently published in *The Invisible Pyramid*. In the midst of the euphoria about the historic American achievement, Eiseley's lectures sound a cautionary note. He wonders why scientists "have proffered us the power of the void as though flight were the most important value on earth."[1] He questions his compatriots' impulse to abandon the sole planet in the solar system that sustains them, quoting, with ironic puzzlement, one of the space agency administrators interviewed for *Newsweek* just after the astronauts' successful return: "'Should man,' this officer said, 'fall back from his destiny . . . the confines of this planet will destroy him.'" (153). If Eiseley were alive today he might be chagrined but perhaps not overly surprised to learn of the various multimillion-dollar projects aiming to send manned flights to the even more distant and hostile destination of Mars.[2] Apparently, the quest for virgin territory, "to boldly go where no man has gone before,"[3] still captures the imagination.

The dream of colonizing Mars is one of the latest avatars of the American love affair with the blank space on the map. The projection into a space designated as empty is still the first step in the cultural fantasy of correcting the errors of civilization (or nature) by starting anew. The imaginary frontier has merely been extended to take in increasingly vaster stretches of the universe. Unexplored planets are held up as potential homes for our species, while we daily befoul the dwelling that we have on Earth. Granted, the specter of the void spurs creativity. One is struck by the ingenuity evidenced in the scientific literature debating how to transport people to the remote edges of the solar system and how to keep them alive once they get there. Imagining new ways to live durably on Planet Earth may seem more mundane, but it is more urgent for our survival.

It is not easy to abandon the idea inherited from the moderns of a world dichotomized into zones of civilization and nature onto which we then project the values of fullness or emptiness. The elegant simplicity of that model of reality has made it a powerful motor for invention as well as for colonial expansion. Viewing the Earth as inert matter to be disposed of for the benefit of humanity avoids the embarrassing question of there being any unforeseen consequences arising when things act according to the trajectories of their own existence;[4] in other words, this dualistic model bypasses a more complex ecological vision of the planet. With the growing awareness that the planet's resources are finite, we clearly need a new model for inhabitation. As the writers studied here reveal, accepting the Earth's infinitely more multifarious and complicated mixedness means giving up the dream of flight, acknowledging what we have done to the places in which we live, and taking responsibility for them. It means refocusing creative energies to take in both sacralized and polluted places, because of course they are linked together. To ignore the seductive appeal of the imaginary blank space on the map is the necessary first step to making life sustainable on our home planet.

After contemplating the call of the void, Eiseley affirms the uniqueness of Earth: "In the entire solar system it alone possesses water and oxygen sufficient to nourish higher life" (152). He movingly concludes his meditation on space exploration by recalling not the triumphant astronauts of Apollo 11, but the "desperate crew" of the maimed Apollo 13 "intent, if nothing else availed, upon leaving their ashes on the winds of earth. A love for earth, almost forgotten in man's roving mind, had momentarily reasserted its mastery, a love for the green meadows we have so long taken for granted and desecrated at our cost" (156). His proposed antidote to the allure of emptiness orients attention back to Earth and its "green meadows." *The Invisible Pyramid* concludes by urging the necessity of turning the clock backward: "Today man's mounting numbers and his technological power to pollute his environment reveal a single demanding necessity: the necessity for him consciously to reenter and preserve, for his own safety, the old first world from which he originally emerged."[5] Though Eiseley's concerns about overpopulation and pollution seem more pressing than ever in the twenty-first century, his nostalgic dream of returning to the garden no longer seems realistic. That "old first world" no longer exists.

Humanity's imprint has altered the planet to such an extent that geologists are now debating whether to acknowledge the beginning of a new geological epoch, the Anthropocene.[6] In this century, the Earth that calls us is not simply the dreamy, opalescent orb that the astronauts photographed from space. Our planet has shown another face: Gaia is not simply beautiful; she can also appear implacable, unpredictable, even vengeful.[7] Rather than idealizing a former, pristine state of nature, we now have to acknowledge how our way of living on the planet has altered it. Still, we have no other place to live; caring for the planet is another way of caring for ourselves. The corrective to our longing for empty space is to admit that we are earthbound. We are always placed somewhere precise, somewhere that asks for our attention, but that emplacement extends farther than our immediate surroundings, stretching beyond us in space-time. Being earthbound entails both a spatiotemporal location and a moral commitment; it means recognizing both one's dependence on the Earth and one's obligations toward it. In assimilating nature to raw material for their use and in imagining that there exist empty spaces for their expansion, the moderns have managed to threaten everything that exists, including themselves. Becoming earthbound means taking into account the activities and interests of our co-tenants. It means opening up the scope of our vision to include not only the other-than-human inhabitants of the planet, but also the ever-proliferating hybridizations resulting from ongoing interactions.

Just how to pay attention to Earth is a controversial issue in environmental studies, however. In *Sense of Place and Sense of Planet*, Ursula K. Heise brilliantly inventories the contradictions in twentieth-century appeals either to a global orientation representing the Earth "in relatively simple and concrete images that foregrounded synthesis, holism and connectedness,"[8] or to a concentration on local issues emphasizing proximity, autonomy, and self-sufficiency, but ignoring both the broader reach of material existence and the migratory patterns of existence.[9] Heise proposes "eco-cosmopolitanism" that explores "by what means individuals and groups have succeeded in envisioning themselves in similarly concrete fashion as part of the global biosphere, or by what means they might be enabled to do so."[10] Does the local diminish in importance in the face of environmental problems that are decidedly planetary? The new writers of place suggest the contrary. In exploring their chosen milieus, they offer distinctive takes on what it means to be earthbound.

While grounding their explorations in particular places, these writers extend their reach to the networks that connect specific localities with far-flung sites and times. While they pay close attention to local biota, they acknowledge the role humans play in the ongoing dynamics of environmental transformation. Meloy describes the introduction of nonnative species into the western deserts; Sullivan notes the way in which human intervention has altered mosquito populations. Their conception of place is much wider geographically than a particular point on a map and more historically informed than the place-specific tradition of nature writing. Localities radiate outward in webs of connections. For Bass and Bowden, the webs are initially personal and autobiographical, though commitment to beloved places pushes them to move beyond the boundaries of the local to defend their chosen territories.[11] The other writers studied here are more intensely aware of the structuring relationships between the local, the national, and the global. In tracing the route from the restaurants of Manhattan to the pig farms and garbage dumps of the Meadowlands, Sullivan critiques a culture of unsustainable consumerism. He also critiques the nation's twentieth-century love affair with pristine wilderness in observing the planes transporting weekend adventurers westward away from the abandoned wastelands close to their homes. Raban tracks the migrations of hopeful homesteaders across continents toward the plains of eastern Montana, drawn by the fantasy of extracting gold from the land. Meloy discovers that a road near her Utah home leads outward to the national sites dedicated to the arms race and finally to Hiroshima and Nagasaki. Solnit covers much more ground than simply the excursions between Yosemite and the Nevada Test Site that structure *Savage Dreams*. She circles through space-time to take in places as distinctive as Thoreau's Concord; Göteborg, Sweden, where Lise Meitner took a life-changing walk with her nephew Otto Frisch; and the South Pacific island of Elugelab, vaporized by a U.S. fusion bomb in 1952. Looking beneath the sign of empty these writers reveal the many ways in which local sites connect to national and international trends and projects. Their books exemplify place-centered forms of ecohistoricism and ecocosmopolitanism.

How does this new literature of place differ from other forms of place writing? In contrast to travel writing, the new literature of place does not offer readers the thrill of vicariously exploring exotic sites. Instead it seeks to strengthen the commitment to the places we call home by encouraging us to know them better. For Bass, Bowden, and Meloy home ground remains fairly restricted, although responsibility ramifies outward toward other places and other beings. For Raban, Solnit, and Sullivan, home has a larger sense; their wanderings take in places that are only vaguely sketched in on most people's mental maps of the nation, and their writing aims to make those places more distinct so that the nation will recognize them. As opposed to geographical studies of place, the new literature does not claim to be objective—quite the contrary: the personal connections the writers establish with their chosen sites are vital. Nevertheless, in contrast to nature writers, whose personal attachment to the land is also primordial, the authors studied here do not relate their exhilarating experiences of self-expansion through encounters in zones beyond the boundaries of human habitation.[12] Their books suggest that there is no "nature" independent of us; we share the planet with everything else that exists, even taking the lion's share.

In gathering scripts centering on their adopted sites, these writers share their painstakingly achieved understanding and invite readers to embrace the tangled realities of their chosen space-times. They ask us to accept that there is no virgin territory where we can escape history. The places they describe are marked by the past but also full of promise for the future. None of the writers offers a remedy for the environmental problems they encounter in the sites they explore, but they take the first step toward solving problems in giving a more honest picture of them. Bass self-consciously parodies the ostrich-like impulses of the wilderness lover in imagining himself holed up in the woods when the neighboring town of Libby "begins to fester and boil" (29). Bowden fantasizes ironically about plans "to blow up the only highway leading to the mountain and then leave the mountain to heal alone" (160). These petulant outbursts aside, the writers studied here move from a vision of the land as divided into zones of purity and pollution to one of complex and interrelated territorial networks. Their protocol for connecting with land that has been treated as empty is first to conduct a reality check of their surroundings by deciphering the accumulated traces of human passage and then to renew their commitment through the encounter with otherness. These encounters foster awareness and responsibility. They usher in an age of retrospection after the age of expansion brought on by the myth of empty.

In the face of planetary threats of environmental catastrophe, the new writers of place choose a specific locality in order to retrace through language the steps that have led to its despoliation and to recommit through language. They stage their physical and intellectual trajectories for readers to follow. They correct the misapprehension that Americans migrate between the apparent "nowhere" of cities and suburbs[13] and remote utopian or dystopian "empty" spaces. It is vital to correct this misperception, since the more detached we are from our environment the more unreal it becomes, and the more powerless we feel to address ecological problems. The new writers of place visit the zones that have been blanked out on the map of America in order to expose the illusion of emptiness. They consider problems of habitation not through abstract concepts like ecology or environment but as concrete cases. In this way they counter the generally accepted tendency to pose the current ecological crisis in terms that overwhelm our capacity to take corrective measures. Looked at on a planetary scale, the threats of global warming, pollution, and loss of biodiversity are frightening, yet individuals are called on to feel personally responsible for circumstances that are far beyond their control. This tends to result in feelings of culpability, powerlessness, and ecological apathy,[14] which only perpetuate the status quo. We are weighed down by the guilt of ecological sins for which there seems to be no redemption, yet disasters are never inescapable fatalities. As these writers show, at every point and at all stages decisions are made, alternatives are open, and actual persons, institutions, and things are involved. In retracing the various stages we see that at each step a disastrous course could have been corrected, except that the myth of empty preempted discussion. The books also show that actions are interconnected, so that a decision made in one place affects another. The key is to assume responsibility as residents of our habitations and to find ways to dialogue with decision makers. The Anthropocene era calls for a new more-than-humanism, not triumphant but shamed, repentant, and resolute.

A new form of inhabitation is also necessary, one that reaches beyond the myth of empty and full spaces. As the writers studied here show, an informed personal attachment to a particular space-time nexus is a stronger and more enduring way of relating to the land than embracing broad cultural value judgments that designate what is sacred or desecrated, wilderness or wasteland. It is certainly less destructive. In order to favor that more respectful attitude toward the land, the new writers, geographers, and historians of place ask us to see the territory as neither blank nor superscripted but instead as bearing the tale-telling traces of countless encounters. The territory thereby becomes readable, interpretable, and ready for responsible habitation. Careful empirical interpretation of the land replaces the sanctification or obliteration of space. Some of the writers suggest ways of breaking with the pattern of conceptually and materially clearing the territory before appropriating it for new projects. Ellen Meloy imagines a mode of settlement that pays careful attention to what was and is already in place. In inaugurating the St. Thomas Aquinas Cactus and Succulent Society (111), she follows in the footsteps of Aldo Leopold, whose *Sand County Almanac* documents his more ecologically responsible way of inhabiting an overexploited site. Rebecca Solnit embraces a more political commitment, joining the activists who walk in the Nevada desert to bear witness that the atomic test site and the surrounding territory are not empty.

The preliminary step toward action involves changing the ways of thinking that have brought about the problem. The new writers of place work toward this by developing an aesthetic of complexity that expresses the interaction and overlapping of their personal and investigative orientations. They refuse conventional discriminations between different forms of discourse, drawing on anecdotes and history books, comparing political decisions and private choices, mixing legends, folklore, and facts. In this way, their texts demonstrate the hybridity of place. By interweaving multiple discourses, they suggest the correspondences and continuities between public and private spheres, between the local and the global, present and past. They figure time not as a forward-extending set of linear occurrences but as a multilayered experience spiraling backward and forward in a complex relation to memory and place. The writers also refuse hierarchical distinctions between human and other-than-human claims to the land, so that Bass's moose, Meloy's lizard, Solnit's blind horses, and Sullivan's mosquitoes can bear witness just as effectively as the human record keepers.

The new writers of place employ the interactive hermeneutic practice that I have called scripting. Favoring the accumulation of multiple discursive folds and layers, scripting can accommodate the heterogeneity that characterizes our existence in space-time. As a practice it is better described as relating than as representing. Representation predicates a split between subject and object and between the word and the world, while relation always implies a less hierarchical pairing—a connectedness and interactivity that is expressed through the synonymy between storytelling and relating. The writers of place shape themselves in their relation to the places they write about. Subject and object co-define each other, except that neither is fully subject or object any longer. Michel Serres's terms "quasi-object" and "quasi-subject" better designate the complementarity of the two positions by questioning the conceptual split between them and suggesting how they are co-created in interaction.[15] The relation is not symmetrical; it involves a distribution of power. Nevertheless, it also implies exchange more than confrontation.

Relating place is a way of connecting with the world. Robert Pogue Harrison even goes so far as to say that our ultimate place of residence is in language:

> Language is the ultimate "place" of human habitation. Before we dwell in this or that locale, or in this or that province, or in this or that city or nation, we dwell in the *logos*.
>
> The Greek word *logos* is usually translated as "language," but more originally it means "relation." *Logos* is that which binds, gathers or relates. It binds humans to nature in the mode of openness and difference. It is that wherein we dwell and that by which we relate ourselves to this or that place.[16]

Though Harrison's perception of existence seems rather too logocentric, language is undeniably one of the ways in which human beings interact with and in the world. My study of the myth of emptiness argues that our problems of habitation derive in part from discourse, and the authors selected for analysis investigate those problems in discourse as well as in the field. They readjust to the land by assuming responsibility for its representation, a process brilliantly figured in Meloy's Map of the Known Universe.

Scripting invites readers to form a personal relation with place through their work of finding coherence in the texts' assembled fragments. Readers and writers work together in restoring lost or broken connections between time and space, humans and nonhumans. Given the heterogeneity of discourses gathered in the new literature of place, readers must decide on the nature of the relation into which they enter. The reading contract in this kind of text is founded on the assumption that the writer is telling the truth, but readers are free to decide on the degree to which its truths are autobiographical, geographical, historical, or philosophical and how to fit these different reading experiences together in responding to the text. N. Scott Momaday describes a deeply satisfying relation to a particular place in these terms:

> Once in his life a man ought to concentrate his mind upon the remembered earth, I believe. He ought to give himself up to a particular landscape in his experience, to look at it from as many angles as he can, to wonder about it, to dwell upon it. He ought to imagine that he touches it with his hands at every season and listens to the sounds that are made upon it. He ought to imagine the creatures there and all the faintest motions of the wind. He ought to recollect the glare of noon and all the colors of the dawn and dusk.[17]

Ideally, the writer transmits this effort of remembering and recollecting with such force that the resulting book allows readers in turn to pay attention to the land, "to dwell upon it." American sites located under the sign of empty are in particular need of attentive consideration. The division of the American territory into zones of emptiness and plenitude has resulted in the inhabitants' misprision and loss of contact with it.[18] The writers studied here respond to this violent ideological separation by considering these misunderstood places from multiple angles and reinscribing them in the continuum of space-time. As readers of these works, we learn of lost or forgotten connections between the land and its people. In following the intellectual, emotional, and spatial trajectories of the literary disclosers, we begin to reconnect with the places in which we live.

New forms of place writing are vital both for the land and for the people. Myra Jehlen has studied how American culture has literally grounded itself in the national soil.[19] For her, America's self-construction as "nature's nation" dates from the moment of Europeans' discovery of the continent,[20] when "personal identity and national identification come together."[21] As long as identity formation depends on a space conceived of as empty, the relation will benefit only the individuals who impose the myth and use it to their ends. The imposition may appear to be ecological in preserving some segments of the American territory in an untouched state. However, this restricted form of conservation functions in disregard of the larger, messier, more entangled community of people, places, and things. The writers examined in this study open up the scope of place writing to acknowledge the histories of violence hidden by projections of emptiness. This more inclusive focus works to complicate and fracture both individual and national identities, but at the same time it enlarges them by including what has been left out in the dichotomous mythical construction of full and empty spaces. In this new literature of place, individuals connect with other members of the community (human as well as other-than-human). America's story becomes more than simply geographical. In the new narratives of space-time, the nation becomes accountable for its history. While this development engages responsibility, it also releases the potential for reconciliation.

NOTES

Introduction

1. See the exhibition catalogue by Katherine Ware, *Earth Now: American Photographers and the Environment* (Santa Fe: Museum of New Mexico Press, 2011).
2. The photograph appeared in the exhibition *This Is the American Earth*, which opened in San Francisco at the American Academy of Sciences in 1955. In 1960 it was featured in the highly successful publication of the same title: Ansel Adams, Nancy Wynne Newhall, and David Ross Brower, *This Is the American Earth* (San Francisco: Sierra Club, 1960).
3. As Ware points out in her introduction to the catalogue:

   By the 1960s, Adams was firmly established as an influential cultural figure and was invited to meet with a succession of American presidents to discuss environmental issues. . . . Adams worked closely with Wilderness Society director William Turnage in the late 1970s to protect Alaskan wildlands and sent a print of his photograph *Mount McKinley and Wonder Lake, Denali National Park, Alaska* to President James Earl Carter. . . . In December 1980, just before he left the White House, Carter signed the largest land preservation act in history, protecting more than 104 million acres in Alaska. Also in that year President Carter awarded Ansel Adams the National Medal of Freedom, and after Adams died in 1984 a mountain and a wilderness area in the Sierra Nevada were named after him in tribute to his work for environmentalism. *Earth Now*, 20–22.
4. Its description, from the *Federal Register Notice*, June 10, 1986, can be found on the National Priorities List website: http://www.epa.gov/superfund/sites/npl/nar207.htm.
5. Ware explains: "After consulting the National Priorities List identified by

the Superfund program for cleanup administered by the Environmental Protection Agency, the artist decided to document the 120 sites in New York considered to be of immediate threat to human and animal populations. Expecting to see withered landscapes and workers in hazmat suits, Toedter instead found that these sites often appeared quite ordinary and were frequently in proximity to playgrounds and homes." *Earth Now*, 122.

6. Ware remarks that "the long views of sweeping valleys and towering mountains, for which he is renowned, seem to place us on the edge of wilderness looking in rather than inside it where the photographer himself traveled." Ibid., 22.
7. I am thinking of Susanne Antonetta's *Body Toxic: An Environmental Memoir* (Washington, DC: Counterpoint, 2001); Janisse Ray's *Ecology of a Cracker Childhood (The World as Home)* (Minneapolis: Milkweed, 1999); and Terry Tempest Williams's *Refuge: An Unnatural History of Family and Place* (New York: Vintage, 1992).
8. I have defined scripting as a literary practice appropriate to the literature of place in "Scripting the Wilderness," Ecocriticism Issue, *Journal of American Studies of Turkey* 30 (2009): 57–72. The term will be explained in chapter 1 and expanded on in subsequent chapters.
9. The genre of nature writing is moving in this direction, taking into account the postmodern interrogation of the split between nature and culture. For example, books by Lopez, Fiennes, and Wheeler centering on the Arctic weave together various kinds of textual references, descriptions of encounters with humans and animals, and observations of the various kinds of economic activities taking place in that fragile and threatened biotope. See Barry Lopez, *Arctic Dreams: Imagination and Desire in a Northern Landscape* (New York: Charles Scribner's Sons, 1986); William Fiennes, *The Snow Geese: A Story of Home* (New York: Random House, 2002); and Sara Wheeler, *The Magnetic North: Notes from the Arctic Circle* (New York: Farrar, Strauss and Giroux, 2011). These works illustrate the difficulty in making distinctions between travel writing, nature writing, and literature of place.
10. Rick Bass, *Winter: Notes from Montana* (New York: Houghton Mifflin, 1991). Subsequent references to the book will be inserted parenthetically within the text.
11. Charles Bowden, *Frog Mountain Blues* (Tucson: University of Arizona Press, 1994). Subsequent references to the book will be inserted parenthetically within the text.
12. Ellen Meloy, *The Last Cheater's Waltz: Beauty and Violence in the Desert Southwest*

(New York: Henry Holt, 1999). Subsequent references to the book will be inserted parenthetically within the text.

13. Jonathan Raban, *Bad Land: An American Romance* (New York: Vintage, 1997). Subsequent references to the book will be inserted parenthetically within the text.
14. Rebecca Solnit, *Savage Dreams: A Journey into the Landscape Wars of the American West* (New York: Vintage, 1995). Subsequent references to the book will be inserted parenthetically within the text and will refer to the 1995 edition.
15. Robert Sullivan, *The Meadowlands: Wilderness Adventures at the Edge of a City* (New York: Scribner, 1998). Subsequent references to the book will be inserted parenthetically within the text.

Chapter One

1. Henri Lefebvre, *The Production of Space*, trans. Donald Nicholson-Smith (Oxford: Blackwell, 1991).
2. Doreen Massey, *Space, Place, and Gender* (Cambridge: Polity Press, 1994), 265.
3. N. Scott Momaday, *The Man Made of Words: Essays, Stories, Passages* (New York: St. Martin's, 1997), 187.
4. Massey, *Space, Place*, 269.
5. "And with certain exceptions modern American writing has been overwhelmed by space. . . . One feels there's nothing but geography in this country, and certainly a geographical history is the only kind it can significantly have." William H. Gass, introduction to Gertrude Stein, *The Geographical History of America, or the Relation of Human Nature to the Human Mind* (New York: Vintage Books, 1973).
6. Edward S. Casey, "How to Get from Place to Space in a Fairly Short Stretch of Time: Phenomenological Prolegomena," in *Senses of Place*, ed. Steven Feld and Keith H. Basso (Santa Fe, NM : School of American Research Press, 1996), 24. He continues: "Minimally, places gather things in their midst—where 'things' connote various animate and inanimate entities. Places also gather experiences and histories, even languages and thoughts."
7. See Bruno Latour's penetrating elaboration of the distinction he makes between reproduction (the way all things subsist) and the chains of reference through which we gain access to them in chapter 3 of *An Inquiry into Modes of Existence: An Anthropology of the Moderns* (Cambridge, MA: Harvard University Press, 2013), 70–95.

8. Robert Pogue Harrison, *Forests: The Shadow of Civilization* (Chicago: University of Chicago Press, 1992), 200.
9. I hope readers will forgive the sweeping generalizations I make in order to sketch the broad outlines of my theory of the representation of place in America. Each work that I study demonstrates the particularity of the places on which it focuses. Taken together, these works illustrate the richness and complexity of America's geohistory. Nevertheless, I hope to demonstrate that there are lines of convergence connecting the representations of place just as there are routes connecting the various sites represented.
10. Obviously I am referring here to the hegemonic cultural tradition, not to writing identified as minor (in Deleuze and Guattari's sense), ethnic, or regional. The latter traditions consciously rewrite the hegemonic American myths. Cf. Gilles Deleuze and Félix Guattari, *Kafka: Toward a Minor Literature* (Minneapolis: University of Minnesota Press, 1986).
11. Such a conception is defended with particular force in the chapter entitled "Building Dwelling Thinking" in Martin Heidegger, *Poetry, Language, Thought*, trans. Albert Hofstadter (New York: Harper and Row, 1971). It is also the conception underlying the traditions of many indigenous oral cultures, according to David Abram, *The Spell of the Sensuous: Perception and Language in a More-Than-Human World* (New York: Pantheon, 1996), 137–179.
12. Barbara Allen, "Shaping and Being Shaped by the Land," in *The Big Empty: Essays on Western Landscape as Narrative*, ed. Leonard Engel (Albuquerque: University of New Mexico Press, 1994), 108.
13. See chapter 5, "Coming Out of the Country: Environmental Constructivism in Western Nature Writing," in Nathaniel Lewis, *Unsettling the Literary West: Authenticity and Authorship* (Lincoln: University of Nebraska Press, 2003), 145–185.
14. See Thomas J. Lyon, ed., *This Incomperable Lande: A Book of American Nature Writing* (Boston: Houghton Mifflin, 1989).
15. This pattern has been convincingly documented in Richard Slotkin's *Regeneration through Violence: The Mythology of the American Frontier, 1600–1860* (Norman: University of Oklahoma Press, 2000).
16. The important revisionary work of historians such as William Cronon, Patricia Limerick, and Donald Worster has certainly played a part in the changing depictions of the American territory.
17. See William Cronon, "The Trouble with Wilderness; or, Getting Back to the Wrong Nature," in *Uncommon Ground: Rethinking the Human Place in Nature*, ed. William Cronon (New York: W. W. Norton, 1995), 69–90.

18. Environmental literature is concerned with making a political point, according to Patrick D. Murphy, *Farther Afield in the Study of Nature-Oriented Literature* (Charlottesville: University of Virginia Press, 2000), 48. Murphy's study highlights the problem of finding terms to categorize writing about place.
19. Laurence Buell, *The Future of Environmental Criticism: Environmental Crisis and Literary Imagination* (Malden, MA: Blackwell, 2005), 63–71.
20. Doreen Massey uses the term "space-time" in *For Space* (London: Sage, 2005), 80. Lefebvre calls attention to the interwoven mesh of tracks made by people and animals leading into and out of villages and towns. *Production of Space*, 117–118. Tim Ingold extends this observation to describe how people and things gather together into "a relational field" that he terms a "meshwork" in "The Wedge and the Knot: Hammering and Stitching the Face of Nature," in *Nature, Space, and the Sacred: Transdisciplinary Perspectives*, ed. Sigurd Bergmann et al. (Farnham, UK: Ashgate, 2009), 149. Such terms help distinguish between earlier conceptions of space and place and the new paradigms offered in contemporary theories. Still, in trying to reconceptualize our insertion in space-time, we constantly wrestle with the words available to us. Annie Merrill Ingram debates the relative merits of the prefixes "eco-" and "enviro-" and acknowledges that they are both "like language itself, anthropocentric" and culturally inflected, in her preface to Nanette Norris, ed., *Words for a Small Planet: Ecocritical Views* (Lanham, MD: Lexington, 2013), x.
21. Buell, *Future of Environmental Criticism*, 70.
22. This is what Patricia N. Limerick is doing in connection with the history of the West in her reading of ghost towns: "The West, these places tell us, is not the region where the pioneers escaped history. . . . It is instead the region where we can most profitably study the interplay of ambition and outcome, the collision between simple expectation and complex reality, the fallout from optimistic effort to master both nature and human nature." "Haunted by Rhyolite: Learning from the Landscape of Failure," in *The Big Empty: Essays on Western Landscapes as Narrative*, ed. Leonard Engel (Albuquerque: University of New Mexico Press, 1994), 38.
23. Massey, *Space, Place*, 268.
24. Edward W. Soja concentrates on Los Angeles in *Thirdspace: Journeys to Los Angeles and Other Real-and-Imagined Places* (Oxford: Blackwell, 1996); David Harvey studies Paris in *Paris: Capital of Modernity* (London: Routledge, 2003); Doreen Massey frequently refers to London in her works.
25. It is interesting to observe how an adjective can in the discourse of ideology be "enriched" in order to acquire the status of a notion through nominal-

ization: "wild" and "wilderness." I will use the nominal form of empty, as in "the empty" and also "the sign of empty."

26. The empty spaces I will treat in this study are somewhat different from the blank spots on people's mental maps that Peter Gould and Rodney White discuss in *Mental Maps* (Harmondsworth, UK: Penguin, 1974), 31–81.The two geographers are interested in the way individuals experience the places in which they live. Although there may be some overlap insofar as people share cultural projections, my own focus is on broader tendencies affecting national policies and mentalities.

27. The text entitled "Des Espaces Autres," published by the French journal *Architecture, Mouvement, Continuité* in October 1984, was the basis of a lecture given by Michel Foucault in March 1967. It can be found online in English and French. http://foucault.info/documents/heteroTopia/foucault.heteroTopia.en.html.

28. Kent C. Ryden, *Mapping the Invisible Landscape: Folklore, Writing, and the Sense of Place* (Iowa City: University of Iowa Press, 1993), 41.

29. Patricia L. Price conducts a study of the U.S.-Mexico borderlands along similar lines but with an emphasis on landscapes that contrasts with the present study's concentration on literary texts. *Dry Place: Landscapes of Belonging and Exclusion* (Minneapolis: University of Minnesota Press, 2004).

30. Doreen Massey's work has been especially helpful to this study, but David Harvey and Edward Soja have also provided important insights.

31. For Australia, see Roslynn Haynes, *Seeking the Centre: The Australian Desert in Literature, Art and Film* (Cambridge, MA: Cambridge University Press, 1998). For Canada, see Robert Kroetsch, *The Lovely Treachery of Words: Essays Selected and New* (Toronto: Oxford University Press, 1989). J. M. Coetzee mentions that the official version of South African history described the interior of the territory as "unpeopled." *White Writing: On the Culture of Letters in South Africa* (New Haven, CT: Yale University Press, 1988), 177. In a discussion of pictorial representations of landscape that offers American, Canadian, and Australian examples, Jonathan Bordo argues that "*the* wilderness prolongs the European imaginary into a 'new world' displacement that severs the land from its occupants." "Picture and Witness at the Site of the Wilderness," in *Landscape and Power*, 2nd ed., ed. W. J. T. Mitchell (Chicago: University of Chicago Press, 2002), 309; italics in the original.

32. A parallel with slavery could be made to illustrate the workings of cultural denial; in the same way that depriving a man of his manhood autho-

rizes subjection, depriving the land of its human definition authorizes appropriation.

33. See David Chidester and Edward T. Linenthal, eds., *American Sacred Space* (Bloomington: Indiana University Press, 1995).

34. See Robert W. Righter, *The Battle over Hetch Hetchy: America's Most Controversial Dam and the Birth of Modern Environmentalism* (New York: Oxford University Press, 2005).

35. For attitudes to the prairies see John Madson, *Where the Sky Began: Land of the Tallgrass Prairie* (Boston: Houghton Mifflin, 1982); Richard Manning, *Grassland: The History, Biology, Politics, and Promise of the American Prairie* (New York: Viking, 1995).

36. Solnit's *Savage Dreams* illustrates how this dual strategy was enacted in Yosemite and the Nevada desert.

37. In a talk discussing the cultural conceptions that foster climate change, David Abram contrasts indigenous people's conception of the air as animated and sacred to the moderns' conception of air as empty space. He argues that in imagining the atmosphere as a void, we find it "a perfect place to throw whatever we hope to avoid, the perfect dump site for the unwanted by-products of our industries." David Abram, "Climate and Psyche," lecture at the Psychology of Climate Seminar, BI Norwegian Business School, Oslo, September 28, 2012, YouTube video, October 3, 2012, http://www.youtube.com/watch?v=TzZ4103VU7M.

38. Here I distinguish the term "inscriptions" (signs serving the strategies of domination) from "traces" (evidence of the resistance of alternative agencies, which in the present context includes the land itself).

39. For example, in *Bad Land*, Jonathan Raban discovers the traces left on the prairie by abandoned farm buildings.

40. This is the case with Robert Sullivan reconstructing the saga of Manhattan's transformations from the demolition rubble sunk in the Meadowlands.

41. James Clifford, "Partial Truths," introduction to *Writing Culture: The Poetics and Politics of Ethnography*, ed. James Clifford and George Marcus (Berkeley: University of California Press, 1986), 22.

42. Ellen Meloy comically demonstrates the limits of her archaeological search when she reveals that the mysterious and threatening yellow rock she has been carrying around on her quest is actually a piece of asphalt from the highway (190–194). With characteristic irony and self-mockery, Charles Bowden relates in the "Heart of Gold" chapter how he follows the gold miners' traces in the Catalinas (13–42).

43. Soja, *Thirdspace*, 34.

44. Bordo, "Picture and Witness," 307.

45. Emmanuel Levinas, *Totality and Infinity: An Essay on Exteriority* (The Hague: M. Nijhoff, 1979).

46. Massey, *For Space*, 180.

47. Patrick D. Murphy, *Ecocritical Explorations in Literary and Cultural Studies: Fences, Boundaries, and Fields* (Lanham, MD: Lexington, 2009), 35.

48. J. Nicholas Entrikin, *The Betweenness of Place: Towards a Geography of Modernity* (Baltimore: Johns Hopkins University Press, 1991).

49. Val Plumwood discusses this split in chapter 4 of *Feminism and the Mastery of Nature* (London: Routledge, 1993), 104–119.

50. Patricia Nelson Limerick, *Something in the Soil: Legacies and Reckonings in the New West* (New York: W. W. Norton, 2000), 213.

51. Bruno Latour, *We Have Never Been Modern* (Cambridge, MA: Harvard University Press, 1993).

52. Harvey, Lefebvre, Massey, and Soja have already been cited.

53. Readers might bear in mind how Karen Barad extends Foucault's insights in her theory of agential realism. She writes: "Discursive practices produce, rather than merely describe, the 'subjects' and 'objects' of knowledge practice." "Posthumanist Performativity: Toward an Understanding of How Matter Comes to Matter," *Signs* 28, no. 3 (2003): 819. She concludes: "The intra-actions of the material and the discursive are the technologies of embodied objectivity—and socially constructed knowledges have real material consequences." "Meeting the Universe Halfway: Realism and Social Constructivism without Contradictions," in *Feminism, Science, and the Philosophy of Science*, ed. Lynn Hankinson Nelson and Jack Nelson, vol. 256 (Boston: Kluwer Academic Publishers, 1996), 188.

54. Paul Klee, *Notebooks, Volume 2: The Nature of Nature*, ed. Jürg Spiller, trans. Heinz Norden (London: Lund Humphries, 1973), 269.

55. I understand "complexity" as Edgar Morin's "*complexité*" that describes a form of apprehension of the real distinct from traditional logic: "Dans la vision complexe, quand on arrive par des voies empirico-rationnelles à des contradictions, cela signifie non pas une erreur mais l'atteinte d'une nappe profonde de la réalité qui, justement parce qu'elle est profonde, ne peut être traduite dans notre logique" (*Introduction à la pensée complexe* [Paris: ESF, 1990], 92; "In complex vision, when one arrives at contradictions by empirico-rational routes, that does not signify error, but the arrival at a deeper

layer of the reality which, precisely because it is deep, cannot be translated into our logic" [my translation]).

56. Mark Tredinnick, *The Land's Wild Music: Encounters with Barry Lopez, Peter Matthiessen, Terry Tempest Williams, and James Galvin* (San Antonio, TX: Trinity University Press, 2005), 89.

57. In his discussion of the ways in which environmental writing can deepen one's sense of place, Lawrence Buell makes the compelling claim that "environmental texts . . . practice restorationism by calling places into being, that is, not just by naming objects but by dramatizing in the process how they matter." I share this perception of the text's performativity; however, his discussion continues with a note of regret—with what he terms "niggling objections"—that I do not share: "Inevitably certain reductions occur: no one can realize (in the full sense) anywhere near the totality of what can be realized about the environment; to set anything down in an essay or a book, one must be rigorously selective." *The Environmental Imagination: Thoreau, Nature Writing, and the Formation of American Culture* (Cambridge, MA: Belknap Press, 1995), 267–268. My discussion of the technique of scripting argues that the effectiveness of evocations of place depends on both their complexity and their incompleteness.

58. The notion of "mental geographies" was suggested by Alison Deming's perceptions of her writings as "geographic and mental habitats located on the borders of change." Alison Hawthorne Deming, *The Edges of the Civilized World: A Journey in Nature and Culture* (New York: Picador, 1998), 10.

59. William James, *The Principles of Psychology*, vol. 1 (New York: Henry Holt, 1890), 243.

60. Massey, *For Space*, 80 (Massey's emphasis).

61. See chapter 3, "Disruptions as Openings," in Wendy Harding and Jacky Martin, *Beyond Words: The Othering Excursion in Contemporary American Literature* (Newcastle upon Tyne, UK: Cambridge Scholars, 2007), 41–63.

62. Derek Gregory, *Geographical Imaginations* (London, Blackwell, 1994), 34.

63. Price, *Dry Place*, 4.

64. Thus I cannot agree completely with Carolyn Merchant's assertion that "the history of spatial changes is a history of power changes." *Ecological Revolutions: Nature, Gender, and Science in New England* (Chapel Hill: University of North Carolina Press, 1989), 50. I would have to qualify it by insisting that changes in power sometimes change the idea of space more than space itself. I hold with Michel de Certeau that place is palimpsestic: "Le lieu, c'est le palimp-

seste. L'analyse savante n'en connait que le texte dernier; encore n'est-il pour elle que l'effet de ses décisions épistémologiques, de ses critères et de ses objectifs" (Michel de Certeau, Luce Giard, and Pierre Mayol, *L'invention du quotidien* [Paris: Union Générale d'Éditions, 1980], 295; "Place is a palimpsest. Scholarly analysis knows only the latest text; furthermore, it produces only the effect of its epistemological choices, of its criteria and its objectives" [my translation]).

65. Massey, *For Space*, 159.

Chapter Two

1. Wayne Franklin discusses this crisis in language in the introduction to his book *Discoverers, Explorers, Settlers: The Diligent Writers of Early America* (Chicago: University of Chicago Press, 1979).
2. Joseph Conrad, *Heart of Darkness* (New York: Garden City, 1916), 5.
3. As the "discoverers" of territories that were new to Europeans, the different colonizing nations laid claim to the lands of indigenous peoples. See Robert J. Miller's discussion of how this "Doctrine of Discovery" was implemented on the North American continent in *Native America, Discovered and Conquered: Thomas Jefferson, Lewis and Clark, and Manifest Destiny* (Westport, CT: Praeger, 2006).
4. While this chapter deals with the evolution of a particular mode of representing the U.S. territory, I subscribe to the view of William Cronon, George Miles, and Jay Gitlin that "we can best know the history of the American West if we read it as a chapter of the much larger history of colonialism." "Becoming West: Toward a New Meaning for Western History," in *Under an Open Sky: Rethinking America's Western Past*, ed. William Cronon, George Miles, and Jay Gitlin (New York: W. W. Norton, 1992), 9. It is curious that the history of the United States is so rarely referred to as a story of colonization. The "larger history of colonialism" would have to include the whole American continent.
5. Perry Miller gives a highly nuanced account of the Puritans' struggles to build cohesive communities in *Errand into the Wilderness* (Cambridge, MA: Belknap Press, 1956). I hope I will be excused for the broad strokes with which I sketch out the different forms that their projections of emptiness and fullness take.
6. John Smith, *A Description of New England (1616)*, online electronic text ed., ed. Paul Royster, Electronic Texts in American Studies, Paper 4, DigitalCom-

mons at the University of Nebraska–Lincoln, http://digitalcommons.unl.edu/etas/4.

7. Ibid.
8. Ibid.
9. Thus, in 1653, Edward Johnson claimed that New England had, "through the mercy of Christ become a second England for fertilness in so short a space that it is indeed the wonder of the world." *Johnson's Wonder-Working Providence, 1628–1651*, ed. John Franklin Jameson (New York: Barnes and Noble, 1959), 210.
10. For a sampling of additional descriptions of America's plenty, see Brooks Atkinson, *This Bright Land: A Personal View* (Garden City, NY: Natural History Press, 1972), 2–7; and Daniel G. Payne, *Voices in the Wilderness: American Nature Writing and Environmental Politics* (Hanover, NH: University Press of New England, 1996) 9–11. Wayne Franklin notes that the lists or catalogues in the early accounts of discovery also had a religious dimension: "Through the very detail of its enumeration it expresses an idea of the American God as the ultimate good provider, as a providential deity in the root sense of the term." *Discoverers, Explorers, Settlers*, 23.
11. William Bradford, *Bradford's History of Plymouth Plantation, 1606–1646*, ed. William T. Davis (New York: Charles Scribner's Sons, 1908), Early Americas Digital Archive, http://mith.umd.edu//eada/html/display.php?docs=bradford_history.xml.
12. Smith, *Description of New England*, 24.
13. Roderick Nash studies the shifting values associated with this icon in *Wilderness and the American Mind* (New Haven, CT: Yale University Press, 1967).
14. In Dwight B. Heath, ed., *Mourt's Relation: A Journal of the Pilgrims at Plymouth* (London: n.p., 1622; Bedford, MA: Applewood Books, 1963), 88–96. Quotations from this text refer to the Applewood edition.
15. In his introduction, Heath attributes the text to Robert Cushman, one of the organizers of the separatists' emigration. Ibid., xi.
16. Ibid., 93.
17. Ibid., 91–92.
18. This argument appears in a number of seventeenth-century texts. Compare John Cotton's words from *God's Promise to His Plantations* (London: William Jones, 1634), 4–5: "In a vacant Soyle, he that taketh possession of it, and bestoweth culture and husbandry upon it, his Right it is. And the ground of this is, from the Grand Charter given to Adam and his Posterity in Paradise, Gen. 1. 28. Multiply, and replenish the earth, and subdue it."

19. See the discussion in Barbara Arneil, "The Wild Indian's Venison: Locke's Theory of Property and English Colonialism in America," *Political Studies* 44 (1996): 60–74.

20. William Cronon discusses this question in the chapter "Bounding the Land" in *Changes in the Land: Indians, Colonists, and the Ecology of New England* (New York: Hill and Wang, 1983), 54–81.

21. Thomas Jefferson, "Notes on the State of Virginia," Query XIX, in *Writings*, ed. Merrill D. Peterson (New York: Library of America, 1984), 290. The notion of land being "locked up" recurs in different forms in the discourse governing land management in the United States.

22. J. Hector St. John de Crevecoeur, *Letters from an American Farmer* (New York: E. P. Dutton, 1957), 75.

23. Ibid., 51.

24. Ibid., 75.

25. Indeed, this reflects changes in the disposition of property in the former British colonies in America. See the discussion of the Northwest Ordinances in Margaret Walsh, *The American West: Visions and Revisions* (New York: Cambridge University Press, 2005), 24–27.

26. The image of the American territory as female is richly documented by Annette Kolodny in *The Lay of the Land: Metaphor as Experience and History in American Life and Letters* (Chapel Hill: University of North Carolina Press, 1975).

27. Thomas Jefferson to James Madison, December 20, 1787.

28. de Crevecoeur, *Letters*, 53.

29. Alexis de Tocqueville, *Democracy in America*, vol. 1, trans. Henry Reeve (New York: Longmans, Green, 1889), 295.

30. Ibid.

31. In fact, Tocqueville echoes a widespread conviction, increasingly bolstered by the burgeoning scientific investigations of extinct species, that the Indians were doomed to die out. His elaboration of this topos of the vanishing Indian contradicts his claim that the continent was initially empty, for he admits that "vast tracts of country . . . were formerly inhabited by powerful Indian nations which are now extinct; I have myself passed some time in the midst of mutilated tribes, which witness the daily decline of their numerical strength and of the glory of their independence; and I have heard these Indians themselves anticipate the impending doom of their race." Ibid., 233.

32. Ibid., 295.

33. For a seminal study of the way in which American writers respond to the idea that their national identity springs from nature, see Perry Miller's *Nature's Nation* (Cambridge, MA: Belknap Press, 1967).
34. Much of Limerick's writing is devoted to critiquing the popular caricature of western history found in dime novels and movies and given an influential degree of scholarly credibility in Frederick Jackson Turner's "frontier thesis." See, for example, her groundbreaking book *The Legacy of Conquest: The Unbroken Past of the American West* (New York: W. W. Norton, 1987). Richard White portrays the contact zone between cultures as a space of exchange and accommodation in *The Middle Ground: Indians, Empires, and Republics in the Great Lakes Region, 1650–1815* (Cambridge: Cambridge University Press, 1991). See also Patricia Nelson Limerick, Clyde A. Milner, and Charles E. Rankin, eds., *Trails: Toward a New Western History* (Lawrence: University Press of Kansas, 1991).
35. de Crevecoeur, *Letters*, 53.
36. For a succinct discussion of some of the questions facing the new republic as a result of the Louisiana Purchase, see D. W. Meinig, *The Shaping of America: A Geographical Perspective on 500 Years of History*, vol. 2, *Continental America, 1800–1867* (New Haven, CT: Yale University Press, 1993), 4–23.
37. Quoted by Jon Kukla in *A Wilderness So Immense: The Louisiana Purchase and the Destiny of America* (New York: A. A. Knopf, 2003), 325.
38. Fisher Ames to Thomas Dwight, October 31, 1803, in *Works of Fisher Ames*, ed. John Thornton Kirkland (Boston: T. B. Wait, 1809), 484.
39. Letter to Christopher Gore, October 3, 1803. Quoted by Kukla, *Wilderness So Immense*, 293.
40. The quotes are taken from the House debate, recorded in the *Annals of Congress*, House of Representatives, 8th Congress, 1st Session, October 1803, pp. 458, 466, 468, 476. http://www.archive.org/details/annalsofcongress10unit. Among politicians, the arguments in favor concerned mainly the utility of the port of New Orleans, but at least one congressman, Samuel Latham Mitchill, looked forward to future expansion, employing a metaphor that naturalizes as it represents: "Must the hive always maintain its present numbers, and no swarm ever go forth?" (480).
41. In a letter to General Horatio Gates, dated July 11, 1803, Jefferson wrote: "If our legislature dispose of it with the wisdom we have a right to expect, they may make it the means of tempting all our Indians on the east side of the Mississippi to remove to the West, and of condensing instead of scattering our population."

42. John O'Sullivan, "Annexation," *The United States Magazine and Democratic Review* 17 (July 1845): 5–10. http://www.historytools.org/sources/manifest_destiny.pdf.
43. Ralph Waldo Emerson, *Nature* (Boston: James Monroe, 1849), 7–8.
44. Henry David Thoreau, "Walking," in *Excursions* (New York: Thomas Crowell, 1913), 154.
45. Henry David Thoreau, *The Journal of Henry David Thoreau*, ed. Bradford Torrey and Francis H. Allen (Salt Lake City: Gibbs M. Smith, 1984), 9:44.
46. This anticipates the celebration of the chaotic vitality of disinherited areas in the new literature of place, as will be seen later in the discussion of Sullivan's *Meadowlands*.
47. Thoreau, *Excursions*, 169.
48. Henry David Thoreau, *The Maine Woods* (Boston: Houghton Mifflin, 1890), 64.
49. Ibid.
50. Ibid., 70.
51. Ibid., 71.
52. Ibid., 64.
53. Ibid., 71.
54. The quote appears on the title page of Henry David Thoreau's *Walden; Or, Life in the Woods* (Boston: Ticknor and Fields, 1854).
55. Walt Whitman, *Leaves of Grass* (Boston: Thayer and Eldridge, 1860), 104.
56. Frederick Jackson Turner, "The Significance of the Frontier in American History" (paper presented at the Meeting of the American Historical Association World Columbian Exposition, Chicago, IL, July 12, 1893).
57. Robert Archey Woods, *The City Wilderness: A Settlement Study* (Boston: Houghton Mifflin, 1899).
58. Ibid., 2.
59. "Wherever pushed to logical conclusion, it makes one millionaire and a million paupers. There is no complete happiness under its blight." Thomas Seton, *The Gospel of the Red Man*, commemorative ed. (Bloomington, IN: World Wisdom, 2005), 127.
60. He finds them "almost without exception treacherous, murderous, worthless, without a shadow of a claim on our respect." Ibid., 112–113.
61. Seton's Woodcraft Indians organization was a model for the Boy Scout movement.
62. Seton, *Gospel of the Red Man*, 113.

63. This turn is already anticipated in the works of James Fenimore Cooper, for example in *The Prairie*, where Natty Bumpo deplores the destruction of the eastern forests.

64. Aldo Leopold, *A Sand County Almanac, with Essays on Conservation from Round River* (New York: Ballantine Books, 1966), 150.

65. Ibid., 156.

66. Ibid., 150.

67. Ibid., 157–158.

68. Jennifer K. Ladino, *Reclaiming Nostalgia: Longing for Nature in American Literature* (Charlottesville: University of Virginia Press, 2012), 97.

69. "Eco-memory" is a term coined by Robin L. Murray and Joseph K. Heumman and cited in Ladino, *Reclaiming Nostalgia*, 228.

70. Angela Miller sums up the situation: "Wilderness was achieved through a willed act of historical erasure. Setting aside public lands protected from development, the creation of the national parks was also premised on the exclusion of any human presence." "The Fate of Wilderness in American Landscape Art: The Dilemmas of 'Nature's Nation,'" in *American Wilderness: A New History*, ed. Michael Lewis (Oxford: Oxford University Press, 2007), 108. See also Benjamin Johnson's essay, "Wilderness Parks and Their Discontents," in the same volume; Mark David Spence, *Dispossessing the Wilderness: Indian Removal and the Making of the National Parks* (New York: Oxford University Press, 1999); Robert H. Keller and Michael F. Turek, *American Indians and National Parks* (Tucson: University of Arizona Press, 1998).

71. These aims are clearly articulated in Frederick Law Olmsted's 1865 report to the Board of Commissioners appointed to oversee the management of Yosemite Valley. Frederick Law Olmsted, "The Yosemite Valley and the Mariposa Big Tree Grove," 1865; reprinted in Lary M. Dilsaver, ed., *America's National Park System: The Critical Documents* (Lanham, MD: Rowman and Littlefield, 1994), http://www.nps.gov/history/history/online_books/anps/anps_1b.htm.

72. John Muir, "The Hetch Hetchy Valley," *Boston Weekly Transcript*, March 25, 1873, Sierra Club, John Muir Exhibit, http://www.sierraclub.org/john_muir_exhibit/writings/muir_hh_boston_25mar1873.aspx.

73. Wallace Stegner, "Wilderness Letter" (letter to David E. Pesonen, December 3, 1960), The Wilderness Society, http://wilderness.org/bios/former-council-members/wallace-stegner.

74. Wilderness Act of September 3, 1964. Public Law 88–77. 88th Congress, S.4., Wilderness.net, http://www.wilderness.net/NWPS/legisact.
75. Quoted in Doug Scott, *The Enduring Wilderness: Protecting Our Natural Heritage through the Wilderness Act* (Golden, CO: Fulcrum, 2004), 7.
76. Quoted in Scott, *Enduring Wilderness*, 23.
77. In "The Trouble with Wilderness," William Cronon argues that one of the consequences of the ideal of wilderness is the tendency to pay less attention to environmental destruction in inhabited areas:

    To the extent that we live in an urban-industrial civilization but at the same time pretend to ourselves that our real home is in the wilderness, to just that extent we give ourselves permission to evade responsibility for the lives we actually lead. . . . By imagining that our true home is in the wilderness, we forgive ourselves the homes we actually inhabit. In its flight from history, in its siren song of escape, in its reproduction of the dangerous dualism that sets human beings outside of nature—in all of these ways, wilderness poses a serious threat to responsible environmentalism at the end of the twentieth century." Cronon, *Uncommon Ground*, 81
78. Soren C. Larsen and Timothy J. Brock, "Great Basin Imagery in Newspaper Coverage of Yucca Mountain," *The Geographical Review* 95, no. 4 (October 2005): 528. By contrast, Larsen and Brock point to Goin and Starrs's findings that residents, especially the Paiute and Shoshone Indians, and sometimes visitors, find aesthetic and spiritual value in the place (519). See Peter Goin and Paul F. Starrs, *Black Rock* (Reno, University of Nevada Press, 2005).
79. For a comparison between European and American land artists, see Mel Gooding and William Furlong, *Artists, Land, Nature* (New York: Harry N. Abrams, 2002).
80. As suggested by the title of his book, *The Void, the Grid and the Sign: Traversing the Great Basin* (Salt Lake City: University of Utah Press, 2000), Fox habitually represents the playas as empty, inscribable spaces; for example, he describes "the smooth off-white surface rolling up to meet us as if it were a sheet of paper in a typewriter" (76). This is a nice image of the desert's availability for art, and also of Fox's own ekphrastic intentions in the book.
81. Ibid., 52.
82. Ibid., 16.
83. Fox describes a conversation with an archaeologist who criticized Heizer's *City* as "a travesty upon the land because it did not serve as a dwelling place." Ibid., 27. "For her, because *City* was not inhabitable it had no utility to soci-

ety, and was thus merely an egotistical desecration of the environment. . . . To the archeologist, *City* was simply the will of one person imposed on the land for his own pleasure" (28).

84. Ibid., 147.

Chapter Three

1. John Muir, *My First Summer in the Sierra* (Boston: Houghton Mifflin, 1911).
2. Ibid., 183.
3. This quotation appears on the cover of the Mariner paperback edition.
4. Bass's subsequent books on the Yaak—for example, *The Book of Yaak* (New York: Houghton Mifflin, 1996) and *Brown Dog of the Yaak: Essays on Art and Activism* (Minneapolis: Milkweed, 1999)—focus more intensely on the way humans have modified its environment. They also take into account the economic dependence of the community on the region's natural resources, offering suggestions for sustainable development.
5. Richard White, "'Are You an Environmentalist or Do You Work for a Living?': Work and Nature," in Cronon, *Uncommon Ground*, 185.
6. Thoreau, *Walden*, 170.
7. Adorno once remarked that "someone who looks upon thingness as radical evil, who wants to dynamize all that exists into pure actuality, tends to be hostile to otherness, to the alien—which has lent its name to alienation, and not for nothing" (Theodor W. Adorno, Negative Dialektik [1966], [Frankfurt: Suhrkamp, 1975], 191; Wem das Dinghafte als radikal Böses gilt; wer alles, was ist, zur reinen Aktualität dynamisieren möchte, tendiert zur Feindschaft gegen das Andere, Fremde, dessen Name nicht umsonst in Entfremdung anklingt). The English is Sven Lütticken's adaptation of the English translation by E. B. Ashton, *Negative Dialectics* (London: Routledge and Kegan Paul, 1990), 191, and is quoted in Lütticken's essay "Art and Thingness, Part Two: Thingification," *e-flux* 15 (2010), note 2, http://www.e-flux.com/journal/art-and-thingness-part-two-thingification/.
8. According to Burke:

   The passion caused by the great and sublime in nature, when those causes operate most powerfully, is astonishment; and astonishment is that state of the soul, in which all its motions are suspended, with some degree of horror. In this case the mind is so entirely filled with its object, that it cannot entertain any other, nor by consequence reason on that object which employs it. Hence arises the great power of the sublime, that, far from being produced by them, it anticipates our reasonings, and hurries us on by an irresistible force. Astonishment, as I have said, is the effect of the sublime in its highest degree; the inferior effects are admiration, reverence, and respect. Edmund Burke, "On the Sublime and Beautiful," in *The Works of the Right Honorable Edmund Burke*, 3rd ed., vol. 1 (Boston: Little, Brown, 1869), 130.

9. For a brief summary see Barbara Novak's discussion of the late-eighteenth-century ideas of the sublime and their transformation in the American context in *Nature and Culture: American Landscape and Painting, 1825–1875* (New York: Oxford University Press, 1980), 34–44.
10. "But let it be considered, that hardly anything can strike the mind with its greatness, which does not make some sort of approach towards infinity; which nothing can do whilst we are able to perceive its bounds; but to see an object distinctly, and to perceive its bounds, is one and the same thing. A clear idea is therefore another name for a little idea." Burke, *Works of the Right Honorable*, 136–137.
11. For a discussion of the way nature writers develop their own subjectivity through their perceptions of the natural world, see Scott Slovic, *Seeking Awareness in American Nature Writing: Henry Thoreau, Annie Dillard, Edward Abbey, Wendell Berry, Barry Lopez* (Salt Lake City: University of Utah Press, 1992). Thomas Bailey discusses some of the ways in which Bass is both inside and outside that tradition in "Rick Bass's *Winter*: Self Discovery in a Cold Place," in *The Literary Art and Activism of Rick Bass*, ed. O. Alan Weltzien (Salt Lake City: University of Utah Press, 2001), 91–101.
12. This immersion in the natural world contrasts with the more detached role that Thoreau assigns himself as "self-appointed inspector of snow-storms and rain-storms." *Walden*, 19.
13. Umberto Eco, *The Role of the Reader: Explorations in the Semiotics of Texts* (Bloomington: Indiana University Press, 1984).

Chapter Four

1. For example, the narrator's mention of the legend of Nueva Mia Ciudad prepares for the indented 1880 account that he subsequently explains he has found "reprinted in a yellow booklet published by a modern-day seeker of treasure" (18).
2. Bowden makes a number of references to Leopold's writings. Michel Serres develops his suggestions for an ethical relationship with the environment

in *The Natural Contract* (Ann Arbor: University of Michigan Press, 1995). Bruno Latour takes up the question of ethics at the end of *An Inquiry into Modes of Existence*, extending it to "quasi objects and quasi subjects together" (456). He urges a new conception of morality in which "every existent" would take into account "the multitude of those, *the others*, that have allowed it to exist and about which it is never very sure that they are not its finality. And it is obviously not a question of human beings alone" (455).

3. Bowden's book could easily serve as an example to expand Leo Marx's thesis in *The Machine in the Garden: Technology and the Pastoral Ideal in America* (New York: Oxford University Press, 1964).
4. See David Wallace Adams, *Education for Extinction: American Indians and the Boarding School Experience, 1875–1928* (Lawrence: University Press of Kansas, 1995).
5. Richard Slotkin claims that "the myth of regeneration through violence became the structuring metaphor of the American experience." *Regeneration through Violence*, 5. Slotkin studies the figure of William Cody extensively in *Gunfighter Nation: The Myth of the Frontier in Twentieth-Century America* (New York: Atheneum, 1992).
6. Jane Bennett, *Vibrant Matter: A Political Ecology of Things* (Durham, NC: Duke University Press, 2010).
7. Bruno Latour has convincingly demonstrated the creative force of the fictional division between culture and nature in *We Have Never Been Modern*.

Chapter Five

1. I am struck by the similarity between Meloy's metaphor and Tim Ingold's description of the gatherings of people and things into a "meshwork." *Nature, Space, and the Sacred*, 149. See also Tim Ingold, *Lines: A Brief History* (London: Routledge, 2007).
2. Following Australian ecocritic Kate Rigby's lead, Tom Lynch explores the ways in which American nature writers go beyond the limitations of "the exploring eye" to engage more fully with what Merleau-Ponty calls "the flesh of the world." This erotic, somatic engagement seems centered largely on enhancing the individual's experience, becoming a more complete form of self-expansion. Nevertheless, as Lynch argues, it clearly fosters deeper attachments to and understandings of specific biotopes. See Tom Lynch, *Xerophilia: Ecocritical Explorations in Southwestern Literature* (Lubbock, TX: Texas Tech University Press, 2008), 177–226.
3. Dianne Chisholm reverses the proposition, seeing the desert dwellers as

cheats. For her, the book "bewails the desert's betrayal by those who claim to husband it, including not only the U.S. industrial-military complex that executes large-scale violence but also small landholders like herself who perpetrate small-scale assaults on fragile desert ecology." "Ellen Meloy's Deep Nomadology (How to Map the Heartland of a Nuclear-Age Desert)," *Rhizomes: Cultural Studies in Emerging Knowledge* 13 (Fall 2006), http://rhizomes.net/issue13/chisholm/chisholm.html.

4. Emmanuel Levinas, *Alterity and Transcendence* (New York: Columbia University Press, 1999).
5. Daniel T. Spencer, "Restoring Earth, Restored to Earth: Toward an Ethic for Reinhabiting Place," in *Ecospirit: Religions and Philosophies for the Earth*, ed. Laurel Kearns and Catherine Keller (New York: Fordham University Press, 2007), 431; italics in the original.
6. Chisholm argues that "Meloy prompts us to profoundly rethink the concept of 'desertification' . . . ; she regards deserts to be alive, if extreme, ecosystems: resilient and fragile, vulnerable yet hardy." "Ellen Meloy's Deep Nomadology."
7. See Latour's chapter 3, "Revolution," in *We Have Never Been Modern*.
8. Meloy alludes here to Mary Oliver's poem "Wild Geese," which can be found in Mary Oliver, *Dream Work* (New York: Atlantic Monthly Press, 1986), 14.
9. Bruno Latour elaborates the concept of the parliament of things in *We Have Never Been Modern* (142–145). In this assembly, the hybrid constituents of existence would be given a voice: "They are all talking about the same thing, about a quasi-object they have all created, the object-discourse-nature-society whose new properties astound us all and whose network extends from my refrigerator to the Antarctic by way of chemistry, law, the State, the economy, and satellites. The imbroglios and networks that had no place now have the whole place to themselves" (144).
10. In this sense, the books discussed in Part III are more like parliamentary forums than personal claims to a relationship with place.

Chapter Six

1. Jonathan Raban was given a copy of the manuscript by one of Percy Wollaston's sons. He then wrote the foreword to the edited version of the memoir. Percy Wollaston, *Homesteading: A Montana Family Album* (New York: Penguin, 1997).
2. Indeed, Raban could be criticized for failing to give attention to the vio-

lence of the policies of genocide and removal practiced against the Indians. These policies led directly to the Homestead Act and the influx of immigrants to eastern Montana. Although the scope of his book is wide, it is by no means as far reaching as that of Solnit's *Savage Dreams*.

3. John Wesley Powell was one of the first to insist that either much larger tracts of land should be distributed or modes of farming different from the homestead model should be adopted in the dry lands of the American West, although his warnings were ignored; see Richard Manning, *Grassland*, 102–109. For a discussion of some of the problems resulting from the policies and practices adopted see Manning, 157–168.
4. See the discussions of landscape in Augustin Berque, *MÉDIANCE: De milieux en paysages* (Montpellier, France: Reclus, 1990); Anne Cauquelin, *L'invention du paysage* (Paris: PUF, 2000); Alain Corbin, *L'homme dans le paysage* (Paris: Editions Textuel, 2001).
5. Deborah Epstein Popper and Frank J. Popper, "The Great Plains: From Dust to Dust," *Planning* 53 (December 1987): 12–18, http://www.csupomona.edu/~tgyoung/rs510/Grt_Plains.pdf.

Chapter Seven

1. In the years since the publication of the book, this has apparently changed somewhat. The park's website announces an oral history project designed to take into account the knowledge of "individuals from park-associated American Indian tribes, including members of both federally recognized and unrecognized tribes . . . [concerning] genealogy, oral or folk history, place names and associated stories, legends, plant and animal recourses [*sic*], religious practices, and other past or present uses of the park." "Oral History," National Park Service, Yosemite website, updated August 10, 2009, http://www.nps.gov/yose/historyculture/oral-history.htm.
2. The book's original subtitle was *A Journey into the Hidden Wars of the American West*.
3. Solnit gives relatively few details concerning the park's creation and management as a public institution. For a much fuller treatment, see Alfred Runte, *Yosemite: The Embattled Wilderness* (Lincoln: University of Nebraska Press, 1990).
4. Cronon, "The Trouble with Wilderness," *Uncommon Ground*, 86. Cronon's influential essay was published shortly after Solnit's book and offers a striking example of the postmodern reevaluation of the concept of nature.

5. Solnit quotes (294) from Bill McKibben, *The End of Nature* (New York: Random House, 1989), 58: "We have deprived nature of its independence, and that is fatal to its meaning. Nature's independence is its meaning; without it there is nothing but us."
6. Alfred North Whitehead analyzes the split between nature and culture beginning in the seventeenth century—the moment of "the great bifurcation"—in the second of his Tarner Lectures, published in *The Concept of Nature: The Tarner Lectures Delivered in Trinity College* (Cambridge: Cambridge University Press, 1920): 26–48. His critique of this conceptual division is fundamental to Bruno Latour's analysis of the anthropology of the moderns in *We Have Never Been Modern* and subsequent books. Anthropologist Philippe Descola also sees the idea of nature's separation from humanity as a recent development of Western culture. He describes other cultural modes of configuring the meaning of humanity and nature in *Par-delà nature et culture* (Paris: Gallimard, 2005).
7. In the chapter entitled "Lise Meitner's Walking Shoes," Solnit discusses twentieth-century developments in scientific thought: "Einstein's Theory of Relativity, Heisenberg's Uncertainty Principle, and Bohr's Principle of Complementarity suggested a subtler model of truth than classical physics and Cartesian philosophy put forward" (140).
8. Rebecca Solnit, *A Field Guide to Getting Lost* (New York: Viking, 2005), 5.
9. See Gilles Deleuze and Félix Guattari, *A Thousand Plateaus: Capitalism and Schizophrenia*, trans. Brian Massumi (Minneapolis: University of Minnesota Press, 1987).
10. See Pierre Nora's influential essay, "Between Memory and History: Les Lieux de Mémoire," in "Memory and Counter-Memory," special issue, *Representations* 26 (Spring 1989): 7–24.
11. See Abram, "In the Landscape of Language," *Spell of the Sensuous*, 137–179.
12. Rebecca Solnit, *Wanderlust: A History of Walking* (New York: Viking, 2000), 8.
13. Solnit makes this claim in the acknowledgments that preface *Savage Dreams* (x).
14. Frost's poem deals with the paradox of a nation of immigrants haunted by their country of origin and detached from the land they claim: "Possessing what we still were unpossessed by, / Possessed by what we now no more possessed." Robert Frost, "The Gift Outright," *A Witness Tree* (London: J. Cape, 1943), 27.
15. This thought-provoking compound structure is found in Karen Barad, *Meeting the Universe Halfway: Quantum Physics and the Entanglement of Matter and Meaning*

(Durham, NC: Duke University Press, 2007), 376. Barad's discussion in the final chapter of her book of the ways in which the brittle star's remaking of the boundaries of its own body challenges conventional ideas of agency and subjectivity seems pertinent to Solnit's realization of her connection to the land.

Chapter Eight

1. Whitehead's theory of "the great bifurcation" is discussed earlier, in chapter 7.
2. Barry Lopez discussed this in a 1998 personal interview with Nicholas O'Connell quoted in O'Connell's book *On Sacred Ground: The Spirit of Place in Pacific Northwest Literature* (Seattle: University of Washington Press, 2003). Lopez explains that his gesture of bowing before the landscape is a way of acknowledging its spiritual dimension and thereby its right to consideration: "If the land is incorporated into the same moral universe that you occupy, then your bow is an acknowledgment of your participation in that universe and a recognition that all you bow to is included in your moral universe. If you behave as though there was no spiritual dimension to the place, then you can treat the place like an object" (141).
3. Meriwether Lewis and William Clark, *Original Journals of the Lewis and Clark Expedition, 1804–1806*, vol. 1, ed. Reuben Gold Thwaites (New York: Dodd, Mead, 1904), 15.
4. Thoreau, *Walden*, 64–65.
5. Robert Sullivan, *The Thoreau You Don't Know: What the Prophet of Environmentalism Really Meant* (New York: HarperCollins, 2009).
6. "By imagining that our true home is in the wilderness, we forgive ourselves the homes we actually inhabit." Cronon, *Uncommon Ground*, 81.
7. Recalling her work as a ranger for the National Park Service, Ladino states that "nostalgia can aid in environmental movements by invoking an organic or unspoiled natural world in order to enlist sympathetic proponents of preservation." *Reclaiming Nostalgia*, xii–xiii.
8. Not surprisingly, Jane Bennett notes the vitality of Sullivan's garbage hills in *Vibrant Matter* (6).
9. Sullivan, *Thoreau You Don't Know*, 190.
10. For Wolfgang Kayser, the conjunction of the mechanical and the organic is a specifically grotesque motif; see *The Grotesque in Art and Literature*, trans. Ulrich Weisstein (New York: Columbia University Press, 1981), 183.

11. “The mind does not long tolerate such affronts to its classificatory systems as grotesque forms present.” Geoffrey Galt Harpham, *On the Grotesque: Strategies of Contradiction in Art and Literature*, 2nd ed. (Aurora, CO: Davies Group, Publishers, 2006), 4.
12. I believe there is a link between the moderns’ process of purification that splits reality into “distinct ontological zones: that of human beings on the one hand; that of nonhumans on the other” (Latour, *We Have Never Been Modern*, 10–11) and their aesthetic preference for unity and purity. The practice of purification helps foster the unacknowledged proliferation of hybrids. Advocating purity as an aesthetic principle helps to occult the existence of hybrids.
13. Robert Pinsky, “Swamp Dreams,” *New York Times* book review, April 19, 1998, New York Times on the Web, http://www.nytimes.com/books/98/04/19/reviews/980419.19pinskyt.html.
14. Sullivan, *Thoreau You Don’t Know*, 306.
15. Ibid., 304.

Conclusion

1. Loren C. Eiseley, *The Invisible Pyramid* (New York: Charles Scribner’s Sons, 1970), 152.
2. One of the more sensational projects for travel to Mars is being masterminded by Bas Lansdorp, a Dutch entrepreneur who has invited candidates for the mission to participate in a TV reality show that will select the winners for a one-way voyage. Among the thousands of candidates who want to make the journey, the majority are apparently American. Adam Gabbatt, “Mars One Says 80,000 Have Applied for One-Way Mission to Red Planet,” *The Guardian*, May 8, 2013, Guardian News and Media, http://www.theguardian.com/science/2013/may/08/mars-one-applications-mission.
3. These words famously describe the mission of the starship *Enterprise* in *Star Trek*. They were spoken in the opening voice-over to the series in the 1960s.
4. The work of Bruno Latour and of the practitioners of Actor Network Theory offers an alternative to the moderns’ dichotomizing vision; see Latour’s discussion in *Reassembling the Social: An Introduction to Actor-Network-Theory* (Oxford: Oxford University Press, 2005). For a provocative exploration of the agency of things, see Bennett, *Vibrant Matter*.
5. Eiseley, *Invisible Pyramid*, 154.
6. Cf. Bruno Latour, “Facing Gaia: Six Lectures on the Political Theology of

Nature," Gifford Lectures on Natural Religion, Edinburgh, February 18–28, 2013. The lectures were recorded and diffused via the Internet. A PDF version of the talks is available for consultation (http://bruno-latour.fr) before their anticipated publication. The Anthropocene would start at the beginning of the nineteenth century, with the changes brought about by the Industrial Revolution.

7. Latour cites Lovelock's warning about Gaia as being "at war" and taking "revenge" on "the humans." Latour, "Facing Gaia," 80.
8. Ursula K. Heise, *Sense of Place and Sense of Planet: The Environmental Imagination of the Global* (Oxford: Oxford University Press, 2008), 63.
9. Ibid., 33–40.
10. Ibid., 62.
11. For Bass this widening of focus comes later in works like *The Book of Yaak* and *Brown Dog of the Yaak*.
12. See my discussion of some nature writers' accounts of crossing the imaginary boundary between the self and the outside world in "Border Crossing in the New Literature of Place," in *Wretched Refuge: Immigrants and Itinerants in the Postmodern*, ed. Jessica Datema and Diane Krumrey (Newcastle upon Tyne: Cambridge Scholars, 2010), 69–83. In *The Land's Wild Music*, Mark Tredinnick gives a less restrictive definition of nature writers' focus: "The world that nature writing engages with is not bounded by society; it extends to the universe that came before, that goes beyond, that contains the human world. . . . It writes ecologies, not just societies" (23). Still, in his subsequent attempt to define nature writing, he seems to suggest that the nature writer passes beyond civilization's boundaries: "To enter into lyric engagement with place is to allow ourselves to become wild. . . . It is to become the green man, Nature's scribe, the shore bird, the dancing woman, the meadow's surrendered soul" (302).
13. James Howard Kunstler characterizes the towns and suburbs in which most Americans live as "the geography of nowhere, that has simply ceased to be a credible human habitat." *The Geography of Nowhere: The Rise and Decline of America's Man-Made Landscape* (New York: Simon and Schuster, 1993), 15. Edward Relph, in the preface to his 1976 study *Place and Placelessness* (London: Pion, 1976), argued that contemporary urban landscapes are increasingly characterized by "placelessness": "the casual eradication of distinctive places and the making of standardized landscapes that results from an insensitivity to the significance of place." Though their terms are sometimes hyperbolic, their critiques are somewhat valid and aimed at raising consciousness

about creating environments that will foster a fuller and richer commitment to community.

14. Joy Williams describes this complex in *Ill Nature: Rants and Reflections on Humanity and Other Animals* (New York: Lyons, 2001).
15. Michel Serres, *The Parasite*, trans. Lawrence R. Schehr (Baltimore: Johns Hopkins University Press, 1982), 225.
16. Harrison, *Forests*, 200. For Harrison, language distances humanity from the world as much as it connects; it defines us as apart from nature: "We are in relation to nature because we are not within nature. We do not intrinsically belong to the natural order (if we did we would not need to discover the facts of life) but find in our relation the terms of our destiny as excursioners on the earth" (222). Characteristic of modern Western thought, this conviction of our separation from nature has been relativized and contextualized in the work of Descola and Latour.
17. N. Scott Momaday, *The Way to Rainy Mountain* (Albuquerque: University of New Mexico Press, 1969), 83.
18. This perception is expressed in different ways by Kunstler, Relph, and Cronon.
19. Myra Jehlen, *American Incarnation: The Individual, the Nation, and the Continent* (Cambridge, MA: Harvard University Press, 1986).
20. Jehlen cites Perry Miller's seminal study of this myth in *Nature's Nation*, but she would put the date of its inception two centuries earlier than he does.
21. Jehlen, *American Incarnation*, 2.

BIBLIOGRAPHY

Abram, David. "Climate and Psyche." Lecture at the Psychology of Climate Seminar, BI Norwegian Business School, Oslo, September 28, 2012. YouTube video, October 3, 2012. http://www.youtube.com/watch?v=TzZ4103VU7M.

———. *The Spell of the Sensuous: Perception and Language in a More-Than-Human World*. New York: Pantheon, 1996.

Adams, Ansel, Nancy Wynne Newhall, and David Ross Brower. *This Is the American Earth*. San Francisco: Sierra Club, 1960.

Adams, David Wallace. *Education for Extinction: American Indians and the Boarding School Experience, 1875–1928*. Lawrence: University Press of Kansas, 1995.

Allen, Barbara. "Shaping and Being Shaped by the Land." In *The Big Empty: Essays on Western Landscape as Narrative*, edited by Leonard Engel, 93–111. Albuquerque: University of New Mexico Press, 1994.

Ames, Fisher. *Works of Fisher Ames*. Edited by John Thornton Kirkland. Boston: T. B. Wait, 1809.

Annals of Congress, 1st–18th Cong., 1st sess.; Mar. 3, 1789–May 27, 1824. Princeton, NJ: Princeton Microfilm, [197-?]. http://www.archive.org/details/annalsofcongress10unit.

Antonetta, Susanne. *Body Toxic: An Environmental Memoir*. Washington, DC: Counterpoint, 2001.

Arneil, Barbara. "The Wild Indian's Venison: Locke's Theory of Property and English Colonialism in America." *Political Studies* 44 (1996): 60–74.

Atkinson, Brooks. *This Bright Land: A Personal View*. Garden City, NY: Natural History Press, 1972.

Bailey, Thomas. "Rick Bass's *Winter*: Self Discovery in a Cold Place." In *The Literary Art and Activism of Rick Bass*, edited by O. Alan Weltzien, 91–101. Salt Lake City: University of Utah Press, 2001.

Barad, Karen. *Meeting the Universe Halfway: Quantum Physics and the Entanglement of Matter and Meaning*. Durham, NC: Duke University Press, 2007.

———. "Meeting the Universe Halfway: Realism and Social Constructivism without Contradictions." In *Feminism, Science, and the Philosophy of Science*. Vol. 256, edited by Lynn Hankinson Nelson and Jack Nelson, 161–194. Boston: Kluwer Academic Publishers, 1996.

———. "Posthumanist Performativity: Toward an Understanding of How Matter Comes to Matter." *Signs* 28, no. 3 (2003): 801–831.

Bass, Rick. *The Book of Yaak*. New York: Houghton Mifflin, 1996.

———. *Brown Dog of the Yaak: Essays on Art and Activism*. Minneapolis: Milkweed, 1999.

———. *Winter: Notes from Montana*. New York: Houghton Mifflin, 1991.

Bennett, Jane. *Vibrant Matter: A Political Ecology of Things*. Durham, NC: Duke University Press, 2010.

Berque, Augustin. *MÉDIANCE: De milieux en paysages*. Montpellier, France: Reclus, 1990.

Bordo, Jonathan. "Picture and Witness at the Site of the Wilderness." In *Landscape and Power*, 2nd ed., edited by W. J. T. Mitchell, 291–315. Chicago: University of Chicago Press, 2002.

Bowden, Charles. *Frog Mountain Blues*. Tucson: University of Arizona Press, 1994.

Bradford, William. *Bradford's History of Plymouth Plantation, 1606–1646*. Edited by William T. Davis. New York: Charles Scribner's Sons, 1908. Early Americas Digital Archive. http://mith.umd.edu//eada/html/display.php?docs=bradford_history.xml.

Buell, Lawrence. *The Environmental Imagination: Thoreau, Nature Writing, and the Formation of American Culture*. Cambridge, MA: Belknap Press, 1995.

———. *The Future of Environmental Criticism: Environmental Crisis and Literary Imagination*. Malden, MA: Blackwell, 2005.

Burke, Edmund. *The Works of the Right Honorable Edmund Burke*. 3rd ed. Vol. 1. Boston: Little, Brown, 1869.

Carson, Rachel. *Silent Spring*. Boston: Houghton Mifflin, 1962.

Casey, Edward S. "How to Get from Place to Space in a Fairly Short Stretch of Time: Phenomenological Prolegomena." In *Senses of Place*, edited by Steven Feld and Keith H. Basso. Santa Fe, NM : School of American Research Press, 1996.

Cauquelin, Anne. *L'invention du paysage*. Paris: PUF, 2000.

Certeau, Michel de, Luce Giard, and Pierre Mayol. *L'invention du quotidien*. Paris: Union Générale d'Éditions, 1980.

Chidester, David, and Edward T. Linenthal, eds. *American Sacred Space*. Bloomington: Indiana University Press, 1995.

Chisholm, Dianne. "Ellen Meloy's Deep Nomadology (How to Map the Heartland of a Nuclear-Age Desert)." *Rhizomes: Cultural Studies in Emerging Knowledge* 13 (Fall 2006). http://rhizomes.net/issue13/chisholm/chisholm.html.

Clifford, James, and George Marcus, eds. *Writing Culture: The Poetics and Politics of Ethnography*. Berkeley: University of California Press, 1986.

Coetzee, J. M. *White Writing: On the Culture of Letters in South Africa*. New Haven, CT: Yale University Press, 1988.

Conrad, Joseph. *Heart of Darkness*. New York: Garden City, 1916.

Corbin, Alain. *L'homme dans le paysage*. Paris: Editions Textuel, 2001.

Cotton, John. *God's Promise to His Plantations as It Was Delivered in a Sermon, by Iohn Cotton, B. D. and Preacher of God's Word in Boston*. London: William Jones, 1634.

Crevecoeur, J. Hector St. John de. *Letters from an American Farmer*. New York: E. P. Dutton, 1957.

Cronon, William. *Changes in the Land: Indians, Colonists, and the Ecology of New England*. New York: Hill and Wang, 1983.

———, ed. *Uncommon Ground: Rethinking the Human Place in Nature*. New York: W. W. Norton, 1995.

Cronon, William, George A. Miles, and Jay Gitlin, eds. *Under an Open Sky: Rethinking America's Western Past*. New York: W. W. Norton, 1992.

Deleuze, Gilles, and Félix Guattari. *Kafka: Toward a Minor Literature*. Minneapolis: University of Minnesota Press, 1986.

———. *A Thousand Plateaus: Capitalism and Schizophrenia*. Translated by Brian Massumi. Minneapolis: University of Minnesota Press, 1987.

Deming, Alison Hawthorne. *The Edges of the Civilized World: A Journey in Nature and Culture*. New York: Picador, 1998.

Descola, Philippe. *Par-delà nature et culture*. Paris: Gallimard, 2005.

Dillard, Annie. *Pilgrim at Tinker Creek*. New York: Harper's Magazine, 1974.

Dilsaver, Lary M., ed. *America's National Park System: The Critical Documents*. Lanham, MD: Rowman and Littlefield, 1994.

Eco, Umberto. *The Role of the Reader: Explorations in the Semiotics of Texts*. Bloomington: Indiana University Press, 1984.

Eiseley, Loren C. *The Invisible Pyramid*. New York: Charles Scribner's Sons, 1970.

Emerson, Ralph Waldo. *Nature*. Boston: James Monroe, 1849.

Entrikin, J. Nicholas. *The Betweenness of Place: Towards a Geography of Modernity*. Baltimore: Johns Hopkins University Press, 1991.

Fiennes, William. *The Snow Geese: A Story of Home*. New York: Random House, 2002.

Foucault, Michel. "Des espaces autres: Hétérotopies." *Architecture, Mouvement, Continuité* 5 (1984): 46–49. http://foucault.info/documents/heteroTopia/foucault.heteroTopia.en.html.

Fox, William L. *The Void, the Grid and the Sign: Traversing the Great Basin*. Salt Lake City: University of Utah Press, 2000.

Franklin, Wayne. *Discoverers, Explorers, Settlers: The Diligent Writers of Early America*. Chicago: University of Chicago Press, 1979.

Frost, Robert. *A Witness Tree*. London: J. Cape, 1943.

Gabbatt, Adam. "Mars One Says 80,000 Have Applied for One-Way Mission to Red Planet." *The Guardian*, May 8, 2013. Guardian News and Media. http://www.theguardian.com/science/2013/may/08/mars-one-applications-mission.

Goin, Peter, and Paul F. Starrs. *Black Rock*. Reno: University of Nevada Press, 2005.

Gooding, Mel, and William Furlong. *Artists, Land, Nature*. New York: Harry N. Abrams, 2002.

Gould, Peter, and Rodney White. *Mental Maps*. Harmondsworth, UK: Penguin, 1974.

Gregory, Derek. *Geographical Imaginations*. London: Blackwell, 1994.

Harding, Wendy. "Border Crossing in the New Literature of Place." In *Wretched Refuge: Immigrants and Itinerants in the Postmodern*, edited by Jessica Datema and Diane Krumrey, 69–83. Newcastle upon Tyne, UK: Cambridge Scholars, 2010.

———. "Scripting the Wilderness." Ecocriticism Issue, *Journal of American Studies of Turkey* 30 (2009): 57–72.

Harding, Wendy, and Jacky Martin. *Beyond Words: The Othering Excursion in Contemporary American Literature*. Newcastle upon Tyne, UK: Cambridge Scholars, 2007.

Harpham, Geoffrey Galt. *On the Grotesque: Strategies of Contradiction in Art and Literature*. 2nd ed. Aurora, CO: Davies Group, Publishers, 2006.

Harrison, Robert Pogue. *Forests: The Shadow of Civilization*. Chicago: University of Chicago Press, 1992.

Haynes, Roslynn. *Seeking the Centre: The Australian Desert in Literature, Art and Film*. Cambridge: Cambridge University Press, 1998.

Heath, Dwight B., ed. *Mourt's Relation: A Journal of the Pilgrims at Plymouth*. Bedford, MA: Applewood Books, 1963. First published 1622, London.

Heidegger, Martin. *Poetry, Language, Thought*. Translated by Albert Hofstadter. New York: Harper and Row, 1971.

Heise, Ursula K. *Sense of Place and Sense of Planet: The Environmental Imagination of the Global*. Oxford: Oxford University Press, 2008.

Ingold, Tim. *Lines: A Brief History*. London: Routledge, 2007.

———. "The Wedge and the Knot: Hammering and Stitching the Face of Nature." In *Nature, Space, and the Sacred: Transdisciplinary Perspectives*, edited by Sigurd Bergmann et al., 147–162. Farnham, UK: Ashgate, 2009.

James, William. *The Principles of Psychology*. Vol. 1. New York: Henry Holt, 1890.

Jefferson, Thomas. Letter to General Horatio Gates. July 11, 1803. *The Writings of Thomas Jefferson*. New York: H. W. Derby, 1861. Project Gutenberg e-book, *Memoir, Correspondence, and Miscellanies, from the Papers of Thomas Jefferson*. http://www.gutenberg.org/files/16783/16783-h/16783-h.htm#link2H_4_0305.

———. Letter to James Madison. December 20, 1787. *The Writings of Thomas Jefferson*. Project Gutenberg e-book, *Memoir, Correspondence, and Miscellanies, from the Papers of Thomas Jefferson*. http://www.gutenberg.org/files/16782/16782-h/16782-h.htm#link2H_4_0119.

———. *Writings: Autobiography; a Summary View of the Rights of British America; Notes on the State of Virginia; Public Papers; Addresses, Messages, and Replies; Miscellany; Letters*. Edited by Merrill D. Peterson. New York: Library of America, 1984.

Jehlen, Myra. *American Incarnation: The Individual, the Nation, and the Continent*. Cambridge, MA: Harvard University Press, 1986.

Johnson, Benjamin. "Wilderness Parks and Their Discontents." In *American Wilderness: A New History*, edited by Michael Lewis, 113–130. Oxford: Oxford University Press, 2007.

Johnson, Edward. *Johnson's Wonder-Working Providence: 1628–1651*. Edited by John Franklin Jameson. New York: Barnes and Noble, 1959.

Kayser, Wolfgang Johannes. *The Grotesque in Art and Literature*. Translated by Ulrich Weisstein. New York: Columbia University Press, 1981.

Kearns, Laurel, and Catherine Keller. *Ecospirit: Religions and Philosophies for the Earth*. New York: Fordham University Press, 2007.

Keller, Robert H., and Michael F. Turek. *American Indians and National Parks*. Tucson: University of Arizona Press, 1998.

Klee, Paul. *Notebooks, Volume 2: The Nature of Nature*. Edited by Jürg Spiller. Translated by Heinz Norden. London: Lund Humphries, 1973.

Kolodny, Annette. *The Lay of the Land: Metaphor as Experience and History in American Life and Letters*. Chapel Hill: University of North Carolina Press, 1975.

Kroetsch, Robert. *The Lovely Treachery of Words: Essays Selected and New*. Toronto: Oxford University Press, 1989.

Kukla, Jon. *A Wilderness So Immense: The Louisiana Purchase and the Destiny of America*. New York: A. A. Knopf, 2003.

Kunstler, James Howard. *The Geography of Nowhere: The Rise and Decline of America's Man-Made Landscape*. New York: Simon and Schuster, 1993.

Ladino, Jennifer K. *Reclaiming Nostalgia: Longing for Nature in American Literature*. Charlottesville: University of Virginia Press, 2012.

Larsen, Soren C., and Timothy J. Brock. "Great Basin Imagery in Newspaper Coverage of Yucca Mountain." *Geographical Review* 95, no. 4 (October 2005): 517–536.

Latour, Bruno. "Facing Gaia: Six Lectures on the Political Theology of Nature." Gifford Lectures on Natural Religion. Edinburgh, February 18–28, 2013. http://bruno-latour.fr.

———. *An Inquiry into Modes of Existence: An Anthropology of the Moderns*. Cambridge, MA: Harvard University Press, 2013.

———. *Reassembling the Social: An Introduction to Actor-Network-Theory*. Oxford: Oxford University Press, 2005.

———. *We Have Never Been Modern*. Cambridge, MA: Harvard University Press, 1993.

Lefebvre, Henri. *The Production of Space*. Translated by Donald Nicholson-Smith. Oxford: Blackwell, 1991.

Leopold, Aldo. *A Sand County Almanac, with Essays on Conservation from Round River*. New York: Ballantine Books, 1966.

Levinas, Emmanuel. *Alterity and Transcendence*. New York: Columbia University Press, 1999.

———. *Totality and Infinity: An Essay on Exteriority*. The Hague: M. Nijhoff, 1979.

Lewis, Meriwether, and William Clark. *Original Journals of the Lewis and Clark Expedition, 1804–1806: Printed from the Original Manuscripts in the Library of the American Philosophical Society and by Direction of Its Committee on Historical Documents, Together with Manuscript Material of Lewis and Clark from Other Sources, including Note-books, Letters, Maps, Etc., and the Journals of Charles Floyd and Joseph Whitehouse, Now for the First Time Published in Full and Exactly as Written*. Edited by Reuben Gold Thwaites. Vol. 1. New York: Dodd, Mead, 1904.

Lewis, Michael L., ed. *American Wilderness: A New History*. Oxford: Oxford University Press, 2007.

Lewis, Nathaniel. *Unsettling the Literary West: Authenticity and Authorship*. Lincoln: University of Nebraska Press, 2003.

Limerick, Patricia Nelson. "Haunted by Rhyolite: Learning from the Landscape of Failure." In *The Big Empty: Essays on Western Landscape as Narrative*, edited by Leonard Engel, 27–47. Albuquerque: University of New Mexico Press, 1994.

———. *The Legacy of Conquest: The Unbroken Past of the American West*. New York: W. W. Norton, 1987.

———. *Something in the Soil: Legacies and Reckonings in the New West*. New York: W. W. Norton, 2000.

Limerick, Patricia Nelson, Clyde A. Milner, and Charles E. Rankin, eds. *Trails: Toward a New Western History*. Lawrence: University Press of Kansas, 1991.

Lopez, Barry Holstun. *Arctic Dreams: Imagination and Desire in a Northern Landscape*. New York: Charles Scribner's Sons, 1986.

Lütticken, Sven. "Art and Thingness, Part Two: Thingification." *e-flux* 15 (2010). http://www.e-flux.com/journal/art-and-thingness-part-two-thingification/.

Lynch, Tom. *Xerophilia: Ecocritical Explorations in Southwestern Literature*. Lubbock: Texas Tech University Press, 2008.

Lyon, Thomas J., ed. *This Incomperable Lande: A Book of American Nature Writing*. Boston: Houghton Mifflin, 1989.

Madson, John. *Where the Sky Began: Land of the Tallgrass Prairie*. Boston: Houghton Mifflin, 1982.

Manning, Richard. *Grassland: The History, Biology, Politics, and Promise of the American Prairie*. New York: Viking, 1995.

Marx, Leo. *The Machine in the Garden: Technology and the Pastoral Ideal in America*. New York: Oxford University Press, 1964.

Massey, Doreen B. *For Space*. London: Sage, 2005.

———. *Space, Place, and Gender*. Cambridge: Polity Press, 1994.

McKibben, Bill. *The End of Nature*. New York: Random House, 1989.

Meinig, D. W. *The Shaping of America: A Geographical Perspective on 500 Years of History*. Vol. 2, *Continental America, 1800–1867*. New Haven, CT: Yale University Press, 1993.

Meloy, Ellen. *The Last Cheater's Waltz: Beauty and Violence in the Desert Southwest*. New York: Henry Holt, 1999.

Merchant, Carolyn. *Ecological Revolutions: Nature, Gender, and Science in New England*. Chapel Hill: University of North Carolina Press, 1989.

Miller, Angela. "The Fate of Wilderness in American Landscape Art: The Dilemmas of 'Nature's Nation.'" In *American Wilderness: A New History*, edited by Michael Lewis, 91–112. Oxford: Oxford University Press, 2007.

Miller, Perry. *Errand into the Wilderness*. Cambridge, MA: Belknap Press, 1956.

———. *Nature's Nation*. Cambridge, MA: Belknap Press, 1967.

Miller, Robert J. *Native America, Discovered and Conquered: Thomas Jefferson, Lewis and Clark, and Manifest Destiny*. Westport, CT: Praeger, 2006.

Mitchell, W. J. T., ed. *Landscape and Power*. 2nd ed. Chicago: University of Chicago Press, 2002.

Momaday, N. Scott. *The Man Made of Words: Essays, Stories, Passages*. New York: St. Martin's, 1997.

———. *The Way to Rainy Mountain*. Albuquerque: University of New Mexico Press, 1969.

Morin, Edgar. *Introduction à la pensée complexe*. Paris: ESF, 1990.

Muir, John. "The Hetch Hetchy Valley." *Boston Weekly Transcript*, March 25, 1873. Sierra Club, John Muir Exhibit. http://www.sierraclub.org/john_muir_exhibit/writings/muir_hh_boston_25mar1873.aspx.

———. *My First Summer in the Sierra*. Boston: Houghton Mifflin, 1911.

Murphy, Patrick D. *Ecocritical Explorations in Literary and Cultural Studies: Fences, Boundaries, and Fields*. Lanham, MD: Lexington, 2009.

———. *Farther Afield in the Study of Nature-Oriented Literature*. Charlottesville: University of Virginia Press, 2000.

Nash, Roderick. *Wilderness and the American Mind*. New Haven, CT: Yale University Press, 1967.

Nelson, Lynn Hankinson, and Jack Nelson, eds. *Feminism, Science, and the Philosophy of Science*. Vol. 256. Boston: Kluwer Academic Publishers, 1996.

Nora, Pierre. "Between Memory and History: Les Lieux de Mémoire." In "Memory and Counter-Memory," special issue, *Representations* 26 (Spring 1989): 7–24.

Norris, Nanette, ed. *Words for a Small Planet: Ecocritical Views*. Lanham, MD: Lexington, 2013.

Novak, Barbara. *Nature and Culture: American Landscape and Painting, 1825–1875*. New York: Oxford University Press, 1980.

O'Connell, Nicholas. *On Sacred Ground: The Spirit of Place in Pacific Northwest Literature*. Seattle: University of Washington Press, 2003.

O'Sullivan, John. "Annexation." *The United States Magazine and Democratic Review* 17 (July 1845): 5–10. http://www.historytools.org/sources/manifest_destiny.pdf.

Oliver, Mary. *Dream Work*. New York: Atlantic Monthly Press, 1986.

Olmsted, Frederick Law. "The Yosemite Valley and the Mariposa Big Tree Grove," 1865. Reprinted in Lary M. Dilsaver, ed. *America's National Park System: The Critical Documents*. Lanham, MD: Rowman and Littlefield, 1994. http://www.nps.gov/history/history/online_books/anps/anps_1b.htm.

"Oral History." National Park Service, Yosemite website. Updated August 10, 2009. http://www.nps.gov/yose/historyculture/oral-history.htm.

Payne, Daniel G. *Voices in the Wilderness: American Nature Writing and Environmental Politics*. Hanover, NH: University Press of New England, 1996.

Peterson, Merrill D., ed. *Thomas Jefferson: Writings: Autobiography; a Summary View of the Rights of British America; Notes on the State of Virginia; Public Papers; Addresses, Messages, and Replies; Miscellany; Letters*. New York: Library of America, 1984.

Pinsky, Robert. "Swamp Dreams." *New York Times* book review. April 19, 1998.

New York Times on the Web. http://www.nytimes.com/books/98/04/19/reviews/980419.19pinskyt.html.

Plumwood, Val. *Feminism and the Mastery of Nature*. London: Routledge, 1993.

Popper, Deborah Epstein, and Frank J. Popper. "The Great Plains: From Dust to Dust." *Planning* 53 (December 1987): 12–18. http://www.csupomona.edu/~tgyoung/rs510/Grt_Plains.pdf.

Price, Patricia L. *Dry Place: Landscapes of Belonging and Exclusion*. Minneapolis: University of Minnesota Press, 2004.

Raban, Jonathan. *Bad Land: An American Romance*. New York: Vintage, 1997.

Ray, Janisse. *Ecology of a Cracker Childhood (The World as Home)*. Minneapolis: Milkweed, 1999.

Relph, Edward. *Place and Placelessness*. London: Pion, 1976.

Righter, Robert W. *The Battle over Hetch Hetchy: America's Most Controversial Dam and the Birth of Modern Environmentalism*. New York: Oxford University Press, 2005.

Runte, Alfred. *Yosemite: The Embattled Wilderness*. Lincoln: University of Nebraska Press, 1990.

Ryden, Kent C. *Mapping the Invisible Landscape: Folklore, Writing, and the Sense of Place*. Iowa City: University of Iowa Press, 1993.

Scott, Doug. *The Enduring Wilderness: Protecting Our Natural Heritage through the Wilderness Act*. Golden, CO: Fulcrum, 2004.

Serres, Michel. *The Natural Contract*. Ann Arbor: University of Michigan Press, 1995.

———. *The Parasite*. Translated by Lawrence R. Schehr. Baltimore: Johns Hopkins University Press, 1982.

Seton, Thomas. *The Gospel of the Red Man*. Commemorative ed. Bloomington, IN: World Wisdom, 2005. First published 1936 by Doubleday.

Slotkin, Richard. *Gunfighter Nation: The Myth of the Frontier in Twentieth-Century America*. New York: Atheneum, 1992.

———. *Regeneration through Violence: The Mythology of the American Frontier, 1600–1860*. Norman: University of Oklahoma Press, 2000.

Slovic, Scott. *Seeking Awareness in American Nature Writing: Henry Thoreau, Annie Dillard, Edward Abbey, Wendell Berry, Barry Lopez*. Salt Lake City: University of Utah Press, 1992.

Smith, John. *A Description of New England (1616)*. Online electronic text ed., edited by Paul Royster. Electronic Texts in American Studies, Paper 4. Digital Commons at the University of Nebraska–Lincoln. http://digitalcommons.unl.edu/etas/4.

Soja, Edward W. *Thirdspace: Journeys to Los Angeles and Other Real-and-Imagined Places*. Oxford: Blackwell, 1996.

Solnit, Rebecca. *A Field Guide to Getting Lost*. New York: Viking, 2005.

———. *Savage Dreams: A Journey into the Landscape Wars of the American West*. New York: Vintage, 1995.

———. *Wanderlust: A History of Walking*. New York: Viking, 2000.

Spence, Mark David. *Dispossessing the Wilderness: Indian Removal and the Making of the National Parks*. New York: Oxford University Press, 1999.

Spencer, Daniel T. "Restoring Earth, Restored to Earth: Toward an Ethic for Reinhabiting Place." In *Ecospirit: Religions and Philosophies for the Earth*. Edited by Laurel Kearns and Catherine Keller, 415–432. New York: Fordham University Press, 2007.

Stegner, Wallace. "Wilderness Letter." Letter to David E. Pesonen. December 3, 1960. The Wilderness Society. http://wilderness.org/bios/former-council-members/wallace-stegner.

Stein, Gertrude. *The Geographical History of America, or, the Relation of Human Nature to the Human Mind*. With a new introduction by William H. Gass. New York: Vintage Books, 1973.

Sullivan, Robert. *The Meadowlands: Wilderness Adventures at the Edge of a City*. New York: Scribner, 1998.

———. *The Thoreau You Don't Know: What the Prophet of Environmentalism Really Meant*. New York: HarperCollins, 2009.

Thoreau, Henry David. *Excursions*. New York: Thomas Crowell, 1913.

———. *The Journal of Henry David Thoreau*. 14 vols. Edited by Bradford Torrey and Francis H. Allen. Salt Lake City: Gibbs M. Smith, 1984.

———. *The Maine Woods*. Boston: Houghton Mifflin, 1890.

———. *Walden; Or, Life in the Woods*. Boston: Ticknor and Fields, 1854.

———. *A Week on the Concord and Merrimack Rivers*. Cambridge, MA: James R. Osgood, 1873.

Tocqueville, Alexis de. *Democracy in America*. Vol. 1. Translated by Henry Reeve. New York: Longmans, Green, 1889.

Tredinnick, Mark. *The Land's Wild Music: Encounters with Barry Lopez, Peter Matthiessen, Terry Tempest Williams, and James Galvin*. San Antonio: Trinity University Press, 2005.

Turner, Frederick Jackson. "The Significance of the Frontier in American History." Paper presented at the Meeting of the American Historical Association World Columbian Exposition, Chicago, IL, July 12, 1893.

Walsh, Margaret. *The American West: Visions and Revisions*. New York: Cambridge University Press, 2005.

Ware, Katherine. *Earth Now: American Photographers and the Environment*. Santa Fe: Museum of New Mexico Press, 2011.

Weltzien, O. Alan, ed. *The Literary Art and Activism of Rick Bass*. Salt Lake City: University of Utah Press, 2001.

Wheeler, Sara. *The Magnetic North: Notes from the Arctic Circle*. New York: Farrar, Strauss and Giroux, 2011.

White, Richard. "'Are You an Environmentalist or Do You Work for a Living?': Work and Nature." In *Uncommon Ground: Rethinking the Human Place in Nature*, edited by William Cronon, 171–185. New York: W. W. Norton, 1995.

———. *The Middle Ground: Indians, Empires, and Republics in the Great Lakes Region, 1650–1815*. Cambridge: Cambridge University Press, 1991.

Whitehead, Alfred North. *The Concept of Nature: The Tarner Lectures Delivered in Trinity College*. Cambridge: Cambridge University Press, 1920.

Whitman, Walt. *Leaves of Grass*. Boston: Thayer and Eldridge, 1860.

Wilderness Act of September 3, 1964. Public Law 88–77. 88th Congress, S.4. Wilderness.net. http://www.wilderness.net/NWPS/legisact.

Williams, Joy. *Ill Nature: Rants and Reflections on Humanity and Other Animals*. New York: Lyons, 2001.

Williams, Terry Tempest. *Refuge: An Unnatural History of Family and Place*. New York: Vintage, 1992.

Wollaston, Percy. *Homesteading: A Montana Family Album*. New York: Penguin, 1997.

Woods, Robert Archey. *The City Wilderness: A Settlement Study*. Boston: Houghton Mifflin, 1899.

Worster, Donald. *An Unsettled Country: Changing Landscapes of the American West*. Albuquerque: University of New Mexico Press, 1994.

INDEX